Strategic Affection?

SOLIDARITY AND IDENTITY

Recent social, cultural and economic developments in Western society are at the basis of increasing cultural and ethnic diversity. People's social and cultural identitities are becoming more varied. What are the consequences of these developments for social bonds and solidarity? Finding answers to this question is the aim of the series *Solidarity and Identity*.

EDITORS OF THE SERIES

Prof. dr. A.E. Komter, Faculty of Social and Behavioural Sciences, Utrecht University

Prof. dr. J. Burgers, Faculty of Social Sciences, Erasmus University Rotterdam

Prof. J.C. Rath, Institute for Migration and Ethnic Studies, University of Amsterdam

PREVIOUSLY PUBLISHED

Minghuan Li, *We Need Two Worlds: Chinese Immigrant Associations in a Western Society*, 1999 (ISBN 978 90 5356 402 8)

Aafke E. Komter, Jack Burgers and Godfried Engbersen, *Het cement van de samenleving: een verkennende studie naar solidariteit en cohesie*, 2000/2004² (ISBN 978 90 5356 437 0)

Clementine van Eck, *Purified by Blood: Honour Killings amongst Turks in the Netherlands*, 2002 (ISBN 978 90 5356 491 2)

Joanne van der Leun, *Looking for Loopholes: Processes of Incorporation of Illegal Immigrants in the Netherlands*, 2003 (ISBN 978 90 5356 600 8)

Marc Hooghe, *Sociaal kapitaal in Vlaanderen: verenigingen en democratische politieke cultuur*, 2003 (ISBN 978 90 5356 643 5)

Aafke E. Komter, *Solidariteit en de gift: sociale banden en sociale uitsluiting*, 2003 (ISBN 978 90 5356 645 9)

Marco van der Land, *Vluchtige verbondenheid: stedelijke bindingen van de Rotterdamse nieuwe middenklasse*, 2004 (ISBN 978 90 5356 678 7)

Frank J. Buijs, Froukje Demant and Atef Hamdy, *Strijders van eigen bodem: radicale en democratische moslims in Nederland*, 2006 (ISBN 978 90 5356 916 0)

Strategic Affection?

Gift Exchange in Seventeenth-Century Holland

Irma Thoen

Amsterdam University Press

The publication of this book has been made possible by donations from the European University Institute, the J.E. Jurriaanse Stichting, Stichting Dr. Hendrik Muller's Vaderlandsch Fonds, and the M.A.O.C. Gravin van Bylandt Stichting.

Cover illustration: Dirck Hals, *A Party at Table* (1626), The National Gallery, London

Cover design: Sabine Mannel, NEON grafische vormgeving, Amsterdam
Layout: JAPES, Amsterdam

ISBN-13	978 90 5356 811 8
ISBN-10	90 5356 811 5
NUR	757

Table of Contents

Acknowledgements

Naturally a work like this can not be completed without the help of family, friends and professional contacts. Some of these people have helped me through their academic knowledge and critical remarks on my work, some of them have inspired me through the discussions we had, and others were there to support and positively distract me. Although it is impossible to mention all these people by name, there are a few that I wish to thank explicitly.

First of all I want to extend my gratitude to my supervisor, Peter Becker. Although his field of expertise does not include seventeenth-century Holland nor gift exchange, he has proved himself willing and able to supervise this book. Secondly, I wish to thank my co-supervisor, Willem Frijhoff. Not only is his knowledge of early-modern Dutch history – and many other things – unsurpassed, the swiftness with which he reads and corrects texts is unequalled.

Other academic contacts that have helped me throughout the years are Ingrid van der Vlis, who helped me with my database project, and Alexander Geppert, who taught me the advantages of a good bibliographical program. I am also indebted to Professor Arjo Klamer and the participants of his 'Value of Culture' seminar as well as to the participants of Frijhoff's 'Cultural History' seminar.

Alexandra van Dongen, curator at the Boijmans Van Beuningen Museum, and Cora Laan are responsible for introducing me to the field of material culture. The Meertens Institute in Amsterdam has welcomed me to do my research on the 'Letters to the Future'. With Rudolf Dekker I discussed ego-documents in seventeenth-century Holland, and with Jeroen Blaak I discussed the same and many other research issues. I also want to thank Jeroen for his hospitality; he was kind enough to share his office with me whenever I was in Holland for one of my 'missions'.

Naturally I also want to thank my parents. They have always been very supportive of me, in every way they possibly could. Still the most important gift they have offered me throughout my life is their faith that I can do whatever I set my mind to. I hope this book is proof that they were right about me all along.

Last but conventionally not least, I want to thank Serge for all his practical and mental support. I could have probably written this book without you, but with you it has been so much more fun and so much more interesting.

Irma Thoen
September 2006

Introduction

When in 1624 Constantijn Huygens was staying in London with an official delegation, he received a number of letters from Dorothea van Dorp.[1] Dorothea lived next to the Huygens family in The Hague and had once been his childhood sweetheart. In these letters she not only kept him informed on the latest gossip of high society in The Hague, but she also urged Huygens on several occasions to have Lady Killigrew, a mutual acquaintance, send her a present.[2] On 24 March Dorothea wrote:

> "I wish lady Killigrew would send me a little golden ring."[3]

A month later she received a number of gemstones from this Lady Killigrew, for which Dorothea thanked her through the mediation of Huygens. In May, Dorothea sent Lady Killigrew a present; a bracelet made of amber. This gift was presumably also offered upon request, for it was accompanied by a letter to Huygens which stated:

> "I am glad there is something she wishes to have from me. This and everything I possess in this world is at her disposal. She will do me great honour by wearing it, with which she will greatly oblige me to her. Tell her that it comes from someone who is more her servant than anyone has ever been, notwithstanding all the people that love her."[4]

These phrases about Lady Killigrew went on for a while, after which Dorothea directed her attentions once more to Huygens himself:

> "I beg you: do not forget the little ring she has promised me."[5]

This begging for gifts seems to suggest that Dorothea was a rather bad-mannered young girl; it is definitely not a way in which one would expect "a humble servant" to behave. Yet Dorothea van

Dorp came from an old, noble family.[6] Her father had played an important role in the liberation of the Dutch from the Spanish, and had made an impressive career for himself in the military. He died as the governor of Tholen, Zeeland, in 1612 and was buried at The Hague. His second wife, Sara van Trello, moved to The Hague after his demise, and brought Dorothea, who was born from his first marriage to Anna Schets, along to live with her.[7] In The Hague they lived at the *Voorhout*, which was then – and still is – a very classy lane in the centre of town.[8] In 1614, the Huygens family had moved into the house next to the Van Dorp residence, which is when the friendship between Dorothea and Constantijn Huygens started.

The Huygens family was part of the regent class of the Dutch Republic. Constantijn's father, Christian Huygens, was one of the secretaries of the Council of State and therewith one of the highest state officials in the Dutch Republic. Constantijn himself was also trained to become a high-ranking government official in due course. His trip to London in 1624 was only one of the starting points of his career. He was a minor delegate of these official state missions to England, but later he followed in his father's footsteps as the secretary to the stadholders, besides which he was also to become one of the more famous poets of that period.[9]

Considering that both Dorothea and Constantijn were members of elite families and their upbringing will have reflected this social position, it is unlikely that their conniving over Lady Killigrew's gifts was just a matter of bad behaviour. Moreover, Dorothea had by this time passed the age of thirty. Her bold insistence on receiving these gifts from Lady Killigrew will therefore also not have derived from childish greed. Besides which, the remark about the amber bracelet suggests that Lady Killigrew herself did not find it inappropriate to indicate what gift she wished to receive from Dorothea. It seems that this behaviour was acceptable between these two upper class individuals and Constantijn Huygens obviously did not object to playing his role in the whole mediation of the exchange of these gifts either.

However, the picture painted here does leave the modern beholder with a somewhat peculiar feeling. There is a sense of inappropriateness to this behaviour, which is caused by Dorothea's explicitness in asking for gifts and her explicitness as to what gifts she wished to receive. Even though this explicitness does exist in contemporary society as such – it is not considered inappropriate, for instance, for children to make a wish list for Christmas – it is generally considered "not done" to ask for a gift. If this does occur at all, it is more likely associated with childish behaviour, begging or corruption than with a friendly exchange of gifts.[10] This implies that the cultural conventions, or rules of behaviour, that surrounded gift exchange in the seventeenth-century may have been rather different from the conventions that apply to contemporary – in the sense of turn of the twentieth century – gift exchange.[11]

Defining the Gift

An analytical reconstruction of gift-exchange practices needs to start with at least a tentative definition of the gift. Interestingly enough, despite all the literature on gift exchange in the social sciences most social scientists do not define their topic of research in full detail. This might seem like a disadvantage, but, on the other hand, it might not be such a brilliant idea to define gift and gift exchange in advance. Since hardly anything is known about gift exchange in seventeenth-century Holland and the assumption is that gift exchange then might have been rather different from gift exchange now, it seems sensible to start off with a rather open frame of mind. Any definition thought up beforehand might impose a contemporary view on the seventeenth-century sources, while the idea behind this research is to study gift exchange as it was perceived by individuals in the cultural context of seventeenth-century Dutch society.

Nevertheless, some reference point is obviously needed, as to what can actually be considered gifts. Gifts in this research include both material gifts, such as objects, food and drink, money and artistic or intellectual gifts, and immaterial gifts, such as hospitality and support.[12] Objects can be any type of gifts in objectified form, be it kitchen utensils or pottery that is used for decoration. Food and drink, in contrast to hospitality, is offered outside of one's own home, whereas hospitality is considered to be all offerings of food, drink and lodging within the confines of the home of the giver. Artistic and intellectual gifts are those gifts that spring from the artistic and intellectual efforts of the giver, be it poems, paintings and prints or treatises and books. Support can be offered in several forms, such as practical, financial and emotional support. Some of these types of gifts may be perishable, like food and drink, while others are more likely to have survived the tests of time, such as silver objects.

The character of these different types of gifts will be further explored in the chapters that follow. The advantage of working with such a broad range of gifts is that it leaves an opportunity to trace the full extent of reciprocal exchange in seventeenth-century Holland. Therewith, it can hopefully offer full insight into how individuals in seventeenth-century Holland used gifts as a means to establish and maintain social ties, and how gift exchange as a system was organised.

If so many different things can be gifts, when does an object or an activity enter the sphere of gift exchange, when the same exact object or activity could also be part of an economic transaction? Undoubtedly the line between gift exchanges and economic transactions is sometimes difficult to draw. The contemporary idea of an economic transaction would be that a certain object, activity or service is exchanged for money, yet in the early modern period an economic exchange may well have involved payment in kind. On the other hand, even today money itself can function as a gift and in those cases it is definitely not seen as a form of payment. Sums of money that grandparents offer their grandchildren on occasions such as birthdays are seen as gifts and not as payment.

So what makes a gift? Where does one draw the line between gift exchange and economic transaction? This all depends on the parties involved. It is a necessity that at least one of the parties involved in the exchange of the gift – either the giver or the recipient – thinks of the gift as such. For it is only by either explicitly or implicitly acknowledging an object or activity as a gift that it becomes one. For that reason, all cases that are considered or referred to as gifts by the seventeenth-century subjects involved will be considered gifts, even when the exchange for the contemporary onlooker seems to have more to do with economic exchange or barter than with gift giving. It is the subjects involved that distinguish gift exchange behaviour from economic behaviour.[13]

One way of doing this is through their discourse on this behaviour. Through the use of words that refer to the exchange of gifts, the actual offering turns into a gift. Words that belong to the rhetoric of the gift in seventeenth-century Holland are *gift*, *geschenk*, *schenkagie* and *gave*, which can all be translated as gifts, and *vereering*, which means honouring by giving.

It is not just the terminology that makes the gift, it is also the context in which something is offered that makes the subjects interpret the offering as a gift. Certain occasions, for instance, are strongly connected to gift exchange rituals and on these occasions it is clear to all parties involved that the things offered on these occasions are gifts. Gifts that guests bring to wedding, for example, are generally acknowledged as such. Nobody will wonder whether these gifts were in fact part of an economic transaction. Over all, one might say that this research deals with all those objects and activities that are offered within a (possible) pattern of reciprocity not as an economic transaction but as a means to establish or maintain social ties.

However, there are also situations that are not obviously connected to gift exchange rituals and that do not include a discourse of gift exchange. Dorothea, for instance, does not use the terminology of gift exchange when she refers to the ring and bracelet she exchanged with Lady Killigrew in her letters to Huygens. Still both Lady Killigrew and Dorothea will have thought of their mutual offerings as a friendly exchange of gifts rather than anything else. As Dorothea mentioned, she thought it an honour that Lady Killigrew would wear a bracelet that she had offered her. So, even though this is not considered gift exchange behaviour in the eye of the contemporary beholder, to Dorothea and Lady Killigrew it was, which poses the question of how this behaviour can be explained within the cultural context of seventeenth-century Holland.

Gifts in Theory

Social relations and instrumentality in the early modern period

Dorothea's behaviour may be explained by the supposed instrumental character of social relations in the early modern period. Several historians have reflected upon the idea that the existence of affection and intimacy within social relations is a modern phenomenon that only began developing in the seventeenth and eighteenth century, and was not necessarily a feature of relations in the early modern period. This lack of affection supposedly applied to relationships within marriage – between husband and

wife; within the family; between parents and children; and between friends.[14]

It has been argued, for instance, that marriages in the early
modern period consisted of alliances between families, rather
than affectionate relationships between husband and wife. Parents looked for partners for their children that would best suit
their family interests in terms of financial gain, career perspec-
tives, status and healthy progeny. In that sense, marriage in the
early modern period was about strategy and allegiance instead of
affection or even love. The ideal of romantic love between spouses
would only develop during the course of the eighteenth and nineteenth century.[15]

The relationship between parents and children in the early
modern period has also been claimed by several authors to be devoid of affection. The high infant mortality rate caused parents
and especially mothers to refrain from developing any feelings for
their children in order not to be hurt when the child died. Not only
was there a lack of general affection for children, they were largely
neglected during their upbringing as such. The idea of the child as
a specific category in need of special care and attention only developed in the course of time, while the concept of motherly love did
not surface until the eighteenth century.[16]

Outside the family, this lack of affection has also been described
by historians. Friendship, for instance, was, like any other type of
relationship, just a means to an end. Friendship was mostly instrumental in character and would just be maintained for the mutual benefit of the involved.[17] The idea of friendship in the modern sense of the word of people sharing certain interests, enjoying
each others company and developing feelings of affection for each
other is considered to be the result of the Romantic era in the
eighteenth century.[18]

One might say that friendship as a system was a type of carpool-
ing. When necessary, people used the social capital of their friends
to obtain whatever it was they needed – be it a favour, a job or a
spouse – and there was a mutual understanding that whenever
their friends in turn were in need of their social capital they would
be reciprocated for the help earlier received. This means that the
offering of support was expected to be reciprocated and while the
reciprocation had not yet taken place, the recipient of the initial
support was "obliged to" his benefactor. If the recipient in time

failed to live up to this expectation of reciprocation, it was likely to bring disgrace.[19]

Naturally, these claims by some historians have been strongly opposed by others who have pointed out that both marital and parental love, and friendly affection did indeed exist before the eighteenth century.[20] Yet, even though there is an ongoing discussion on parental love, emotions and friendship in the early modern period, there seems to be a general agreement that instrumentality can be considered a prominent feature of Dutch society in the seventeenth and eighteenth centuries. As Frijhoff and Spies stated in their *1650 Bevochten Eendracht*: "Friendship in the early modern period was a notion that not so much expressed an affective tie as an instrumental one, even though affection was decidedly part of proper friendly intercourse."[21] Friendship – in the broadest sense of the word including both family relations and friendship proper – consisted of a form of solidarity between individuals and groups with coinciding interests, who depended on each other for practical help and moral support.

However well argued and convincing some of these views are, the generalisation that social relations in the early modern period are predominantly instrumental is in some respects rather problematic. First of all, this generalisation – by describing general patterns of human relations – seems to deny the fact that there are real human beings involved in these relationships who might offer different meanings to their behaviour than historians do. Or, in other words, the patterns that can be described with the benefit of hindsight were not necessarily intentional patterns for the individuals that constitute these patterns. Two individuals who get married, just get married and do not therewith intentionally establish a particular marriage pattern, even though later on the marriages of a great number of individuals might add up to a pattern. The bride and groom might, consciously or unconsciously, be adjusting to social conventions, but the objective analysis that can be made of this behaviour does not necessarily coincide with the subjective experience of the couple involved. This probes the question of whether these individual human beings then interpreted their social contacts in the same instrumental manner as historians do now. Did early modern individuals ascribe the same instrumental meanings to their behaviour within social relationships as contemporary historians do?

The second problem with these instrumental views of social relations in the early modern period is that by defining these relations as instrumental it is suggested that this instrumentality is typical for the described period and for that period only. Whereas some historians have just analysed the early modern period and have come to the conclusion that this – in social terms – was an instrumental period, others have actually explicitly argued that there has been a development from instrumental to affectionate ties. Whether implicitly or explicitly, in both cases the stress is on change rather than continuity, on historical development rather than anthropological perpetuity and the standard by which this change is measured is usually – but never explicitly – the society of which the author himself is part.

Yet, one might wonder whether social relations then were actually so different from social relations now. If one takes contemporary marriage patterns, for instance, it becomes clear that most individuals, even though they have the freedom of choice, still marry within their own peer group, which consists of people with the same level of education and same social status. This would imply on an analytical level that they, like seventeenth-century individuals, are mostly concerned with maintaining their social capital, while, in fact, the contemporary discourse on marriage is one of love and affection. This probes the question of whether the instrumentality of social relations is really typical of the early modern period.

These two questions – the one on the individuals interpretation of his social behaviour and the other on instrumentality as a typical trait of early modern social relations – direct the attention to yet another question: the question of how one can answer these questions. How can the meanings that individuals ascribed to their social behaviour and their social relations be researched? And how can one know that instrumentality is typical for the early modern period? These two questions require two different approaches in answering them. The first approach needs to offer an opportunity to deal with individual social behaviour in the early modern period and the ways in which relationships in that period were maintained and interpreted, while the second question implies a need for comparison. It is only by comparing levels of instrumentality in the early modern period with those of another period that the supposed instrumental character of the former can be established. But first and foremost, a vehicle is needed through which social relations – in any period, but the early modern period in particular – can be studied.

In this research, the exchange of gifts is taken as the vehicle through which the character of social relations in seventeenth-century Holland is analysed. This choice for gift exchange is manifold. First of all, gift exchange is a phenomenon that until recently has largely been ignored by cultural historians of the early modern period. Works have been published on related themes such as marriage exchange, charity and credit.[22] Still there is only one cultural/social historical research document that deals with the phenomenon of gift exchange in the early modern period: Natalie Davis's *The Gift in Sixteenth-Century France.* [23]

This lack of historical interest in gift exchange is rather surprising, since there has been considerable interest in historical anthropology (or anthropological history) over the last decade and traditionally, the gift has always been a very prominent topic in the field of anthropology.[24] Therefore, it would have seemed unavoidable that the gift as a historical research topic would have gained momentum sooner than it eventually did. However, this means that, especially within the historiography of the Dutch Republic, the field of gift exchange is a largely unexplored territory and therewith an exciting voyage to embark upon.

The Dutch Republic experienced its Golden Age during the seventeenth-century. It had freed itself from the Spanish domination, overseas exploration brought relative wealth, and the arts and sciences blossomed in the Dutch climate of relative tolerance. The Dutch were known as a bourgeois and Calvinistic people who enjoyed making money more than spending it, which makes their gift exchange behaviour especially interesting. Even though the Dutch Golden Age has always been an epoch of great interest to historians and art historians alike, relatively little has been written on and is known about the exchange of gifts in seventeenth-century Holland.

This is surprising in the sense that, in general, every possible topic of Dutch society in that period has been covered; monographs have been published on subjects ranging from Dutch humour to civil servants and from widows to friendship associations.[25]

There are, however, a number of Dutch studies that deal with the exchange of gifts in a more indirect manner. These either use theoretical notions from gift exchange theory to study more or less institutional forms of exchange, like charity, and the ways in which poverty was dealt with by seventeenth-century individuals.[26] Or they discuss the exchange of gifts as a part of a larger concept such as friendship in the early modern period.[27] Furthermore, there are a number of older works, from the turn of the century, that deal with daily life among "our Dutch ancestors" that refer to events and occasions in this period that involved the exchange of gifts, such as birth and calendar feasts.[28] However, before sailing off to the rather unexplored island of gift exchange in seventeenth-century Holland, the rather over-explored concept of the gift and gift-exchange in the social sciences deserves some attention.

Gift exchange and the social sciences

Ever since the publication of Marcel Mauss's *Essai sur le Don*, gift exchange has been a topic of great interest in the social sciences.[29] It is a popular research theme in fields ranging from cultural anthropology to sociology and from social psychology to consumer research and within all of these fields of study, Mauss is referred to as the initiator of gift-exchange research.

As with the discussion on the existence of affection in early modern relationships, when it comes to the development of gift exchange through time there seem to be two streams within gift-exchange theory. One of these favours the discontinuity and the other the continuity of the gift exchange system. In the first case, it is claimed that the gift exchange system over time has been overtaken by an economic system of market exchange. According to this view "gifts historically performed primarily economic functions".[30] It is acknowledged that gift exchange does still exist today but it is more or less considered only a remnant of days gone by. The idea is that, over time, the gift system was largely overtaken by the market system.

Others have adhered to a more continuous view in which the gift exchange system proceeds to exist next to a system of market exchange. According to this view gift exchange is still very much alive and has its own (social) function within the larger context in which these systems exist.[31] Authors like Macharel have argued that even "in industrial societies where most exchange is governed by the market, entire sectors of social life are ruled by the gift".[32]

This is also a statement to the effect that money and gifts are actually not only able to but actually exist side by side, and perform their own specific roles as well. This coincides with Natalie Davis's remark that more recently a new generation of anthropologists and historians have emerged who claim that "rather than a gift system eventually being superseded by a market system, gift elements persist with new connections and consequences".[33]

As will be shown throughout this research, the latter view that gift exchange is a system with a continuous role within the history of human society, seems to be the most convincing. Here gift exchange is considered an anthropological given. As is stated in the *Encyclopaedia of Human Emotions* "giving and receiving is a practice common to all cultures in the world".[34] It is a phenomenon that exists in any time and place, irrespective of the level of economic development of the society under scrutiny. The gift system exists parallel to the economic system and is not a replacement of it, nor a contradiction to it. The two systems may interfere and influence each other in certain instances, but, in general, the gift system is a system with its own specific function within human society.

This specific function within society is largely caused by one of the features of gift exchange that social scientists generally agree upon. Gift exchange is commonly accepted as a means to establish and maintain social ties, but not only that: Gifts are also viewed as a sign of the existence or coming into existence of a social tie.[35] As Schmied has put it in his work on giving as a form of social practice: "*Geschenken dienen [...] dem Ausdruck, der Bestätigung oder Bekräftigung sozialer Beziehungen*".[36] A slightly more down to earth statement that basically comes down to the same thing is Cheal's remark that "gifts are the cement of social relationships".[37] As such, gifts serve as a good means to study social relations in the early modern period: they were a tool in the maintenance of these relationships and at the same time an indication of the existence of a relationship.

The question is how gifts actually function as the cement which holds society together. According to Gouldner, it is the principle of reciprocity that makes the exchange of gifts possible.[38] This norm prescribes that for each gift offered there must be a gift returned. It therewith helps individuals to initiate a relationship by offering the first gift, because due to this norm they can be certain that their initial efforts will be reciprocated, and through this norm existing relationships are further stabilised by the offering of more gifts. Therewith the norm of reciprocity makes it less risky for individuals to initiate and maintain a relationship: through the norm of reciprocity, the recipient is always socially bound to reciprocate received attentions.[39] This doesn't mean, however, that for every gift offered there has to be a gift of equal form and value in return, or that reciprocity has to be balanced under all circumstances. Instead, it is through the expectation of reciprocity by the donor and the feeling of obligation to reciprocate by the recipient that the relationship is maintained. People are bound together by the expectation of reciprocity.

It is exactly this feature of gift exchange that makes it such a suitable vehicle for studying social relations. Naturally, the assumptions that gift exchange is a means to establish and maintain social ties and that reciprocity is a basic principle of its functioning, stress the instrumental character of gift exchange as a social act. In that sense, one might assume that this research could be concluded right here and now: if one studies social relations through the exchange of gifts and one assumes that the exchange of gifts is instrumental by nature, then it seems obvious that social relations are likely to be instrumental as well. However, authors like Bourdieu and Komter have offered an opportunity to interpret gift exchange behaviour in a broader sense than just instrumental interpretations. As Komter argues, with reference to Bourdieu, a vital part of (contemporary) gift giving is that:

> Gift giving, though in many cases objectively fitting within a pattern of reciprocity, is subjectively felt to be essentially a non-economic, spontaneous and altruistic activity, meant to communicate personal feelings instead of being a exchange transaction.[40]

In short, a distinction is made between the subjective experience of gift exchange behaviour and the objective analysis that can be made of this behaviour. This seems to differ from what happens in the historic discipline. Whereas some historians – when they discuss social relations in the early modern period – assume that individuals were then following the patterns that are now described in their writings, social scientists consider the possibility that whatever they describe as a pattern does not necessarily coincide with the individual's interpretation of his behaviour. The idea that there might be a difference between the objective patterns of human behaviour and the subject's interpretation of this behaviour actually does seem to be rather fruitful. If this applies to contemporary gift exchange, why wouldn't it also apply to social relations and the exchange of gifts therein in the early modern period? In that case, Dorothea may not have considered her own behaviour, as described in the beginning of this introduction, as obviously instrumental as historians and other contemporary onlookers might.

But if gift exchange as a social act is an anthropological given then why does Dorothea's behaviour seem so out of the ordinary for contemporary onlookers? This is explained by the fact that even though gift exchange is a phenomenon that exists in any place and time and is therewith invariant, the rules and regulations, or cultural conventions that surround the exchange of gifts are dependent upon the specific cultural context in which the exchange takes place.[41] Dorothea's behaviour obviously does not live up to the expectations that contemporary onlookers have of proper gift exchange. Their expectations are based on the cultural conventions that surround the exchange of gifts in contemporary society, but the example of Dorothea shows that seventeenth-century gift exchange may have been organised quite differently.

These conventions usually consist of unwritten rules and are usually followed unconsciously.[42] As Malinowski put it in his *Crime and Custom in Savage Society*:

> Though no native, however intelligent, can formulate this state of affairs in a general and abstract manner, or present it as a social theory, everyone is well aware of its existence and in each concrete case he can foresee the consequences.[43]

Although this remark neither refers to Western nor to contemporary society, social scientists who deal with contemporary Western gift exchange often reflect upon this issue in the same manner. Gift exchange and the unwritten rules that determine it have both been barely reflected upon by the individuals involved. They deal with their exchange of gifts in a rather subconscious manner.[44] Gift giving belongs to the sphere of practical knowledge: without knowing the exact rules, we know how to play the game.[45]

This, however, has not stopped other social scientists from trying to describe or specify the rules of the game. Caplow, for instance, has filtered out a number of the unwritten rules that regulate Christmas gift giving from the ways in which people celebrate Christmas in Middletown.[46] An example of one of the rules he describes for Christmas gift exchange is what he calls the Gift Selection Rule. This rule prescribes that the gift should demonstrate the giver's familiarity with the recipient's preferences. Furthermore, it should surprise the recipient by either expressing more affection for or knowledge of the recipient than could be expected and lastly, the gift should be scaled in economic value to the emotional value of the relationship.[47] Caplow convincingly argues that this system of rules is enforced by the participants without them being aware of it and without reference to a system.[48] Caplow's findings also reveal that a distinction should be made between the subjective experience of gift exchange and the objective analysis that can be made of it.

In fact, the aforementioned quotation by Komter is not only a good example of the distinction between subjective experience and objective analyses, it also nicely shows what some of the conventions are that apply to contemporary Dutch gift exchange. It says that subjects experience their gift exchange behaviour as a non-economic activity instead of as an exchange transaction, it is felt to be spontaneous and altruistic, and meant to communicate personal feelings.[49] Analytically, there is a lot to be said against this subjective view of gift exchange. Although the subjects do not experience their offerings of gifts as being part of an exchange transaction, the offering of a birthday gift to a friend does, however, bring with it the expectation that this same friend will offer a gift in return when the time comes.

Moreover, it is difficult to maintain that gifts are generally offered spontaneously and out of one's free will. Although the subject may experience his offerings this way, there are cultural conventions that prescribe on what occasions gifts should be offered in order for the subject to remain a respected member of his social circle. In contemporary society it is considered unheard-of to attend a wedding party without offering the happy couple a gift, and parents who refuse to give their children gifts for Christmas or St. Nicholas, the Dutch counterpart, will not be highly regarded by their social environments. In that respect, a lot of gift-giving occasions have a rather obligatory character.

Even the type of gift that is supposed to be offered on certain occasions does not leave a lot of room for spontaneous interference. When one is invited for dinner in the Netherlands, a guest should bring flowers, a nice bottle of wine or chocolates, but it is unlikely and unnecessary to bring anything more costly or substantial. With respect to cultural conventions, it is interesting to note here that in Italy the offering of a bottle of wine at a dinner party would be regarded as an insult. It would imply that one does not trust the host to select a good wine for his guests to have with dinner.

These obligatory features of gift exchange can probably be traced in seventeenth-century exchange as well as other periods. However, there seems to be this convention, especially in contemporary exchange, of denying these obligations and requirements, at least in the dominant discourse of gift exchange.[50] Another convention that is typical for contemporary exchange is the idea that gifts are expressions of personal feelings towards the recipient. It remains to be seen whether this was also a cultural convention in seventeenth-century gift exchange. Moreover, even for contemporary gift exchange this is a convention that is more part of the discourse on exchange than of the actual exchange practice. But this will have to be explored further in later chapters.

Gifts as instruments or tokens of affection?

Given the invariable character of gift exchange over time as a system of practical knowledge, the goal of this research is to describe the otherwise unwritten rules, or cultural conventions, that gave shape to gift exchange in seventeenth-century Holland. My approach is basically analytical.

On one level of analysis, the exchange of gifts and the cultural conventions that underpin it will be analysed on the basis of the practices of gift exchange. The practices of gift exchange are constituted by the occasions on which individuals in seventeenth-century Holland were exchanging gifts, the gifts they would exchange on these occasions, and the networks in which these exchanges took place. So, in fact, the practices coincide with the question of who was giving what to whom on what occasions.[51]

On a second level, a "discourse analysis of gift exchange" deals with the ways in which individuals in seventeenth-century Holland dealt with the exchange of gifts in words.[52] This can be traced through the sources they have left behind, and how gift exchange and related topics are discussed and referred to in these sources.

The ways in which gift exchanges leave traces in historic sources is important in this respect, as is the way in which the individuals who have left these sources discuss the exchanges they have ventured into. These references can help determine whether individuals in this period perceived their gift exchange behaviour as instrumental in keeping up their social relations, or whether to them it was a matter of sympathy or affection to offer gifts to friends and family. Attention will also be paid to related topics like gratitude and reciprocity.

The third level of analysis is a comparison of seventeenth-century and contemporary gift exchange. It is striking to realise that our otherwise rather subconscious knowledge of contemporary gift exchange conventions seems to surface in contrast to the behaviour exposed by Dorothea. It is not that her behaviour enables the contemporary onlooker to make these otherwise unwritten rules explicit, but at least it makes him aware that this is not how it is done in contemporary society. Therefore, in order to establish the peculiarities of seventeenth-century Dutch conventions on gift exchange, they are confronted with contemporary conventions of gift exchange. It is through comparison – or rather confrontation – that the familiarities and peculiarities of seventeenth-century gift exchange behaviour become the clearest.

The purpose of all this is to find out whether gifts in seventeenth-century Holland were mere instruments or whether they were conceived as tokens of affection, and how the gift's various roles intermingled. Another question that will be answered is in what way this was typical for Dutch society in that period as compared to gift exchange in contemporary Dutch society. It is presumed that an analysis of gift exchange in this way also offers an insight into the character of social relations in the seventeenth century. In that sense, this research might help nuance the existing view of the calculating early modern individual, while at the same time, contribute to the existing knowledge of gift exchange as a social practice.

Sources and Methodology

The question remains how these practices of, and discourses on, gift exchange in seventeenth-century Holland can best be studied. Several different types of sources have been considered in this respect, ranging from written documents, to visual sources to material objects. Some of these turned out to be more fruitful than others. However, the main interest in this research are the ways in which individuals in seventeenth-century Holland used gifts as a means to establish social ties, and to analyse how they experienced this exchange of gifts and what unwritten rules applied to this social practice. Since individual exchange is central to this research, it needs to be based on sources that actually offer an insight into the daily life and practices of individuals during this period.

As such, this research excludes other types of exchange that are of a more institutional nature, like diplomatic exchange and charity.[53] With that, it also excludes those sources that would provide information on these types of exchange, like official reports of diplomatic delegations or the records of poorhouses. The main body of research material consists of egodocuments. Other than that, use has also been made of seventeenth-century literature like plays and emblem books, material objects, and probate inventories.

Egodocuments

What Dutch historians have come to refer to as *egodocuments* are in fact exquisite sources for the purpose of this research. The term "egodocument" was introduced by Jacob Presser in 1958 and refers to a diversity of sources, such as diaries, autobiographies, memoirs, travel reports and letters, which have in common that they are written from an I- or We-perspective. These are documents in which the author reveals something about himself, his actions or his feelings.[54] Initially, historians were rather sceptical about the possibilities for this type of source. Even the introduction to a special issue on egodocuments in the *Tijdschrift voor Geschiedenis* included a statement to this effect:

> The historian who occupies himself intensively with research based solely on egodocuments for an extended period of time, will not estimate the possibilities [they offer] for acquiring true knowledge, or for reconstructing the past very highly. He will easily generalise his findings and will turn to a form of historic scepticism.[55]

Even though the authors of this statement acknowledged that in most other written documents the author, either directly or indirectly, also reveals something about himself and therewith may be deemed less objective than generally assumed, they went on to argue that the common difficulty with egodocuments is that it is impossible to distinguish between *Dichtung* and *Wahrheit*, or fiction and fact. The authors claimed that since these egodocuments were so obviously subjective they should only be used in cases where no other form of historical evidence existed.

Nevertheless, in the article that followed this introduction, Von der Dunk did state that historians could not do without the historic individual. The discipline of history became, in the period from 1920 to 1970, more and more anti-individualistic. Most of the research focused on the social, economic and demographic aspects of the past, and the individual had been largely neglected in that process.[56] Von der Dunk, however, believed that the historic individual deserved more attention. This renewed interest in the individual gained ground when the focus of some historians turned from socio-economic history to the history of mentalities and cultural history. Their interest in the history of daily life resulted in a renewed attention for the individual, the ways in which he perceived his life, and the sources he left behind.[57]

In that respect, egodocuments are indeed very welcome sources in this research. It is not that other sources are lacking, but for the purpose of the questions posed in this research, the subjective character of these sources is an advantage rather than a disadvantage, especially because the interest is not only in the practices of exchange, but also in the meanings that seventeenth-century individuals ascribed to their gift-exchange practices.

However useful these sources are, Dutch egodocument expert Rudolf Dekker has rightly argued that it is important to be aware of how the specific documents came about and why they were written in order to interpret this material in a sensible manner.[58] Diaries, for instance, originally had a business-like character. They derived from the petty cash books people kept to keep track of their receipts and expenditures. Sometimes printed almanacs provided opportunities for their owners to take notes as well.

These notes were initially short and very "matter of fact", but in the course of the seventeenth century, they became more personal. The seventeenth century is generally seen as a period of transition from the external diary, with a function in the public life of the writer, to the internal diary that helped the writer to deal with his or her mental well-being. This was caused by developments in the religious sphere and spirituality in general. Religion became to be seen as a matter of someone having a personal relationship with God and keeping a diary was an introspective means of maintaining this relationship. It was only in the eighteenth century that the diary evolved into the *journal intime*, which was used as a means of acquiring self-knowledge.[59]

A more profane reason for keeping a diary was as a support for one's memory. People used their diaries later in life as a source for writing their memoirs or autobiographies. This is shown by the accurate knowledge of dates. It was in any case uncommon to write notes in a diary on a daily basis. The diary of David Beck, which serves as one of the main sources for this research, is a welcome exception to this rule.

However, some diaries are themselves based on earlier notes. Most of the remaining diaries are the neat versions of earlier records.[60] Of course, this makes these diaries less spontaneous accounts of the past than expected. In writing the neat version at a later time, people had the opportunity to revise certain aspects or take into consideration later developments. The notes on which these diaries were based have usually not survived.

Autobiographies, meanwhile, have a rather different background; they originally functioned as chronicles. Some of them were related to oral traditions: in earlier texts, people appear to have written down what they traditionally would have told. Autobiography did not develop until the sixteenth century as a specific genre with its own forms and rules.[61] This development coincided with the gradual construction of the concept of individuality and the growing awareness of time. [62] Another factor was the growing internalisation of the faith, which by that time was a requirement for all confessions.[63]

In general, the character of autobiographies is more public than that of diaries, even when the document is written by hand. The text is constructed more consciously since the author wishes to present himself in a certain way towards his readers and he also makes more use of contemporary literary traditions. [64] This is even more obvious in the case of printed autobiographies. Before the nineteenth century, however, it was considered inappropriate and a sign of vanity to have one's autobiography published.[65] Seventeenth-century autobiographies that have survived in print were usually printed after the author had died.

The development of these types of egodocuments has often been connected to the process of individualisation and the rise of the bourgeoisie. Dekker, for instance, argues that, on the one hand, the bourgeoisie supposedly had a stronger need for self-reflection and a more profound sense of individuality than other social groups. However, on the other hand, he claims that a lot of these documents were written to bridge the gap between two generations. In that sense, they seem to reflect a traditional awareness of the family more than any modern sense of individuality.[66]

Kooijmans has taken this family connection even further by claiming that diaries were used to keep track of the social capital of the family. According to him, diaries were first and foremost tools for the bookkeeping of this social capital. The information registered in a diary consisted of services received and rendered. The diaries were used to balance debits and credits on the level of social capital and were left to the next generation as a way of accounting for the activities developed by the author in order to sustain and acquire social capital.[67] Although Koijmans's analysis is convincing to a certain extent, it does ignore the complexity of the meaning given to these practices by early modern individuals.

Letters naturally have a different character altogether. They were semi-public in the sense that they were intended to be read by another party and therewith public by nature, but then again in a private form. They were usually addressed from one individual to another, although it seems that it was not uncommon for the recipient to share the letter's contents with others as well.

Writing letters was one of the few available means of distant communication in the early modern period. Mail was usually delivered on horseback, but in the Netherlands, the barge was another common mode of delivery.[68] Although one might expect differently, mail was in some ways delivered faster than in modern times. An example from the diary of David Beck shows that mail could go back and forth by barge on a day between Delft and The Hague.[69] This would nowadays take at least three days in the Netherlands. Over longer distances, however, mail delivery would obviously take days or even weeks.

Mail delivery depended partly on professional mail deliverers, who were either city officials or worked for merchant houses, and partly on personal services and consequently on the willingness of the person involved.[70] Preferably one would ask a friend or acquaintance to hand over the letter to the recipient, but even then confidentiality was not guaranteed. Since envelopes did not yet exist, people were obliged to fold and glue their letters in such a way that others could not peek at their contents. Another means of keeping one's correspondence private was by using foreign languages like French and Latin. This at least ensured that uneducated people would not be able to read them. On the other hand, it was quite normal for the upper-classes to write in French and for scholars to discuss intellectual topics in Latin. One other practical disadvantage of corresponding was the fact that it was relatively expensive. This was due both to the deliverance fees and the fact that paper was costly.[71]

In their correspondence, individuals were limited to social and cultural conventions, which could be learned through manuals of letter writing. One of the more popular manuals of the period was the *Nederduytse Secretaris oft Zendbriefschrijver* written by Daniel Mostaert. This manual was commissioned by the council of Amsterdam for which Mostaert was a secretary.[72] One of the rules was that the recipient was to be addressed with his or her proper title. Even friends would not address each other by their first names. The result of this was that letters tended to leave a very formal impression. It was also a convention for people to put a lot of effort into elaborate and artistic introductions and farewell formulas. And even between introductions and farewells one can distinguish a number of conventions, such as the habit of humiliating oneself in respect to the other as part of the modesty ritual.[73]

These conventions can be seen as a complication when one wants to use these letters as a source, but this is only the case when these letters are considered a form of spontaneous and direct expressions of affection, which would be as anachronistic as thinking of the gift as a means of expressing purely personal feelings. It is exactly these types of conventions that make the difference between one culture and the other. Gifts and letters (or at least communication) are universal, it is how people in different periods and societies deal with these "normalities" that make them so interesting for the cultural historian.

Still, the interpretation of letters does leave the historian with some complications. First of all, the writer and the recipient may refer to letters which have not survived or are otherwise unknown to the researcher. Secondly, their use of words and references depends largely on a commonly shared context and past, which the historian is not likely to know. Thirdly, the correspondents have probably left a lot of things unsaid that may be obvious to them, but not necessarily to an outsider.

Case studies

This research is based on a number of case studies of seventeenth-century Dutch individuals who have all left behind egodocuments of some sort, be it diaries, autobiographies or letters. The choice of individuals was obviously based on the question of availability of sources, but furthermore it was assumed important that the individuals involved would be of different social, economic, religious and status-backgrounds, since this should offer a broad overview of all the different aspects of gift exchange practices. In this way differences and similarities of gift exchange practices within different social environments could be detected.

Unfortunately there are too few letters by Dorothea van Dorp still remaining to have a chance of focusing on her gift exchange behaviour any further. As a matter of fact, in general, there are only a few egodocuments produced by women available from this period, and those are not necessarily useful within the framework of this research. This is due to several factors. First of all, the literary practices of women were very different than those of men. Whereas men were largely writing and corresponding in the (semi-) public sphere, women were writing largely within the private sphere. Moreover, the chances of a man's egodocument being preserved over time is presumably higher than those written by women. Thus, it is men who emerge as central to this research.

Schoolmaster David Beck, stadholder Willem Frederik van Nassau-Dietz, bailiff Pieter Corneliszoon Hooft, and furrier Herman Verbeeck will play the most prominent roles. Nevertheless, their sources will be complemented and contrasted with egodocuments by women like Maria van Reigersberch and Tesselschade Roemers Visscher, but also by other types of sources such as seventeenth-century biographies, material objects, poetry, and probate inventories. This should allow for a very broad view of seventeenth-century gift exchange practices and the way they were conceived by the Dutch.

In the following paragraphs some of the main characters of this research will be introduced in order to give some idea of who they were, what they did in life, and what type of sources they have produced.

David Beck

David Beck (1594-1634) was a protestant schoolmaster of German descent who left a diary for the year 1624, when he was living in The Hague.[74] He was born in Cologne in 1594 as the son of Stephan Beck and Sara van Arschot. Around 1612, the Beck family moved from Cologne to Emmerich, after which, in 1617, David moved to The Hague. In The Hague, he started a French school and married a woman named Roeltje van Belle. They had three children: Adriaan, Sara and Roeltje. The latter was born in December 1623, and her mother died soon after the delivery.[75] After her mother's death, the infant was placed with a wet nurse. The other two children remained with their father. David's sister Diliane took care of the household after her sister-in-law died, but she probably lived with David before this period as well. The last member of the Beck household was David's younger brother Abraham. Abraham, however, caused more trouble then he was worth, which led David to place him as an apprentice in one of the Eastern provinces of the Republic. This turned out to be a very short-term solution, however, since literally before David knew it, his young brother had fled Arnhem and had returned to The Hague.

So, when David started his diary on 1 January 1624, he had just become a widower. This might suggest that the diary is filled with the lamentations of a man who has just lost his wife and who is writing to come to terms with the bereavement. This however, is not the case. His suffering over the death of his wife is a regular theme in the diary, but it is not central to the diary, nor was it his motivation for writing it. More than anything else the diary deals with David Beck's daily life. On certain occasions David does dwell upon more personal matters, but in general, the diary is rather more descriptive than personal. As he himself wrote on the front page, it was meant as a "journal or daily history", and "a description of the year of our Lord 1624".[76] He wished to describe all of the striking things that occurred over the year and especially his own "wheelings and dealings, and everything that has happened to me and (and mine)".[77] He claims he has written the diary "with great diligence", to keep as "a sweet memory for my beloved children as a mirror of my life".[78]

The descriptive character of the diary is also manifested in the way the entries are composed. Beck writes in a certain format. He starts off every single entry in his diary with the weather conditions. Other issues are described as they happen, such as the latest news and gossip. He wrote down who came to see him, whom he went to see, whom he had dinner with and whom he met during his daily strolls through town. He also noted the letters he received and sent, the books he read, and the poems he wrote. Furthermore, he mentions when he went to church and what psalms he sang. Births, weddings and funerals are also noted. A typical diary entry is the one for 2 February:

> Den 2. Mild weather with fair sunshine and sometimes snowing, thawing in the morning a little. Wrote 1 poem and 2 ABC poems. Was visited in the evening by mr. Paulus van der Dussen accompanying me 1 hour or 2 by the fire, drinking together a pitcher of Breda beer who told me that the lay reader[79] was going to be my neighbour and had rented in the gate behind the Mirror; after that accompanied him to his door at the market, and went to visit Breckerfelt to see his drawings; from there I went to mother's for a talk and stayed there for dinner, coming home round the hour of ten; drawing up this and the other and going to bed around the hour of eleven.[80]

In general, the diary is very descriptive. In that respect it is more of a chronicle than a *journal intime*. Reading through these matter-of-fact notes on the weather and daily activities is not half as exciting as one would expect when going through another's personal writings. This is because of the general nature of diary writing at the time. Today diaries tend to reveal more personal emotions, while originally they were kept to note very basic information. For the purpose of this research, however, the descriptive nature of this diary is quite helpful. Even though it is not obvious at first glance, this entry offers several references to gift exchanges between Beck and his social environment: Beck had dinner at his mother-in-law's house , while he offered hospitality to Paulus van der Dussen in the form of some beer while talking by the fireplace. As it turns out, the Beck diary includes descriptions of these – sometimes very modest – exchanges on an almost daily basis.

Although this diary is certainly not a very personal account of his life, it does not necessarily mean this diary is nothing more than an account book. Although services received and rendered and gifts and counter-gifts are noted, it seems hard to believe that this diary was intentionally written to keep track of the social capital of the Beck family. One could claim that a family of modest means such as the Beck's had no need to keep track of their social capital, but that seems an invalid argument. Every family, whether of aristocratic, patrician or bourgeois descent, will have felt the need to hold on to their social position. In order to do so one's social capital had to at least remain stable, but preferably rise. In that respect, Beck would have had just as valid a reason to keep a diary as stadholder Willem Frederik van Nassau-Dietz.

The concept of social capital, however, is a concept that is used by scholars who want to make sense of everyday life in the past and need certain analytical tools to do so.[81] On an analytical level, diaries can serve as a source for tracing social capital and the way people behaved in order to maintain it. But on the level of day to day practices, these diaries and this behaviour were not necessarily intended as such. The maintenance of what historians have come to call social capital was, for a seventeenth-century individual, whether aristocrat, regent or schoolmaster, just a part of his everyday routine, as it probably is for individuals in contemporary Western society as well.

If David Beck considered his diary as a mirror of his life, this research accepts it to be a mirror of his life. The exceptional thing about this particular mirror however, is that it does in fact offer a view of every single day of that full year. In that respect, it offers a wonderful insight into both the daily gift exchanges that David ventured into as well as the exchange practices that surrounded occasions that were connected to the calendar year.

As he mentions in his 1624 diary, David Beck also kept a diary for the year 1623. And he might have even kept diaries for other years as well, but unfortunately these have not survived. This is a pity, because later diaries might have explained why he only remained in The Hague for such as short period of time, since he moved to Arnhem in the beginning of 1625, after having applied for a job there in the course of 1624. In Arnhem, he obtained the position of schoolmaster at a French school. Later on, Beck's friend Herman Breckerfelt and his wife also moved to Arnhem. Beck remarried in 1630 with Geertruijt Jansdr Noot. They had three more children.

Pieter Corneliszoon Hooft

Unlike David Beck, who was of a rather modest background, Pieter Corneliszoon Hooft (1581-1647) was the son of a rich, Reformed merchant who had climbed his way up the regent echelons of Amsterdam after the purges of the civic administration in 1578. At this time, Amsterdam had joined the Revolt against Spain, one of the consequences of which was that Catholic regents were expelled from office allowing new (non-Catholic) regent families to emerge.[82] These new regents were usually wealthy Calvinist merchants. Pieter himself was to become a merchant as well, but as it turned out he was more inclined to study, and write poetry. He was sent to Leiden University to study law. This paid off, for Hooft became the first burgher to obtain the position of high bailiff, an office which was traditionally occupied by the nobility.[83]

As the bailiff of Muiden, he served as the highest civic and judicial authority in the region and was responsible for the prosecution and detention of criminals, and the requisition of men and arms in times of war. Another professional obligation was the maintenance and improvement of Muiden's castle, which was an important stronghold in the province of Holland's line of defence. During his term in office, the enemy threat was, however, only felt twice – in 1624 and 1629 – which meant that life in general in Muiden was relatively quiet.

This allowed him to spend a lot of time on his writings. In the early years, Hooft wrote and published numerous poems and several plays. He preferred to write in the vernacular and actually made a strong effort, in co-operation with Joost van den Vondel and others, to improve Dutch to classic Latin standards. Later in life, his focus turned from poetry to prose. He published a biography of Henry IV of France and finally published his *Nederlandsche Histoorien* in 1642.[84] Through the mediation of his friend Constantijn Huygens, who was by that time secretary to the stadholder, Hooft was allowed to dedicate this magnus opus to Frederik Hendrik.[85]

In later centuries, Hooft became more noted for his interesting circle of friends than his actual writings. In the summer, he would be joined at the castle of Muiden by scholars, artists and other interesting people from upper-class Dutch society, such as Huygens, Tesselschade Roemers Visscher, Barlaeus, Bredero and even Grotius. This group was supposedly called the *Muiderkring*, or at least it was introduced as such in the nineteenth century by Busken Huet in his *Land van Rembrandt*.[86] From Hooft's correspondence it is clear however that although some of these people were actually friends, while others, like Grotius, may have visited Muiden once, this social circle was not as tight as Dutch schoolchildren have been taught over the last century.[87]

The correspondence of P.C. Hooft covers a period of nearly half a century from 1599 to 1647 and was published in three volumes between 1976 and 1979 by Van Tricht.[88] This publication covers a total of over 1300 letters, including all of the known letters written by and to Hooft, letters written by his closest relatives and letters about Hooft written by others. The letters were exchanged between Hooft and his relatives, friends, poetic colleagues and the people he was corresponding with in his capacity as bailiff. Thus they cover many topics as well as any conceivable kind of social network. It even includes angry letters that he sent to his former servant.

Not only do the letters give an interesting view of the different social networks Hooft was involved in, they also give an indication of the type of gift exchanges that took place within these networks. Letters were not only a means of communication as such, but they were also a means to invite people, or to accompany a present. Moreover, they were used to express gratitude for any received present, support or service, or even for expressing disappointment when an expected gift or amount of gratitude was not offered or was not up to the expected standards.

Hooft was mingling with the political and culture elite of that day. Due to his position as a bailiff and his literary successes, Hooft found himself in social circles that most people could only dream about. Obviously there were people with a less impressive social background than Hooft's. Yet, like Hooft, these people were also part of various networks, and would exchange gifts as a means of maintaining their social ties within these networks. In that respect, it is also worthwhile looking at the way individuals of modest means dealt with the exchange of gifts.

Herman Verbeeck (1621-1681) was a descendent of refugees from the Southern Netherlands. Unlike most refugees from the Southern Netherlands, the Verbeeck's did not leave for religious reasons – they were Catholic – but for economic reasons. The family moved to Amsterdam where Verbeeck's father worked as a furrier. In that sense he was only an artisan, but even though Verbeeck suggests otherwise in his autobiography, it seems that the family was rather well off. [89] Verbeeck's education gives clues in this direction.[90]

When he was five years of age Herman began receiving tuition in reading and writing. This in itself was not exceptional for children of artisans, but since he was Catholic he probably attended more expensive private classes taught by Catholic schoolmasters.[91] When he completed his basic schooling he went to Latin school. This was a type of school that, together with the illustrious schools and academies, offered further education in Latin.[92] After three years, his father decided that it was time for Herman to become an apprentice in his fur shop. Herman's elder brother was by that time already working for their uncle who was a merchant. This left Herman to take over the family business after his father's death. After managing the shop for four years he decided to sell it. This transaction earned him quite a lot of money, which enabled him to buy both a house and a share in another shop.

In the meantime, Herman had been introduced to Clara Molenaers, whose father owned a grocery shop. Since father Molenaers did not have any sons and two of his other daughters had pursued the religious life, only Clara could provide him with a suitable successor. She therefore decided to marry Herman and have him buy part of the shop. The other half remained in the hands of the Molenaers family. Business was not booming, however, and in 1656 he was forced to find another means of earning an income. He and his family moved in with his mother-in-law and while his wife took care of the business, Herman studied to become a bookkeeper. After this occupational shift, Verbeeck sold the shop and began working as a bookkeeper for his brother-in-law, who owned a merchant house. In the course of two years, he was hired and fired twice, after which he decided to try his occupational luck elsewhere.

This time he opted for a career as a broker at the Exchange. The number of brokers dealing at the exchange was limited and the places were allocated by one of the four burgomasters of Amsterdam.[93] This meant that Herman had to find a patron who would plea his case with the burgomaster in charge, for he was not in a position to address the burgomaster directly. So he turned to Mrs. Breen, who used her contacts with Mrs. Van Vlooswijck, the wife of an Amsterdam burgomaster. In 1658, he took the oath of the broker's guild. There were several advantages to being a member of a guild. It not only provided a relatively good income but it also offered financial assistance in times of illness. This suited Herman fine because he had some severe health problems. On the other hand the position involved a certain amount of investment: Members not only paid an initiation fee, but an annual contribution as well, and they were obliged to attend funerals of other guild members.[94]

The financial advantages notwithstanding, Herman's income did not improve much over the following years. This was due both to the fact that the relatives he depended on for his transactions as a broker saw their business decline, and to the fact that he suffered from his health again. This made Clara decide to once more be the main breadwinner of the Verbeeck household. Herman bought another shop for his wife to manage, whilst he decided to become a clerk. Through the mediation of another female friend he was offered a position. Within a year, however, he turned ill after which he was fired once more. He spent the rest of his life ill until his death in 1681.

Herman Verbeeck's autobiography is, like David Beck's diary, a unique document in the sense that it is written by a person of relatively modest means that was not part of the regent class of Dutch society. Verbeeck's autobiography was probably based on notes he had taken earlier and was written in verse. A short quote from the first section of his autobiography which describes "his free state" is a representative sample of the work:[95]

> It was then the Lords day, the second fifth hour,
> counted past midday sun, that many a man sours,
> the tenth month and one and eight and twenty days
> that I, wretched man, appeared on which heavy burden lay...

This slightly negative account of his day of birth is typical of the autobiography, which starts with his birth on 28 November 1621 and ends in April 1664 and is divided into five sections, each of which describes a different stage in his life. The first section includes his youth, the other parts describe his married state. Beside the autobiography, the manuscript also includes a play and some occasional poetry from his hand, which shows that Verbeeck, like so many of his contemporaries, had an interest in poetry. However, the fact that his plays were never staged and his poetry never published, may serve as an indication of their artistic quality.

Verbeeck seems to have identified strongly with the biblical figure of Job, which results in a life described as a true threnody of unfortunate incidents and accidents. Each of the five sections in his autobiography were preceded by the motto: "*Vita hominis est milita super terram*". He ended each section with the phrase: "*melior mors vita*", which goes to show what a positive view on life he wished to present in this document.[96]

Blaak, who edited the publication of the autobiography, claimed in his introduction that the reason Verbeek wrote it were twofold. First, it was supposed to be a justification of the way his life had evolved and the choices he made along the way. This was especially directed at his brother, who had done far better in life and seemed to look down on him for that reason.[97] Second, it was a means of comforting himself because the writing gave him an opportunity to be in direct communication with God.[98] This relates to Kooijmans's suggestion of the bookkeeping character of this type of documents. The autobiography offers no evidence that Verbeeck wrote it for posterity, but there is no evidence to the contrary either. Another point that might support this bookkeeping characterisation is the fact that Verbeeck titled his work *memoriaal*, a term originally used in accountancy.

Obviously, this autobiography does not provide an overview of Verbeeck's daily gift-exchange practices and it is clearly not an objective description of his life. Still the document *does* offer an opportunity to analyse how Verbeeck wished to present himself and what gifts – or lack of them – he thought necessary to mention in his autobiography in order to establish the required "presentation of self".

Unlike Herman Verbeeck, count Willem Frederik van Nassau-Dietz (1613-1664) was a man of power, even though he never gained as much power as he had hoped.[99] Willem Frederik was stadholder in the province of Friesland from 1640 until his tragic death in 1664. In this position he was the highest-ranking official and the most important dignitary in Friesland. His tasks as stadholder consisted of overseeing the administration of justice, appointing judicial officers and magistrates and he carried military responsibility in his province. He was also responsible for maintaining the Reformed Church in his province.[100]

On a more personal level he had other duties, however. Willem Frederik was born a Nassau, as was Frederik Hendrik, the stadholder of Holland and the most powerful figure in the Dutch Republic at the time. Frederik Hendrik was a cousin of Willem Frederik's late father, and belonged to the more eminent Orange branch of the Nassau family. If, however, this branch were to die out, there was a fair chance that Willem Frederik would gain command of the Dutch army and would become the stadholder of *all* the provinces. For this to happen, he would have to play his cards right. He thus became a man with a mission: he had to ensure enough support throughout the country to emerge as the logical successor if stadholder Frederik Hendrik's only heir, Prince William, should die without having a son. It was not an unlikely scenario, since Prince William's health was rather poor. To gain this support Willem Frederik needed to obtain a prestigious position in the army and, preferably, also marry one of Prince William's sisters.[101]

This left him with some lingering difficulties. First of all, Frederik Hendrik and his wife Amalia van Solms preferred that their daughters marry men of international power and reputation. Even more importantly, Frederik Hendrik had wanted to become stadholder of Friesland himself after the death of Willem Frederik's older brother, Hendrik Casimir I, who had held this office before him, but by the time he reached Friesland, Willem Frederik had already been sworn into office. Frederik Hendrik was not amused and, was certainly a man to hold grudges.[102]

For several years, then, Willem Frederik spent a large part of his time at the stadholder's court in The Hague, spending only his winters in Friesland, in an attempt to once more gain favour with the stadholder. He even voluntarily joined the latter's military campaigns. Despite his efforts it would be a long time before he was back on friendly terms with Amalia and Frederik Hendrik. In the end, however, he succeeded. Although the eldest daughter betrothed the elector of Brandenburg, Willem Frederik managed to marry the second, Albertine Agnes. Unfortunately, Willem Frederik's efforts did not quite pay off in the end: he never became the stadholder of Holland. In 1664, he accidentally shot himself in the mouth whilst cleaning his rifles. He died a few days later from his injuries.

His courting of the stadholder's daughters are among the many things he noted in his diaries, which cover the period 1643-1654.[103] Willem Frederik kept his diaries in a number of almanacs. The notes he took were relatively short and to the point, especially in the early years. He took notes on where he had been, whom he had seen, and what had been discussed, but he seldom revealed his personal reflections on anything that he had experienced. Later on he would sometimes describe his days more elaborately and in more detail, and he was more prone to reflect upon personal matters like his good intentions for the new year.[104] His notes deal both with the personal and the more professional sides of his life, which is regarded by Kooijmans as nothing more than a form of "double entry bookkeeping".[105] Supposedly, Willem purposefully wrote down what services he received and what services he rendered in order to keep account of his social debts and credits. An example of the type of entries is his description of 20 August 1646:[106]

> Slept in, went to eat with H.H. [prince William of Orange], where the marshal de Gramont ate. After the meal we played, and I lost 663 crones, prince William 200 pistols, Desloge 300 pistols, and Roquelore won 800 pistols. I ate with prince William in the evening, and played till four, yet nobody won anything.

Unfortunately, Willem Frederik was not in the habit of writing daily in his diary, but his diaries cover so many years that they include references to almost every type of occasion from calendar feasts to rites of passage. Moreover, since he was dividing his time between his own court in Leeuwarden, Friesland, and the court of Frederik Hendrik in The Hague, his diary offers insight into a number of different social networks. These include his contacts with the other courtiers in The Hague, his political allies in Friesland, and his servants in Leeuwarden. Naturally, he also maintained a social life both in The Hague and Friesland. Thus these diaries offer an opportunity to study the gift-exchange practices of the rich and powerful, while at the same time enabling a comparison of these practices with those of other, more common, Dutch diary keepers.

A comparison in time

The egodocuments of these four individuals together with additional materials from other individuals, as well as other types of sources, should offer an opportunity to describe practices and discourses of exchange in seventeenth-century Holland. They provide information on the social networks in which gifts were exchanged, the types of gifts and the occasions for exchange within the different networks. Furthermore, they suggest what these exchanges of gifts may have meant to the individuals involved and what roles these gifts played in certain specific relationships. They show how gifts and their exchange were discussed among seventeenth-century individuals.

Yet what this source material does not offer is an opportunity to establish whether gift exchange, and therewith social relations, in the seventeenth century were as instrumental as other historians have led us to believe. My hypothesis is that seventeenth-century gift exchange may have been instrumental, but not exclusively. That is to say, that gifts exchanged in the seventeenth-century involved both instrumentality and affection, and that these concepts were not mutually exclusive, but rather interdependent. I also presume that this coexistence of instrumentality and affection within social relations is not typical of seventeenth-century Dutch society, but that it is a general feature of social relations in any given time and place.

To establish this, a comparison with another society or time period is obviously needed. This is done by comparing seventeenth-century to contemporary gift exchange.[107] This comparison is made on the basis of secondary gift-exchange literature and the empirical evidence it offers on gift-exchange practices and discourses in contemporary society. Furthermore, it is based on a very specific type of source that gives insight into both the practices of exchange as performed by certain contemporary individuals and the way in which they refer to their gift-exchange behaviour.

This source material consists of *Brieven aan de Toekomst* (Letters to the Future), which is a collection of 50,000 letters written by ordinary Dutch individuals on 15 May 1998. The letters were written as a result of a highly publicised appeal to the Dutch public by the Meertens Institute (the institute for Dutch ethnology), the Nederlands Centrum voor Volkscultuur and the Nederlands Openlucht Museum Arnhem.[108] The public was requested to describe their day's activities, as well as their thoughts and concerns for 15 May as a means of obtaining source material for future researchers in the field of ethnography and the history of daily life. The letters were catalogued and are being kept by the Meertens Institute in Amsterdam.[109]

Most of the participants in fact did supply the requested full descriptions of daily life for that particular day. The emphasis in most of these letters is on the daily routines of the writers involved. They describe what time they got up, when they had their morning pee and what they ate for breakfast. They noted what they did during the day, whom they met in person and whom they spoke to on the phone. They mention what newspaper they read and what the latest news was. Frank Sinatra had died that night, for instance, which is slightly unfortunate for it results in people endlessly noting his demise and commenting on his talents – or lack of them – as an entertainer.

In that sense, these letters are more like the diary of David Beck in terms of their contents; more descriptive notes than actual letters in the sense of communications between two people. The letters offer a glimpse into the lives and practices of Dutch individuals in contemporary society and therewith they also give an interesting insight into the gift exchanges that these individuals ventured into.

A total of 280 letters from this collection has been used in this research to analyse whether the writers actually refer to the exchange of gifts at all, and if so, what practices they describe and what discourse they use to describe these practices of gift exchange. The letters that were analysed were all from the provinces that are currently called Zuid- and Noord-Holland, which coincide with the seventeenth-century province of Holland.[110] One hundred letters were picked randomly out of a total of 50.000 to obtain a better overview of the character of the letters. The other 180 letters were pulled from the total because of the references these included to feasts, rituals and festivities.[111]

Naturally descriptions that only deal with one day do not give a clear overview of all the occasions that may involve gift exchange in contemporary Holland. For example, the letters hardly make any references to calendar feasts. Yet the letters do deal with occasions ranging from daily exchanges to rites of passage, such as weddings and funerals. Moreover, the letters include references to all possible types of gifts from objects to food. In that sense, they reveal certain patterns of gift exchange in contemporary Holland.

This information from the Letters to the Future is compared with the results from the analysis of the seventeenth-century material. It is not meant to describe an evolution from a gift exchange system to a system of market exchange, nor to show that social relations have evolved from the instrumental to the affectionate. Instead, the idea is to point out the differences in gift exchange patterns between these two periods. The results clearly show that certain aspects of this phenomenon do change over time. Therewith the research becomes more historical. Meanwhile, the similarities in gift exchange patterns offer evidence that gift exchange is indeed an anthropological invariant.

There are certain other advantages that this comparison has to offer. First, by showing that the individual's experience of exchange in contemporary society does not necessarily coincide with the analysis that can be made of that exchange, it can be made clear that even though historians have labelled their behaviour thusly, individuals in the seventeenth-century did not necessarily think of themselves as being self-interested creatures.

Second, what the comparison enables me to do, which would otherwise be impossible, is show that the supposed instrumental nature of social relations in the early modern period is not necessarily typical for that period at all. Of course, this point can also be made by stressing the altruistic evidence that the seventeenth-century sources offer, but this would not be fully convincing since evidence for both the self-interested and the altruistic is easily found in this source material. The interesting thing is, however, that the same applies to the contemporary source material. The Letters to the Future also include references that stress the affectionate character of the gift exchange, while at the same time, some individuals seem to be quite aware that the exchange of gifts as well as social relations, involve certain levels of self-interest.

The overall point of this research is that self-interest and altruism are not necessarily mutually exclusive concepts within the exchange of gifts or the maintenance of social relationships. In both periods, these two concepts go largely hand in hand when it comes to the exchange of gifts or the maintenance of relations in general. There is, however, a big difference between the discourses that surround the exchange of gifts in the seventeenth century and contemporary society. Whereas the seventeenth-century discourse within social relationships was largely one of honour and obligation, the contemporary discourse on gift exchange is largely implicit and one that is expressed in terms of affection.

Part I: Practices of Gift Exchange

Daily Hospitality

A sketch of seventeenth-century gift exchange: The case of David Beck

It seems fruitful to start off this research by offering a broad out-line of general patterns of gift exchange in seventeenth-century Holland. The sketch that follows here serves as a means of point-ing out possible patterns of gift exchange by a seventeenth-century individual. It does not draw on the pretext that this person's gift behaviour is representative for the whole Dutch population of that period. It rather offers an initial opportunity to map what the pos-sible occasions for and networks of exchange were in this period, and what types of gifts were exchanged in these instances. Or to put it differently, it answers the question of "who was giving what to whom and on what occasion", at least for the case of David Beck in 1624.

Whereas Natalie Davis focuses on four "prescriptions of human exchange", Christian charity, noble liberality, exchange between friends and generosity among neighbours in sixteenth-century France, this sketch largely confines itself to exchanges within friendship – in the sense of both family and friends – and other individual relations with, for instance, neighbours and profes-sional contacts.[1] This is the result of the choice of sources, as well as the character of Dutch society in that period. A diary, like David Beck's, does not necessarily include references to charitable offer-ings, especially since he also kept a cash book which suggests that he might have noted his charitable contributions there. Further-more, the Dutch Republic is generally seen as a *burgerlijke* society in which the nobility occupied a weak position.[2] Since David Beck lived in The Hague, he did occasionally come across the nobility such as the stadholder, Prince Maurits of Orange, and the Winter King of Bohemia, who had sought refuge in the Republic, but a burgher like Beck predominantly had contact with other burghers in his personal life. The diary therefore is unlikely to refer to noble liberality. What it does provide, however, is a great number of references to exchanges within his circle of family and friends.

This description of gift exchange practices provides a general outline of seventeenth-century exchange-patterns, which leaves an opportunity to focus on some specific aspects of seventeenth-century gift exchange in the chapters to follow.[3] The goal of this chapter is to analyse what the common gifts, occasions and networks of exchange were for David Beck and other individuals in his social environment. The material from the David Beck case is complemented by findings from other case studies as a means to obtain a broader view of practices of gift exchange in seventeenth-century Holland. Yet the main focus in this chapter remains on David Beck and his family and friends. Thanks to the comprehensiveness of this diary, several different types of occasions, gifts and networks can be analysed. Furthermore, its comprehensiveness also allows for a more or less quantitative analysis of the most common occasions, gifts and networks of exchange.

Expectations and disappointments

Despite the very thorough character of this egodocument, the first reading of Beck's diary turned out to be quite a disappointing experience. All the occasions at which one would expect an exchange of gifts hardly played a role in the life of David Beck and his family and friends. His birthday, for instance, did not turn out to be a day of festivity and an exchange of gifts. He did not receive more visitors than usual, nor was there any special food or drink prepared for the occasion and he certainly was not offered any big and expensive gifts.

It is not that he was unaware of his birthday, because on the eve of that day he mentioned that it was "the last day of his youth", implying that he was turning 30 the following day. This, by early-modern standards, meant that Beck had passed his youth and could now convincingly consider himself to be an adult man. He "ended his youth" by writing the tenth lamentation on the death of his wife, which started with the line "With my youth, joy has flooded from me", on which cheerful note he went to bed that night.[4] The lack of festivity surrounding his birthday the next day may be explained by the fact that David Beck was still mourning the death of his wife, who had died in December 1623.

This could also justify why his son's birthday was also not celebrated. Beck's son Adrian turned five on 20 September 1624 "around one" in the morning, and there was no mention of any special activities on his birthday either. Beck did commemorate the event by addressing a few lines in his diary to his son's progress in school. He commented that little Adrian could "write a fair hand with perfect letters", and described his son as a "comical chatterbox" and a "witty but rather wild boy", but this was the only attention his son's birthday received.[5] The birthdays of his daughters were hardly reflected upon. The birthday of his baby daughter Roeltje was referred to in the diary, but his daughter Sara's birthday is not mentioned at all.[6] This suggests that birthdays were not especially festive occasions for the Beck family, at least not in 1624. However, this supposed lack of birthday festivities in the case of David Beck was in fact not a result of a period of mourning. Stadholder Willem Frederik was not in the habit of celebrating his birthdays either.[7] Willem Frederik kept diaries for years, and he noted his date of birth diligently.[8] Mentions of his birthday were initially very matter of fact. He just barely mentioned what age he had turned and went on to describe his daily events.[9] His birthdays passed in a very ordinary manner, and he did not receive any special visits or gifts.

Later on, he began paying more attention to his birthdays, not so much by actually celebrating them but rather by commemorating the event in a more spiritual manner. On these days he dwelled upon God's grace, his spiritual and moral shortcomings or progress over the last year, and his intentions of doing better next year. But in neither case did his birthday give rise to any special activities.[10] The fact that these descriptions of his birthdays became more elaborate was actually a result of the way his style of writing changed over the years. In the first period, Willem Frederik's writings were quite short and matter of fact. Only in later years did he develop a style that was more elaborate, personal and reflexive.

In other words, when it came to birthdays during this period, it seems that many considered them to be occasions for reflection rather than festivity. This might have been the influence of Calvinism on the daily life of the Dutch burgher. As Van Alkemade discussed in his *Nederlands Displegtigheden* (1732), which was a more or less historic account of Dutch table practices, the celebration of birthdays was an old tradition – both in Eastern and Western countries – that had been deemed inappropriate by Calvin.[11] Or rather, for Calvin, the feast in itself was not so much inappropriate as the fact that mankind was incapable of celebrating these events without surrendering itself to "wantonness, dissolute joy and excessiveness".[12] Calvin preferred that mankind solemnly celebrate the occasion, because this day "admonishes every one of us to thank God, by whom we are created" and therewith left an opportunity to commemorate all idleness of the last year and to recommend oneself in God's grace and protection.[13] In this respect, Beck and especially Willem Frederik may have been living up to Calvinist standards by not celebrating their birthdays joyfully.

Still, the birthdays of the daughters of Frederik Hendrik, stadholder of Holland and Zeeland, were supposedly celebrated with dissolute joy and excessiveness, since Willem Frederik does note in his diary that he was to attend a ball for the birthday of one of the princesses.[14] This is in accordance with Van Alkemade's observation that stadholders in Holland still celebrated their birthdays in a festive manner, especially by having birthday dinners "among the great".[15]

This might suggest that birthdays were occasions that, at least by the common folk, were celebrated less frequently during the seventeenth century because of Calvinist influences.[16] Nevertheless, in the course of the century, the celebration of birthdays underwent a revival and became more common among upper-class burghers. This is revealed, for instance, through the inventory of early-modern occasional poetry of the Royal Library in The Hague.[17] This inventory includes all of the pre-1700 occasional poems in the collection of the library that were written to commemorate important events in the lives of private individuals, such as weddings, funerals and promotions. The catalogue includes only four poems that were written on the occasion of birthdays and all of these birthday poems stem from the second half of the seventeenth-century.[18]

However, the unexpected lack of examples of birthday festivities goes to show that one should not depend too much on expectations based on contemporary gift-exchange practices when it comes to historical research: one may end up with very disappointing birthday experiences. But then again, if not with birthday presents, what gifts did David Beck and his social circle exchange?

In fact, David Beck's diary includes plenty of references to many different occasions of exchange and many different types of gifts. In the entire diary of 365 days, a total number of about one thousand instances of gift exchanges are mentioned. This includes both gifts that Beck himself offered and received, but also gifts exchanged by others in his environment. This means that an average of at least two gift exchanges occurred every single day, which implies that gift exchange was an activity that was part of the day to day contacts that Beck maintained. This indicates that the exchange of gifts was indeed a daily practice. So, while Davis argues that "*many* presents changed hands irrespective of the rhythm of season and rites of passage", I would claim that *most* gifts were exchanged irrespective of these occasions.[19]

Naturally, a distinction should be made regarding the types of gifts exchanged. It would be a mistake to think of these gifts as presents in the sense of material objects that were exchanged on special occasions. Instead, most of these gifts were of a rather humble character, both in terms of economic value and in terms of symbolic meaning, and these gifts were mostly offered on a day to day basis as a matter of course instead of on specific festive occasions. Yet, the significance of these "small" exchanges should not be underestimated, both in the sense of what they meant for David Beck and the function they performed for social cohesion.

Daily hospitality in the life of David Beck

As it turns out, daily exchange, in the sense of a spontaneous offering that is not connected to any particular ritual occasion, is by far the most important occasion for the exchange of gifts. A vast majority of the gifts exchanged, according to David Beck's diary, consists of hospitality.[20] This is unexpected in the sense that hospitality for most individuals, then and now, is offered rather subconsciously, as a matter of course. It is usually not the first thing that springs to mind when one thinks of gift exchange. If gift exchange can be considered a phenomenon that is part of every day life, that is hardly reflected upon, this is even more true for the offering of hospitality. But however neglected hospitality is in people's minds, it is a gift that is of major significance in the maintenance of social relationships.

The hospitality exchanged in David Beck's diary consists of food, drink and a place to stay. The distinction between these types of hospitality seems rather unnecessary, since they end up largely coinciding. If lodging was offered for the night, it either went without saying that the guest would also be offered a meal and something to drink, or it was the result of the guest having stayed for dinner in the first place. And when Beck and his friends had dinner it was obvious that this included wine or beer.

However, the type of hospitality that was offered depended largely on the level of intimacy between host and guest. Wine or beer might be offered to any acquaintance, be it family, friend or a professional contact who passed by the house for a chat. A meal might be offered to any relative or friend, whereas a place to stay was only offered to close relatives and friends.

Within David Beck's social setting, but also in the life of stadholder Willem Frederik, for instance, it was very common to have meals with guests. These could either be relatively modest meals with friends or relatives who just happened to be in the home when the evening meal was served, or quite extensive dinners for invited guests. These occasions might consist of quite a large number of people, which might include both family and friends, but also friends and family of friends and family. In that sense, Beck and his environment were rather indiscriminate in who was invited on these occasions. This resulted in numerous dinner parties with many guests. The meals could have a rather festive character and although the food was not necessarily exquisite, the wine would usually be plentiful.

Furthermore, people would not just be invited for evening meals, but might also join in for lunch or even breakfast.[21] It was quite common to have a guest for lunch, and even organised luncheons were nothing out of the ordinary. Breakfast, however, was hardly ever an organised event to which large numbers of people were invited.[22] Breakfast guests were more likely to be people individuals who had stayed overnight or people who came round to Beck's house early in the morning in order to inform him of the latest news.

In general, many of the dinners and other meals were spontaneous events. Whenever a relative or close friend happened to be around during meal times, it went without saying that they could join the meal. In this respect, it is true that Dutch spontaneous hospitality was limited to those one was close to, while more distant relations were only invited for dinner.[23] Still, spontaneous hospitality among close friends and relatives was not something David Beck and the people in his environment wasted words on; it was just a matter of course that was hardly reflected upon. Occasionally Beck would also pass by the house of friends around dinnertime in order to invite them to his house for dinner, or vice versa.[24]

On other occasions, people would bring food from home to their host when they were spontaneously invited to dinner. When Beck was invited to eat at his mother-in-law's one evening, for instance, he sent someone to his house to pick up a smoked sausage.[25] On another evening when his friend Breckerfelt showed up at dinnertime, Beck sent his sister Diliane to fetch Breckerfelt's wife as well.[26] The latter had already prepared their evening meal, which led her to decide not to let it go to waste and so she brought it along to Beck's place. The four of them ended up having a very nice meal together.

According to Beck, this resulted in a "very sweet and enjoyable" evening, but even if he had refrained from any comments, the fact that the Breckerfelts joined the Becks for dinner when they had already prepared their own meal suggests that these spontaneous dinners were indeed enjoyable occasions. If these had just been social obligations, the Breckerfelts could have easily refused this invitation with the excuse that they already had a meal waiting for them. In that sense, this example nicely shows that hospitality was not only an instrument in the maintenance of social relationships, but was also something enjoyable of its own accord.

Interestingly enough, Beck only mentioned the food he ate in the company of others be they guests or hosts. On the one hand, the fact that he only described these meals may be explained by the notion that it was a means for David Beck to convince himself that he had indeed been either well-received or had received his guests well. On the other hand it was not as if he *always* described the food served on occasions of shared meals, thus it may have been that he only described those meals he particularly enjoyed.

His descriptions of these meals offer a nice overview of the kind of food Beck and his social environment offered their guests. Some foods or dishes were related to specific times of the year. A dish like hotchpotch was served regularly throughout the year, but was especially popular during the *harst*, an event that will be discussed later. Another type of food connected to a particular occasion was pancakes. These could indeed be eaten on other occasions as well, but were the traditional foodstuff of Carnival dinners. Unfortunately, Beck did not note what meals were served by his hosts during the fairs. This not only suggests that there was no particular culinary tradition related to the annual fairs, but also that the food was not the most significant aspect of the hospitality being offered on this occasion. As will be shown later, although many meals were shared with family and friends during the fairs, the importance of these fairs for Beck lay in the offering of hospitality, in the sense of providing family and friends with a place to stay, rather than the offering of food.

In general one might say that fish – be it cod, haddock or the occasional pike – was quite commonly offered to guests, but poultry and ham were also not out of the ordinary.[27] Furthermore, Beck also did not seem to mind having to eat meals that consisted of vegetables such as salads, beets, cucumbers, or beans, occasionally offered with eggs.[28] Another popular meal consisted of cabbage or turnips with *speck* (bacon).[29] Every once in a while, the host might generously serve both sausage and *speck* with the cabbage.[30] Some of the more interesting combinations of foodstuffs mentioned by David Beck are a "hotchpotch of veal with a tasty pike" and "a good ham with a tasty pike".[31]

An example of how these joint meals were organised is when Beck invited some people over for a luncheon. The Friday before this particular lunch, Beck went round town to deliver invitations to his friends and relatives. He invited his late wife's uncle and aunt, a sister of the uncle, his mother-in-law and his friend Breckerfelt and his wife for lunch for that Sunday.[32] On Saturday, the ham was prepared. When it was done, Beck and his sister tasted a piece of the ham to make sure that it was actually good enough to be served to their guests. The verdict was positive: it tasted excellent, but Beck added that his appetite may have been aroused by drinks he had had earlier that day after a funeral.[33] The next day, the invitees arrived for lunch and they "were on a nice ham, very sweet with each other, singing psalm 42 while they ate".[34] His guests did not leave until four o'clock in the afternoon, which is an indication of the party's success.

This was not the end of the ham, however. On Monday evening, Beck picked up Breckerfelt and his Jenneke at their home and had them over for "cold ham", which turned out to be another enjoyable dinner. After dinner they once again sang psalms and Herman and Jenneke stayed until ten thirty.[35] Three days later, Beck's piece of ham was again a cause for joy. Beck's brothers, Hendrik and Steven, joined him for a lunch of "the heel of our ham", with which the brothers drank a good pitcher of wine that Steven had brought along. The Beck brothers were "sweet and delighted", which shows that a nice piece of ham could go a long way.[36]

Another act of generosity presented itself when Beck was offered a rabbit as a gift by his mother-in-law. David had his sister make a big rabbit pie and invited his friend Breckerfelt and his wife, her mother, his own mother-in-law and her sister over to his house the next day in order to eat it. Cynically speaking, this could also be explained as a cheap means of offering hospitality; offering a gift that one had received from another party earlier.[37] However, Beck did not have access to any cooling system and any meat in his house, unless it was preserved, could only be kept for a short while. By eating the rabbit with friends and relatives, he could make both a good impression, and consume the entire rabbit. This instrumental interpretation, however, does not take into account Beck's good intentions in offering a meal to friends and relatives. Offering a received food-gift to family and friends was actually a kind way of sharing received generosities. Actually, the rabbit pie meal turned out to be a rather pleasurable experience. Beck and his company were "sweet and cheerful" and sang psalms after they had finished their lunch.[38]

This alliance of worldly and more or less spiritual pleasures was nothing out of the ordinary. In fact, Beck would often sing psalms after dinner, sometimes with his sister and when his friend Breckerfelt had stayed for a meal he usually joined in for a tune as well. This may have been a matter of adapting to the rules of the host on Breckerfelt's part, but singing psalms was not just a religious practice but also a social activity that was considered enjoyable. Furthermore, psalms were also sung during dinner parties that involved invitees other than just the usual family and friends.[39] Even Beck's tailor was happy to sing along.[40]

Drinks

In contrast to meals, drinks were not something one would be invited to. It seems that in the early seventeenth-century there was no drinking equivalent for dinner parties. This did not, however, prevent people from drinking extensively, but they drank either during the course of a meal, or spontaneously without any prior invitation. Only funerals offered attendees the opportunity to consume generous quantities of wine which did not necessarily include food, or so Beck's diary suggests.[41] Although other sources, like probate inventories and Van Alkemade, imply that meals were indeed offered to people who attended funerals, Beck never makes mention of meals after a funeral, even though he had attended several during the course of the year.[42] He does, however, regularly note that he had drinks at a funeral, which makes funerals one of the few occasions where Beck and his friends and relatives drank extensively without necessarily having a meal with it.

However, it was common knowledge that visiting the homes of family or friends would likely be rewarded with the offering of at least one drink of, most likely, beer or wine, but occasionally stronger drinks like lemon, anise or clove liquors were offered. It was unusual for Beck and his friends to drink large quantities of wine, beer or liquor on these occasions. The drinks were offered as a matter of course and kindness, and were meant to accompany the visit and were not central to the visit as such.[43] The point of these house calls was to inquire after somebody's health, to ask or offer information and news, or to request the occasional favour.

When visitor and host were not more than acquaintances, the host usually only offered one drink, if any at all. Beck, for instance, was offered a drink when he was ordered round to the homes of parents of future pupils. They contracted him to give their children lessons and usually offered him a drink of wine after this had been arranged.[44] Although sharing a drink was traditionally part of signing a contract and may have been part of the economic or judicial sphere, this drink can still be considered a gift. Having a drink together was the one feature of the contract process that helped personalise the business arrangement.[45] Through the ritual of sharing a drink, the parties involved were not only judicially obliged to each other, but also personally, which probably made the contract even more binding.

Unlike visits to relative strangers, house calls to friends often led to an invitation to stay for a meal. The manner in which Beck referred to these spontaneous invitations is quite interesting. Whenever Beck was invited to stay for dinner with the families of close friends, he usually noted – quite neutrally – that he had stayed for dinner or that he had been their guest.[46] This changed, however, when he was invited to dinner at the home of those from whom he had not expected to be invited. These occasions, as will be shown later, were discussed by Beck in such a manner that he expressed – in quite an implicit way – how he had been honoured by the invitation.

Accommodation

As mentioned earlier, lodging for the night, or a couple of nights, was generally only offered to close relatives and friends.[47] This usually happened on special occasions when relatives or friends were visiting from out of town, like for instance, during the annual summer fairs that occurred in most Dutch towns. On those occasions it was not uncommon for Beck and his friends to spend several nights at the homes of relatives or friends. This hospitality during fairs will be discussed further in the chapter on calendar feasts. Yet there were also other occasions when Beck and his social environment could count on each other's hospitality. When David's brother Hendrik became the father of a baby girl, for instance, David left The Hague that same afternoon for Delft to congratulate his brother. Both David and his friend Breckerfelt, who had travelled with him, were offered a meal as was the custom, after which they spent the night and returned to The Hague the next morning.[48]

Beck and his friends not only visited family and friends in other towns for special occasions such as calendar feasts or births, but they also travelled to other, nearby towns like Delft, just to have an evening meal. Since it was usually impractical to return home after dinner (the gates closed at a certain hour and/or there had been heavy drinking), they used these occasions to accept the hospitality offered by their host. David and his brother Hendrik often spend the night at one another's home. This was not always an altogether agreeable experience since the guests and the host often ended up having to share the same small bed.[49]

Although an offer of lodging was usually due to travel difficulties late at night, a bed was sometimes also offered to people living in the same town. Beck's friend Breckerfelt, for instance, often slept at Beck's place when his mother-in-law from Arnhem was visiting.[50] Although it is tempting to ascribe this need for hospitality to an aversion for his mother-in-law, it was more likely due to the fact that his house was just too small to accommodate more than two people. When his wife's cousin visited later that year, Breckerfelt again made use of Beck's hospitality.[51]

Beck's children sometimes also took advantage of this "in-town" hospitality. They occasionally spent the night at their grandmother's house just for fun, but on other occasions, these visits had a more practical reason. When Diliane, Beck's sister, who usually took care of the household, was away on a short vacation, Beck's daughter Sara stayed at her grandmother's house for the entire time her aunt was away.[52] Supposedly Beck found it too difficult to take care of both his young son and daughter.[53] This seems likely in his case, because it is clear from his diary that he was not very involved in the raising of his children. He was certainly interested in their general wellbeing, but this did not include any particular efforts on his part. All of the tasks that were normally done by the housewife, like preparing meals and caring for the children, were left for Diliane.

Another reason for relatives like "sister" Eva, the wife of his brother Hendrik, to impose on Beck's hospitality was the plague. The disease was raging through the Republic at the time, but especially in Delft the loss of human lives was enormous. When her lying-in period after the birth of her baby daughter had ended, Eva spent some days in The Hague at Beck's house to avoid the terror and the likelihood of her becoming sick herself.[54] Her husband Hendrik did not join her, but this did not seem to pose a problem for David. Eva, it seems, was naturally privy to enjoying the hospitality he offered and , she was also welcome to join any meal that Beck was invited to by others. Beck and his sister-in-law had lunch with Anna van Overschie, Beck's mother-in-law, and Herman Breckerfelt and his wife invited them for dinner.[55]

The foy, or farewell dinner

As mentioned earlier, breakfast was seldom an organised event to which people were invited. The one exception was the breakfast that Beck organised as a *foy*, or farewell meal, for Jenneke Arents, an acquaintance from Arnhem, and his younger brother Abraham.[56] Both Jenneke and Abraham were bound for Arnhem on 18 March 1624. Jenneke was to return to her hometown after visiting friends and family in The Hague and Abraham was sent to Arnhem to start an apprenticeship with Herman Jansz, Breckerfelt's uncle. Beck invited friends and relatives to eat breakfast and say their farwells to Jenneke and Abraham. This farewell offering was quite common but usually consist of a dinner party rather than a joint breakfast.

A *foy* could be organised whenever people visiting from out of town were about to return home.[57] It served as an opportunity to say goodbye to all the friends and relatives the guest would leave behind, but it was also something more. It was also a means of reciprocating the hospitality the guest had received from both the host and those who had been kind enough to invite the guest for a meal during his or her stay. If the guest had been in town on business, his business acquaintances were also invited to say their farewells. This was the case, for instance, when Silber von Silbersteyn, a Bohemian nobleman and chamberlain to the Winter King of Bohemia, was about to leave The Hague after having spent some time at the house of Beck's uncle. According to Beck, "another chamberlain of the King of Boheemen, and the King's kitchen-master, as well as uncle and aunt were also held as a guest".[58]

The meal usually took place at the host's home , but the *foy* itself was paid for by the guest as a means of repaying the host's kindness. This arrangement sometimes caused serious trouble. During the first two months of the year, Beck's uncle, or rather the uncle of his late wife, Adrian van der Cruijsse, was hosting a certain nobleman whom Beck referred to as Bilsen.[59] David had occasionally encountered this nobleman when he had visited his uncle. Most of the time David just chatted with his uncle and the nobleman, but occasionally, much to his honour, Beck had been invited to join them for dinner as well.[60] On one occasion, however, the nobleman himself invited Beck to stay, which Beck considered to be a great privilege – as was usually the case when somebody of status wished to enjoy his company.[61]

When Bilsen was bidding his farewells at Van der Cruijsse's house, he invited some guests for dinner, including Beck. Or so he thought, for when he arrived at his uncle's place his aunt begged him to leave. It appeared she had actually invited Beck without Bilsen's knowledge and since the party was rather overcrowded as it was, Beck's attendance would not be appreciated. Although Beck went home to have a good laugh about this ordeal with his sister Diliane and Breckerfelt, the situation was of course rather embarrassing. His aunt was obviously also quite discomfited by this turn of events; "in order to make amends" she felt obliged to invite Beck over for dinner the following evening. "In her own name and not at Bilsen's expense", Beck added wryly.[62]

Beck ended his notes for that day with the statement that even though he and Breckerfelt probably had a more modest meal and less beer to drink than they would have had at the Bilsen party, Breckerfelt and Beck enjoyed themselves more. Although this may be interpreted as a way of coming to terms with the embarrassment in a positive way, one cannot help but wonder whether Beck was still somewhat displeased with the situation. In fact, when his uncle stopped by Beck's house the next day to invite him once more, Beck declined graciously.[63]

Hospitality at Calendar Feasts

Besides the hospitality offered on a daily basis as a matter of course, or spontaneously, there was also the ritualised hospitality that was offered on ceremonial occasions such as calendar feasts and rites of passage. This type of hospitality was the result of events in the course of the year or in the course of a lifetime that were cause for celebration, or – in case of death – mourning. Especially for the study of calendar feasts David Beck's diary is an exceptionally rich source. Since it covers a full year it gives wonderful insights into the ritual feasts that Beck and his circle celebrated. Unlike what was suggested earlier, the fact that Beck was still in mourning did not prevent him and his household being in an occasional festive mood. As a matter of fact, calendar feasts were the second most important occasion for the exchange of gifts after daily exchanges of hospitality, and hospitality was the most common gift offered during these calendar feasts.

New Year's Day

According to Natalie Davis, the most important gift-exchange day in sixteenth-century France was New Year's Day. On this day "the great" offered *étrennes*, or New Year's gifts, to "the small". These gifts usually consisted of small amounts of money.[64] As noted in the works of Cats and Bredero, the Dutch counterpart of these *étrennes* were called *Nieuwe Jaer,* which could be offered either spontaneously or upon request.[65]

Although this type of gift is described in David Beck's diary, it cannot be said that New Year was a grand occasion for gift exchange. The first of January 1624 was actually quite an ordinary day for David Beck. He was not hung over, otherwise he would have mentioned it as he did on other occasions. He just went to church, which he did frequently, had lunch with Breckerfelt, which was nothing out of the ordinary, and met with some friends in the evening, which was also not exceptional.

The only indication that New Year's Day was actually a special day, was that his son Adrian went to his grandmother's and his uncle's house to show them his New Year's ABC-letters. Van Alkemade suggests in his *Nederlandse Displegtigheden* that this writing of New Year's letters was an old tradition that even in his time – the early eighteenth century – was still practiced. Early eighteenth-century youth were still in the habit of writing letters on "Holidays, New Year's and *Kermissen*" to offer to elderly, guardians and friends.[66] These writings presumably included best wishes for these "elderly" people and functioned as proof of the youngster's progress in school, which would be rewarded by the "elderly" with a small gift.

Whereas Van Alkemade mentions that these New Year's writings were a tradition among youngsters, Beck himself also rose to the occasion. On 2 January, Beck spent his afternoon binding one of his printed poems which he then sent to the aforementioned Silber von Silbersteyn, as a "New Year" together with another poem, which was dedicated to the nobleman.[67] In France, but as this example suggests presumably also in Holland, writers saw New Year's Day as a good occasion to dedicate their work important people.[68]

Initially Beck does not leave any clues as to his motivation for offering these poems to this nobleman. Only later in the year does it become clear what Beck's intentions were with this gift. On 22 March, Von Silbersteyn summoned David Beck to come to his uncle's house. It was the last day of Von Silbersteyn's stay in The Hague and he bade his farewells by offering a *foy.* It turned out to be a rather enjoyable evening. By the time Beck left, Silbersteyn had offered him two *rijksdaalders,* to which Beck added in his diary "because I occasionally did something for him".[69]

The fact that Beck noted the payments he received for performing some tasks for this nobleman in his diary and not just in his account book is probably due to the fact that he was honoured to be in contact with such a noble person. His diary offers other occasions at which Beck seems to be flattered by his contacts with the rich and famous. Beck duly noted whenever he saw an important person. He made notes on how "his Excellency", stadholder Maurits of Orange, was receiving guests with fireworks, or how he had attended the funeral of Christian Huygens.[70] Beck also had a keen eye for the Winter King of Bohemia, who had sought refuge in The Hague in 1621. His contacts with the chamberlain and the cook of the king have already been mentioned, yet Beck also had a chance to see the King and Queen of Bohemia eat and visit their garden.[71] Frederik Hendrik, the later stadholder, was seen making an outing with the Winter King.[72]

However, despite these New Year's gifts, New Year's Day was generally not an event that was celebrated in the company of family and friends. A more impressive outburst of gift exchange, or – more specifically – exchange of hospitality, occurred around Shrovetide, or Carnival.

Vastelavond

The first mention of *vastelavond*, or carnival, in David Beck's diary is on Thursday 15 February, when his brother Hendrik was visiting David in The Hague. Hendrik passed by their uncle Adrian van Overschie's house to invite him for *vastelavond*. The actual celebration did not take place until the following Sunday, when David visited his uncle to invite him and his family on behalf of Hendrik for the "feast of his recovered health".[73] This expression referred to the fact that he had recently been seriously ill and presumably thought that a carnival dinner would be the ideal occasion to lift his spirits. Later that day, David and his uncle Adrian walked from The Hague to Delft, where Hendrik was expecting them "with devotion". That evening, Hendrik, his wife Eva, her relatives, their friend Jan de Grave, uncle Adrian and David had a nice dinner of "exquisite fare and delicious wine", after which David and Adrian spent the night at Hendrik's house. David referred to this day as "the first day of *vastelavond*".[74]

The next day, David returned to The Hague to discover that his sister Diliane was offering a lunch of pancakes to "7 or 8 guests" including the wet nurse with her daughter and David's daughter Roeltje, David's mother-in-law, his sister-in-law Jaccomijntje, two of his brothers-in-law and his friend Breckerfelt. That afternoon Diliane left for Delft taking Beck's daughter Sara, Breckerfelt and Jaccomijntje, the half sister of David's late wife, with her. They were all invited "for pancakes with the other young folk" at Hendrik's place. One might say that Hendrik went to great lengths to celebrate his "recovered health", or rather, that he showed great hospitality on this *vastelavond*. In the meantime, David's young son Adrian had his own social obligations. He was invited to eat pancakes at the house of Jacob Corneliszoon, an acquaintance of the family.[75]

The following day was a nice and quiet day for David, because his sister was still in Delft and his son Adrian had spent the night at his grandmother's house. But on the 21 February, or "Ash Wednesday in the Papacy" as Beck called it, it was David's turn to host some carnival bustle in his house. That afternoon Beck, Hendrik, his wife Eva, Breckerfelt and David's mother-in-law "pancaked and drank a good pitcher of wine" together, while young Adrian once more had his own party at his uncle Simon's house. Daughter Sara and David's younger brother Abraham were invited to have pancakes at the house of Jan Willemszoon "the chimneysweep".[76] These were the last of the *vastelavond* celebrations.

Beck's descriptions of his *vastelavond* activities show that carnival was an occasion when Beck and his peers showed great amounts of hospitality.[77] They offered food and drink to large groups of friends and relatives, and also offered a place to sleep when necessary. Not only was the hospitality great in terms of the number of people – David usually mentions only the invitees, not the people that were part of the household and thus automatically part of the celebration – but also in the sense that it was indiscriminate. It was not that total strangers were welcome to join the party, but any close friends of the invitees, who themselves were always relatives or close friends, were indeed also welcome to attend. David's in-laws and friends were invited by both Diliane and Hendrik, even when David himself did not join the party. This is a pattern that is also evidenced during other festivities connected to the calendar year as well as in their daily hospitality.

So Beck and his family and friends literally went back and forth eating and drinking at each other's homes, yet what is especially striking about these vastelavond celebrations is that they ate the same food on almost every single occasion: pancakes, pancakes, and more pancakes. Beck even referred to this ritual as "going pancaking". It is interesting to note that stadholder Willem Frederik described exactly the same ritual in his diaries.[78] During Shrovetide the stadholder, like the schoolmaster David Beck, regularly ate pancakes in the merry company of nice ladies and also occasionally invited others over to eat pancakes at his court in Leeuwarden. In his case, it was not uncommon for these gatherings to last till two or three in the morning. This shows that "pancaking" was not only a matter of popular amusement.[79]

Another striking thing is that David's children, Sara and Adrian, appeared to have a social life of their own. They were invited to their own carnival parties to which they were not chaperoned by their father, nor by Diliane. This would not have been so surprising if it weren't for the fact that these children were still very young; Sara was born in either 1621 or 1622, which made her no older than three years of age, while Adrian, had yet to turn five. On one occasion, Sara is joined by her uncle Abraham. This, however, does not suggest that she was in good hands. Abraham was probably no older than twelve years of age and, as can be gathered from David's worries about him, was not a terribly responsible young man. This is not to say that David did not take good care of his children, because in these instances they were probably in the good care of their grandmother, or the adults who had invited them.[80]

Kermis

An even more important calendar feast in terms of displaying hospitality amongst David Beck and his circle was the annual *kermis*, or fair. Every summer each town and village in the province of Holland hosted a *kermis*, which usually lasted a week or longer.[81] These *kermissen* originally coincided with the birthday of a church's patron saint or the consecration day of that church, but over time they expanded beyond a mere celebrated mass, into a more profane affair in markets and inside inns.[82] However, as Haks has pointed out, relatively little is known about the social function of these fairs.[83] Beck's diary is important in this respect: it gives a good overview of how Beck and his social circle celebrated these events. In fact, Beck and his friends were clearly in the habit of going to fairs and used the opportunity to visit friends and family.

The *kermis* period in The Hague lasted from the end of April to mid-May, right before Ascension. In the Beck household, this period was initiated by Diliane, who cleaned the house for the upcoming *kermis* "for all these weeks".[84] It is not surprising that this type of spring cleaning actually coincided with the *kermis*, because during this period Beck and his family entertained a lot of guests, some of whom also spent many a night at their house.[85] The more official commencement of *kermis* took place on the evening of 30 April by the placement of the May tree in front of the town hall and on 1 May when city officials read the specific *kermis* bylaws aloud.[86]

On 3 May, Beck wrote a letter to his sister-in-law Anneke in Leiden to invite her to the *kermis* in The Hague. There is no evidence that she actually accepted this invitation because at no point in the following days does Beck mention her visit. He did, however, receive the company of his cousin Jan Mannes. Jan arrived on 4 May and stayed with the Beck's till the 9th.[87] On 5 May, Beck celebrated *kermis* at his house with his cousin Jan, his mother-in-law, his brothers Steven and Hendrik, and uncle Adrian. The other members of the household probably attended the party as well. After lunch, they all went for a walk through town to see "the *kermisses* at the town hall and the court".[88] The *kermis* in The Hague distinguished itself from the other fairs because the stadholder of Holland resided there. This meant that the fair was celebrated beyond just the town halls, but also at the court of the stadholder. In fact, that day the *Haagse kermis* was not only visited by the likes of David Beck and his friends but also by the King and Queen of Bohemia and their retinue. Furthermore, in later years, the princesses of Orange were also in the habit of attending the fair, as was noted by stadholder Willem Frederik.[89]

The evening after this big luncheon, both cousin Jan and brother Hendrik stayed overnight at David's house. The following day they again visited the fairs. Here Beck ran into David du Prez, a schoolmaster colleague from Leiden. Beck invited Du Prez to join him, Hendrik, and Jan for lunch at his house, after which he left "to care for his table and to expect his guests with devotion".[90]

That night both Jan Mannes and Hendrik again spent the night at Beck's house. The following day Hendrik returned to Delft. This does not mean that peace had returned to the Beck home, because that same day they again had a number people drop by for lunch: Beck's mother-in-law, Breckerfelt, the wet nurse and her daughter, Beck's daughter Roeltje, brother Steven and cousin Mannes. In the evening Beck and his cousin were both invited to have dinner at the home of Beck's mother-in-law. Two cousins of Beck's late wife also attended this dinner.

On 8 May, Beck once more had friends over for lunch, and in the evening he and his cousin were once again invited to dinner. This time at the home of uncle Adrian. This was the last night that Jan Mannes spent at David's house. The next morning Beck, brother Steven, cousin Mannes and uncle Adrian had breakfast at Beck's house, after which Mannes bade his farewells and returned home. This is not to say that the *kermis* was over, however. David Beck noted in his diary "on dito (because of the weather) there was almost as much *kermis* as the first day".[91] Yet, these were indeed the last days of *kermis*. On 12 May, Beck and his sister had dinner at the home of Herman Breckerfelt and his new wife. After their meal, the four of them took a walk round the fair stalls and even though Beck noted that half of the stands were still there, this was the last mention of the *Haagse kermis*.[92]

Nevertheless, not long after the *kermis* in The Hague ended the *kermis* in Leiden began. On the morning of 18 May, Beck received a letter from his brother Hendrik stating that he intended to go to the *kermis* in Leiden the next day. For some reason this plan did not happen, and Beck decided to go by himself on the 23rd. This was no small undertaking: David woke up at four in the morning in order to take the cart to Leiden one hour later. This trip took some three hours, with Beck arriving in Leiden around eight in the morning. He spent his morning "taking many a walk through and through the city seeing the fair stalls on and under the town hall".[93] In the afternoon, he had lunch with David du Prez, who therewith reciprocated Beck's hospitality during the *Haagse kermis* here in Leiden. Beck had also received a lunch invitation at the home of Johannes Meurskens, a professor at the university of Leiden and master of Beck's sister-in-law Anneke, who had invited Beck's uncle Adrian as well.[94] Beck did not attend this lunch, but did pass by Meurskens's house for a drink later that afternoon. He returned to The Hague that evening.

While the *kermis* in The Hague ended with Ascension, the *kermis* in Leiden ended with Pentecost on 25 May. This did not mean, however, that people had to wait long for the next *kermis* because on 27 May the fair in the nearby village of Scheveningen commenced. Beck did not attend the *kermis* himself, but noted that during one of his walks he ran into "a mass of *kermis* guests by cart and on foot" that had fled the *kermis* because of unexpected bad weather.

Because Beck was such a great fan of "celebrities", he also noted that the king and queen of Bohemia and "almost all the greats" had visited the fair in Scheveningen as well.[95] This reveals that, like the pancaking ritual, the calendar feast of *kermis* also provided entertainment to the upper crust of Dutch society. But P.C. Hooft's letters make it clear that to him the *kermis* in Amsterdam was a good occasion for inviting his friends from Amsterdam over to his castle in Muiden to avoid the terrible *kermis* bustle.[96] As such, this occasion could be used as a means of distinction.

The reason why Beck himself did not necessarily feel the need to attend the Scheveningen fair is that he didn't have any relatives or friends there. However interesting these fairs may have been, the *kermis* for Beck and his friends was mostly a social event. They used the *kermis* as an opportunity to visit friends and family in other towns; the stalls were appealing as such, but the main point of interest during the *kermis* season was visiting or receiving friends and family from other towns. Another opportunity presented itself in June, when the fair in Delft took place. Brother Hendrik sent David a poetic invitation in entitled "The Delft *kermis* cart", with which "he invited us and all friends to the *kermis*".[97]

As with any other festivity, this *kermis* celebration at Hendrik's place was no small affair. On 16 June, Hendrik and his wife Eva were joined for lunch by David, Steven, Breckerfelt, uncle Adrian, Diliane, Adrian Jr., and Sara from The Hague, Eva's father, mother and brother from Delft and a sister and brother-in-law from Rotterdam. Presumably, this party included Hendrik's three children as well, which would add up to a total number of seventeen attendees. Hendrik Beck and friends "tried to put a dash" on the event until four in the afternoon. After which David visited some other acquaintances in Delft, to have a chat and a drink.[98] Unlike his sister and his children, David did not remain in Delft overnight. However, a couple of days later he returned to Delft to visit the *kermis* once more, and on that occasion he did make use of Hendrik's hospitality.

Then from mid-June until mid-September there was no mention of further fairs, until the fair in Amsterdam. Beck wrote that he intended to go to this fair in order to "visit acquaintances and friends".[99] On 20 September, Beck sent his luggage to Amsterdam along with a letter to his cousin Pieter Beck to inform him of his arrival. The following day Beck left very early by barge. In Leiden, he met his brother Hendrik, who was travelling to Amsterdam from Delft. They arrived in Amsterdam around four in the afternoon where they first joined their cousin Pieter for lunch. After lunch they walked around Amsterdam and stopped by to greet some other friends. In the evening, they were treated to a nice dinner of "cooked and baked" food, wine and beer and Portuguese bread which, according to Beck, was exceptionally delicious.[100] Beck remained in Amsterdam until 24 September, passing the time by visiting friends and other acquaintances, and having nice lunches and dinners. These dinners must have been quite lavish at times, since David and his brother on several occasions skipped lunch because they were expecting to be served an extravagant dinner in the evening.[101]

In Amsterdam Beck received a note that the ordinary *kermis* in The Hague had been cancelled by the States General, because "there was not one stall", which was probably due to the plague. According to David, however, this cancellation did not prevent people from "having guests, walking around and idling away for two or three days".[102] This seems a rather interesting observation by a man who himself had just spent days on end being a guest, walking around and being idle.

Yet the *kermis* did dramatically upset the daily routine. Beck, for instance, noted that during the fair in The Hague, he gave his schoolchildren some days off, since most of them were not attending school anyway. Once the Scheveningen fair had begun he did the same, because few students came to school "due to the nice weather and the *Schevelingsche kermis*".[103] During the fair in Delft, school attendance was very low as well.[104] The *kermis* season was basically a period of leisure, socialising and fun, entailing lots of social functions, nice food and the occasional drink. At the same time, it was a period when "normal" life was put on hold for an extensive period of time.

The importance of these fairs for Beck and his circle was the opportunity they offered to visit and receive family and friends from other towns. That these friends and family were welcome to stay at one's house and come for dinners went without saying, as did the fact that this hospitality would be reciprocated at the following opportunity such as the next *kermis*. But those who stayed behind could also get lucky. On 26 September, David's luggage from Amsterdam arrived. It included cakes, which he gave as presents to his children, his mother-in-law, Jaccomijntje, Breckerfelt's wife and Diliane.[105]

The Harst

Another important ritual connected to the calendar year noted in Beck's diary was *harst*, which consisted of dinners during the ox market period in November. Generally speaking, November was slaughter month, when people would buy the meat they needed for the coming season.[106] The meat was preserved for storage during the winter. Beck's friends and relatives who had purchased an ox or pig were in the habit of inviting friends and relatives to consume meals prepared from the freshly slaughtered animal. These dinners were usually attended by many guests who would be invited beforehand, and the dinner would include not only meat but also copious amounts of wine.[107] Beck attended several of these *harst* dinners during this period.[108]

The ox markets in The Hague took place every Monday during November, which also coincided with the pig markets.[109] The first big ox market in The Hague in 1624 took place on 28 October. Beck gave his pupils the day off for the occasion, which was to his own convenience as well. In the early morning, he walked around the market with Breckerfelt and an uncle of his late wife. Later that day he returned to view "the market, the ox market and the pig market" once more.[110] On 4 November, the second ox market took place, which once again resulted in low school attendance. Later that day, Jaccomijntje passed by to tell Beck that his mother-in-law had bought an ox together with Van Ruyven, one of her neighbours. The ox would be slaughtered later that day. That afternoon, Beck visited his mother-in-law "to see the ox". This was not just a matter of looking at the animal, but was also a ritual. The observers would inspect the ox and compliment the new owner on his choice of animal. The owner would in turn offer drinks to the observers as an offering of thanks for the compliments.[111]

After the animal was slaughtered, the real work – and the real fun – started. First the various sections of the animal's meat had to be preserved. Beck mentions methods like the salting and smoking of the meat, as well as the making of sausages. This coincides with preparation methods in one of the few Dutch seventeenth-century cookbooks, *De verstandige kock of sorghvuldige huyshoud-ster*.[112] This book included a chapter on *The Hollandtse Slacht-tijdt*, in which instructions were given on "how one can provide oneself with a stock of meat before the winter".[113] Recipes were offered on how to salt and smoke meat and on how to make sausages.[114] However, those parts of the animal that could not be preserved had to be eaten straight away, so as not to let precious food go to waste. Therefore, slaughter month coincided with numerous feasts, at which a hotchpotch of meat would be eaten and large quantities of wine would be consumed. Both the feasts and the food served could be referred to as the *harst*.

Beck received his first *harst* invitation on 6 November. After buying provisions for making candles from "the smear of her ox", Beck's mother-in-law made a short stop at Beck's home to invite him to dinner that evening.[115] Unfortunately, David did not elaborate on the event any further. He did, however, when he was invited to his brother Hendrik's *harst* a couple of days later. When David and Breckerfelt left for Delft, the weather was so bad that "one wouldn't even send a dog out", to which Beck added that *"amor vincit omnia"*. And for good reason, because when they arrived at Hendrik's house the blazing fire was so big that one could have easily "roasted half a cow" next to it. Beck and company spent a very merry evening with "brother's hotchpotch, sausages and knickknacks from the cow and the pig".[116] Another merry occasion was the *harst* at the home of David's tailor, Beerent Zwidde, who, like David, had just been widowed. The mourning did not necessarily result in a less festive *harst* dinner, however. After dinner, the company was in an "elated mood" with lots of singing, dancing and jumping.[117] David did not return home until two o'clock in the morning, by which time he was pretty inebriated. The next morning, David was not feeling too well due to the amounts of wine he had consumed the night before, and so he refrained from eating until dinnertime.[118]

The last ox market of the year in The Hague was on 11 November, or so David noted. But this did not mark the end of the *harst* period, because David subsequently attended at least four more *harst* dinners. The last one of these took place on 28 November. Furthermore this "last ox market" did not keep him from requesting that his mother-in-law buy him some beef two days later.[119] On 17 November, he passed by her house again in order to discuss the meat she was going to buy him on the ox market the next day.[120] In the end, it was Jaccomijntje who bought and deliverd the requested 75 pounds of beef to his home. That same evening the meat was salted by an "old salter", who took about an hour to finish his job. In the meantime, Beck played his violin and had a chat with the old man. The old salter must have been a pretty efficient character; later that month, David sold a pot full of the remaining salt to Breckerfelt, to salt his own meat with. The salting was not the end of the meat preparations, however. The meat was first smoked in Beck's fireplace and on 23 November, David called upon his brother Steven to carry the cured meat to his mother-in-law's house to hangup.

Not only was the slaughter period a period of hospitality, it also resulted in offerings of food. On 18 November, *moeijtgen* Lijsbeth, the wife of uncle Adrian, brought David a "hotchpotch of their slaughtered ox".[121]

Sinterklaas

On the evening of 5 December, Beck noted in his diary that "according to the rule of the papacy" it was *Sinterklaas* evening.[122] He complained about the noise made by the youngsters in the street who were "buying, selling and walking around".[123] These youngsters were obviously visiting the *Sinterklaas* market held on the eve of the day of death of St. Nicholas. This market sold toys and foodstuffs related to the celebration of *Sinterklaas*. Naturally these markets also offered an opportunity for the young to mingle and be merry.[124]

Beck's remarks suggest that he was not too keen on the celebration of Sinterklaas. St. Nicholas was a Catholic saint, whose death was commemorated by the offering of small presents to children and the exchange of *Sinterklaas* cookies and marzipan amongst adults. But after the Reformation this feast was considered part of the "popish superstition" by Dutch Calvinist government officials, who occasionally made an effort to banish this practice.[125] One would expect that Beck, as a practising Calvinist would subscribe to this idea and would refrain from celebrating *Sinterklaas* altogether.

However, in spite of his initial reluctance towards *Sinterklaas*, the following day, Beck noted that his brother Steven and Jaccomijntje, on behalf of Beck's mother-in-law, had that morning passed by his house to offer his children their "Sinterklaas goodies".[126] Unfortunately, Beck did not describe what these goodies consisted of, but these were traditionally special cookies, candy and small toys. Bredero wrote a play in which one of the characters sums up a number of typical gifts such as "peperhouses", which was a type of gingerbread, a club with a top, and apples stuffed with coins.[127] These gifts were distributed in the children's shoes which were placed next to the fireplace. Children believed that *Sinterklaas* filled their shoes by lowering his gifts down the chimney.[128]

Thus it seems that whatever his personal feelings were towards the celebration of *Sinterklaas*, it did not prevent his children from receiving their *Sinterklaas* gifts. The same is true for the event of *vastelavond* which was also prohibited by the authorities because it was associated with popish superstition, and yet was enthusiastically celebrated by David Beck and his friends, most of whom adhered to the Reformed faith while some were members of the Calvinist Church. This shows that the official banning of Catholic traditions was not necessarily adhered to in everyday life, not even among Dutch Calvinists.[129]

Christian holidays?

In contrast to this phenomenon it is interesting to note that Christian Holidays played only a small role in David's life, at least in terms of gift exchange. This is not due to a lack of faith on Beck's part, however. He was in fact a practising Calvinist as a member of the Reformed church in The Hague, and he attended the main service in the Grand Church almost every Sunday.[130] He also regularly attended other services, read the Bible and enjoyed spending his evenings singing psalms with Breckerfelt and his sister Diliane.

Moreover, it is not that he was unaware of these holidays because he was. He diligently recorded the arrival of Easter, Ascension, Pentecost and Christmas – on 7 April *"Paeschen"*, 16 May *"hemel-vaerts-dag"* and on 26 May *"pinsterdag"* – but as far as we can gather from the diary, these were not days of celebration for Beck and his friends.[131] Beck reserved these days for church attendance. He usually went more than once, except on Ascension when he went to see a doctor in the afternoon to have himself purged. On Easter Sunday, Beck noted that he, Diliane, and Jaccomijntje had taken Holy Communion.[132] This was the first communion for the girls, and Beck had been preparing them for it the week before.[133] But other than these remarks, these days did not receive any special attention in his diary.[134]

During the Christmas season, Beck and his brother Steven were in Amsterdam for a couple of days to visit family and friends.[135] They stayed at their cousin Pieter Beck's house. On Christmas day they attended church three times, but other than that, the diary does not provide any clues that this was an exceptionally festive period of the year. There were no special Christmas visits, no gifts exchanged and no special dinners arranged. The one special dinner Beck does mention was on 28 December, which Beck explicitly referred to as their *"foij"*.[136] This dinner did not have anything to do with Christmas, and was a farewell for their friends in Amsterdam.

All in all it seems that even though Beck was a practising Calvinist, he did not consider Christian holidays as occasions for the exchange of festive hospitality or presents. In that respect, it is possible to conclude that when it came to Christian holidays, Beck and his social circle subscribed to basic Calvinist preferences by celebrating these events in a solemn and reflective manner. Christian holidays meant attending church and reading the Bible, but they were not considered occasions for festivity or socialising. These holidays belonged in the sacred sphere. But when it came to the more worldly (or Catholic) festive traditions, Beck and his family and friends did not consider it inappropriate to celebrate in a more worldly fashion. In that respect, one might say they had a double standard; the Christian holidays had a spiritual character, while Catholic traditions were part of the festive calendar and were celebrated as social events. The same holds true for stadholder Willem Frederik who also seemed to enjoy the festivities surrounding calendar feasts like carnival, but when it came to

Christian holidays, preferred church attendance and reflection over festivity.[137]

Patterns of exchange connected to the ritual year

Certain patterns of exchange can be gathered from David Beck's diary. It reveals that the calendar feasts in David Beck's life largely took place within the confines of private homes.[138] Beck does occasionally refer to some celebrations on the streets of The Hague, like, for instance, the planting of the May Tree in front of town hall or with *Sinterklaas,* and he did visit the *kermis* stalls. But it seems that the actual public feasts were reserved for adolescents and at no point did Beck appear to take part in any of these events. Still Beck and his family and friends did enjoy organising private dinner parties on occasions like Carnival and during the *harst* period. Although it was not uncommon for out-of-towners to spend the night, these events focused mostly on the dinner itself and the food and drink. This is true for the *harst* dinners organised specifically around the animal slaughters in November, as well as the carnival meals that mostly consisted of pancakes.

The annual *kermis,* or fair, on the other hand, was an event at which an offer of lodging to out-of-towners was the main point of interest. Since the fairs moved from one town to the next, they afforded people the opportunity to visit friends and family all over the country. People usually stayed with close relatives, who provided lodging for a number of nights and this hospitality also offered them a chance to visit other relatives, friends and acquaintances in town. In that sense, the *kermis* functioned as an occasion to reacquaint themselves with friends and family who lived further away and with whom contact on a daily basis was impossible. The hospitality Beck offered his relatives would naturally be reciprocated whenever there was a fair in their hometown.

Even though calendar feasts were celebrated in private homes, this did not mean that Beck and his relatives were particularly selective in whom they invited for these occasions. They might invite up to ten or even more people to the house, not including household members themselves. The majority of the invitees consisted of next of kin and close friends, but it was not uncommon for these guests to bring family and in-laws and some close friends. This would generally not be considered an insult and definitely seems to have added to the merrymaking.

The importance of these calendar feasts should not be underrated. Carnival, the *kermis* and the *harst* were quite extended periods during the calendar year in which normal life was for a large part put on hold. These were occasions for intense socialising both with family and friends, which included offerings of food, drink and lodging. There were no strict obligations as to who was obliged to organise parties; this was left to personal incentive. It was clear that those who were willing and able to offer a dinner would enjoy organising one and that those who were invited enjoyed attending these events, even though it was also clear that any hospitality received was in due time to be returned. This reciprocal duty was not so much regarded as an obligation, but more as matter of course. In that sense calendar feasts seem to have been an enjoyable and benign means of maintaining relationships with family and friends. As will be discussed later, other types of occasions and relations sometimes brought obligations that were less enjoyable and less free.

Now let's end the discussion of the important calendar feasts in David Beck's life where we started: New Year's Eve. When travelling back from their visit to Amsterdam, David's brother Steven fell off the carriage and broke his leg. On the last day of 1624, his master Riccen came to visit the unfortunate man and offered him a basket of goodies. However much Steven would have appreciated this gesture, it does leave the historian with a problem. Would this gift be considered a New Year's gift in the style of the French *étrennes*, or a form of charity for the sick? It is impossible to tell. This just goes to show that diaries, however interesting and insightful, do have their disadvantages as a source for historic research: there is always the possibility of coincidence.

Hospitality and Rites of Passage

Calendar feasts were not the only type of ritual occasions that coincided with the offering of hospitality. Rites of passage such as christenings, funerals and weddings were also events when hosts offered dinners and drinks to relatives and friends. Obviously, a diary like David Beck's only offers information on these kind of events upon occurrence, and unfortunately 1624 was not a very busy year in terms of births, marriages and deaths, at least for the Beck household. However, Beck does mention a number of weddings and Beck's sister-in-law did give birth to a baby daughter.

Unexpected engagements

One of the most intriguing events with respect to gift exchange that surrounded rites of passage in David Beck's diary is the wedding of his best friend Herman Breckerfelt. For some reason Beck was not aware of the intended marriage of his friend, and when it finally happened he neither attended nor offered any proper gifts. On 18 March 1624, Beck noted in his diary that in the morning he had attended the, earlier-mentioned, farewell breakfast of his young brother Abraham and a female acquaintance, Jenneke Arents. Jenneke, who was from Arnhem, returned home after having spent some days in The Hague to visit friends. To David's surprise he was informed later that day that Breckerfelt had actually joined Jenneke to go to Arnhem. Initial surprise notwithstanding, Beck and his sister Diliane soon agreed that Herman must have departed for Arnhem "to contract a marriage", the lucky woman in this case being Jenneke.[139]

A little over a week later, Herman returned to The Hague and informed David that he had indeed become engaged to be married to Jenneke Arents.[140] The next morning, Herman and David spent an hour discussing the intended marriage. This must have been either very early or David had slept late, for he mentions still being in bed while talking to his friend. On 31 March, Breckerfelt's marriage was announced in church for the first time.[141]

The next day "bridegroom Breckerfelt" passed by to talk to David. This time he needed David's help because he had to have his wedding suit made, but did not have the means to pay for it. He asked David whether he could arrange for him to get an agreeable price for his fabrics. A couple of days later, Breckerfelt was still in turmoil, according to Beck, he was "moneyless, half desperate [...] and full of heavy thoughts".[142] One of his troubles was that he had rented a new house and workshop beginning in May, but his new landlord refused to allow an extra person stay in the house, unless Breckerfelt was willing to pay extra rent.

On the 18 of April, Breckerfelt eventually left for Arnhem to be married to his Jenneke. It seems that neither Beck nor any other friends of Herman's from The Hague went to Arnhem to attend the wedding. They did discuss the event extensively, but this was done to tease Jaccomijntje, who supposedly had a soft spot for Breckerfelt.[143] Herman Breckerfelt and his new wife did not return to The Hague until 6 May. When they finally did, Beck and Hendrik hurried to the newlyweds' home to give them a warm welcome. Whether this did Jenneke any good is uncertain, because, according to Beck, she was "melancholically sad and half sick from the changes and the loneliness".[144]

Although David Beck and Herman Breckerfelt can be considered good friends, there is no sign that David in any way took part in the wedding celebrations. Breckerfelt's brother Jan had also stayed in The Hague, while the wedding ceremony was taking place in Arnhem. Both David and Jan did send the newlyweds a letter to congratulate them, but other than that it seems they did not offer Breckerfelt any particular gifts. According to Beck, his letter was "sweet and poetic", which suggests that it was actually more of a poem than a letter proper.[145]

Hospitality at birth

Unlike Breckerfelt's marriage, the birth of Beck's new niece was an important event that was celebrated quite extensively. In general, there were several festive moments that surrounded the birth of a child in the seventeenth century. The first of these was the actual birth itself, which was followed by a dinner on the birthday for close family and friends. After the dinner, a number of other dinners followed which allowed relatives from out of town to join in the festivities. Furthermore, there was the christening of the child, which was followed by a dinner and then some festive event would also take place after the churching of the mother.

On 4 March 1624, Beck received a short note from his brother Hendrik in Delft. The note had been written at around six in the morning and said that Hendrik's wife Eva had been in labour since two o'clock that morning.[146] These must have been exciting hours for Hendrik, because while his wife was giving birth there was really not much he could do. In the early-modern period, the delivery of a child was – under normal circumstances – handled by women only.[147] Usually the mother of the mother-to-be was sent for with the first signs of labour as were the midwife and any other possible female helpers, usually relatives and neighbours.[148] According to the letter, Eva could count on the support of several women during her delivery as well, since Hendrik had informed David that his wife was "among the women". So Hendrik just sat in his office and wrote notes to inform other relatives of the situation.

This was obviously the male task during the delivery. For instance, Pieter Teding van Berkhout, a Dutch regent, made notes of his wife's delivery in his diary on 6 April 1670. According to these notes, her labour pains started at one in the morning, but since the pain was still bearable in those first few hours, the couple did not inform anyone until five. When they finally did, one of their aunts and a sister arrived quickly "at their bed" and prepared everything for the birth. His wife, however, remained in labour for another few hours. By quarter to one in the afternoon, they decided to call for further assistance, which consisted of another aunt, five female cousins, one neighbour and the midwife. Around seven that evening, his wife delivered, "by God's grace", a "stout" daughter, which brought the father "no small pleasure", or so he himself noted. An hour later, the new mother was ready to go to bed and the infant was swaddled and ready to be shown to the world. Pieter had invited some friends and relatives over for dinner and they were merry till around midnight.[149]

Immediately after the delivery, Pieter sent a servant to The Hague on horseback with letters to inform family and friends of his good fortune. The first of these were addressed to his father, his father-in-law, one of his aunts and one of his uncles. He spent the next morning writing more letters. All in all, he wrote fifteen other people in five different cities. These were, in turn, requested to spread the news among another forty acquaintances.

In Hendrik's case, all went well: In the afternoon of that same day David received a message that at one o'clock, his brother Hendrik had become the proud father of a baby daughter.[150] This was obviously a reason for celebration and in the evening David and Breckerfelt left for Delft to visit the new parents. They arrived just in time for dinner.[151] After dinner, the men spent some time in Hendrik's office where they reread letters that David had sent to Hendrik over the last few years. These were cause for great laughter, especially since they included some drollery involving Breckerfelt. After midnight, the men went to bed. The three men shared one bed, which led Beck to remark that they "were packed in like herrings". David was especially unfortunate, since he ended up in the middle.

Neither Beck nor Teding van Berkhout mentioned what was served to the guests on this occasion, but traditionally this would have been *ypocras* or *kandeel*, a drink consisting of sugared wine with a cinnamon stirring stick.[152] According to Hieronymus Sweerts, the author of a satiric work on the ten joys of marriage, the wine that was served was an issue of considerable honour for fathers. In fact, when P.C. Hooft once wrote his brother-in-law Joost Baeck requesting that the latter order wine for him, Hooft referred to the wine he had recently drunk at his sister's maternity visit of as being the best wine he had drunk in years.[153] Unfortunately, his sister's baby died soon afterwards and the wine served at the funeral was of lesser quality. This lead Hooft to comment in another letter to Baeck that the quality of the wines served differed as much as "life and death".[154]

Four days after the birth of Beck's niece, she was christened. Beck did not attend this event himself, but he noted that his brother Steven went off to Delft that day to stand as a witness or *compeer* as Beck put it.[155] But three days later "sister" Jaccomijntje, the bastard sister of his late wife, went to Delft to become godmother to the child and to attend the *blymael*, or "happy meal", which was given to celebrate the event with neighbours and friends.[156]

This seems a rather awkward situation: Both Steven and Jaccomijntje were becoming godparents to the child on totally different days. The first explanation for this might be that Jaccomijntje was in fact only a half-sister of Beck's late wife and that she therefore was attending the christening of a relative from the other side of her family. However, archive material does not suggest that there were any other christenings she could have attended.[157] Moreover, even though Jaccomijntje was a bastard child, her social life was fully integrated into that of her stepmother and her relatives, which also included the Beck brothers. In fact, the Delft archives show that Stephen Beck and Anneke Pieters were the only witnesses at the christening of Sara Beck, daughter of Hendrik Beck and Eva Aelbrechts Schoonhave.[158] And according to the archives, Sara was christened on 9 April, which is one day later than Beck claimed in his diary. These are all rather confusing events, with no (obvious) explanations.

However, the celebrations for the birth of Hendrik's daughter went on, because three days later Beck himself went to Delft once more to have *kandeel* – this time he does mention it – at Hendrik's place.[159] These ongoing celebrations of births were satirised by the aforementioned Hieronymus Sweerts as being one of the "joys" of marriage, which suggest that they were at least fairly common. It is not clear whether the people that enjoyed the hospitality of the proud father and mother actually brought any gifts. Beck, at least, did not mention bringing any gifts on any of the occasions that celebrated the birth of his niece. Nevertheless, it seems likely that at least his brother Steven would have brought the child a present at some point during the course of the first year. He was after all the godfather and *pillegiften*, the gifts offered by godparents were considered among the most important gifts an individual received in the course of a lifetime. These *pillegiften* and the meaning ascribed to them in seventeenth-century Holland will be discussed later.

Support at death and drunkenness at funerals

Death was obviously a major theme in David Beck's diary because his wife had just died a few weeks before he started his diary.[160] As mentioned earlier, it is not that David spent a lot of words on his bereavement, but he does occasionally comment on his late wife's qualities. On 8 January, for instance, he passed some time waiting for his uncle Adrian van der Cruijsse whilst talking to his uncle's mother-in-law. Beck accompanied her for over one and half hours and they discussed "several edifying matters, as well as my first date with my beloved R. of blessed memory, and of her talents and Christian virtues".[161]

Furthermore, Beck seemed extremely pleased when Daniel de Kempenaer, a poet who had just written an epitaph upon the death of some baron, promised to write Beck an epitaph for Roeltje. De Kempenaer was presumably not the only poet that made this promise; Beck mentioned that many of his other friends had done so as well.[162] Beck himself used much of his spare time in 1624 to write a lamentation upon the death of his wife. He finished the neat copy of this "Lamentation on the Death of Rolande" on 10 October, which he then brought to his mother-in-law to offer as a gift.[163] In that sense, the death of his wife was indeed an important theme in Beck's life in 1624.

However, it was not only the demise of his wife that received attention in Beck's diary. He duly noted all of the deaths and funerals in his diary, both of people he knew personally and of people that were in the public eye. This included the demise of Christian Huygens, Constantijn Huygens' father. On 7 February, Beck noted that "this day (or hereabouts) died the secretary Huygens".[164] The secretary was buried shortly afterwards, on which occasion Beck noted that "the secretary Huijgens was buried here this afternoon in the grand church with a great following of grand masters and lords, among whom the prince of Orange".[165] Another funeral that made a big impression on Beck was that of Ursula von Solms, daughter of count Johan Albert von Solms, who according to Beck was buried "magnificently".[166]

As a matter of fact, death was all around in the year 1624, especially during the summer months when the plague remained a constant threat. The mortality rate was particularly high in the cities of Delft, Arnhem and Leiden, or at least this much is noted in Beck's diary.[167] On 1 August, Jaccomijntje returned from an overnight stay in Delft in the course of the morning. By the time she had left Delft, 42 people had already been buried that day.[168] This naturally meant that people were scared and any hint of disease was regarded with great fear. When some of cousin Overschie's acquaintances were diagnosed with the plague he was very upset and asked for Beck and some others to join him for dinner "to comfort and accompany" him and his anguished family.[169]

This anxiety did not always turn out to be necessary. Beck's brother Hendrik was quite "worried and disturbed" when Herman Arents, Breckerfelt's brother-in-law with whom Hendrik had just spent an evening, appeared to have symptoms of the disease. But shortly thereafter, Herman was feeling his old self again. This was of great relief to Hendrik as well. This relief must have been short lived for the fear of the plague remained ever present during these months.[170] Entire families were swept away by the disease: husbands and wives, children and servants.[171] As Beck wrote in Delft "one heard nothing but complaining, sighing, bells chiming and talking of dying and death" and people did nothing but "going and coming to bury the dead".[172]

The plague did not only have an emotional effect on the lives of Beck and his circle, it also had practical consequences. Beck's school, for instance, was "half empty" during these months since parents kept their children at home.[173] Some families even decided to temporarily relocate to avoid coming into contact with the lethal disease. Beck's sister-in-law Anneke, who was the maid of a well-to-do family from Leiden, moved with the entire household to the neighbouring village of Wassenaar just to be on the safe side.[174] The family head, Johannes Meurs or Meursius, was a professor at the University of Leiden and the fact that he would be fined for leaving the city of Leiden without permission obviously did not keep him from seeking refuge in quieter Wassenaar. The brother of David's neighbour who was a student in Leiden also sought refuge outside this university town. He fled to his family's home in The Hague.[175] Another one of the unfortunate repercussions was that the *kermis* normally held in The Hague in September was cancelled, as was discussed earlier.[176]

Naturally, Beck did not just take notes on disease and death, he also occasionally attended funerals as well. He attended some of these funerals in order to pay his last respects to someone he had been familiar with and to offer support to the mourning family. But it seems that occasionally Beck also attended funerals on the request of more or less distant relatives that asked him to join them as chaperone to these funerals. In these cases, Beck himself was not close to the deceased or the bereaving, but went along to offer his relatives support. This support may have been practical as well as emotional: In these cases, he was sometimes also asked to arrange the barge or carriage that would carry the party to the funeral.[177]

Another funeral he attended was the one for his neighbour Neeltje Jans on 8 June.[178] She had died two days earlier after having been ill for 30 hours. Beck was one of the first to hear about her demise because the crying of Neeltje's beloved had awoken him early on the morning of 6 June. Since he couldn't get back to sleep after hearing the news, he went out that early morning to inform his mother-in-law, Jaccomijntje and others of the sad demise of his neighbour. So, 6 June turned out to be a rather sad day, because that same afternoon, Beck visited Daniel della Faille, the boyfriend of one of the neighbour girls, who was lying at home "sick to death". Beck joined Daniel's neighbours and friends in prayer, after which he left.[179]

This offering of comfort and company to the sick, the dying and the bereaving was quite common. When the wife of his tailor and friend Berent Zwidde was severely ill and about to die, Beck went over to their home to try to comfort her by saying a last prayer with her. Later that day, he returned only to witness her last sigh and fall "blissfully asleep in the Lord".[180] After the death of Zwidde's wife, Beck visited him a number of times "in his loneliness" as a means of offering comfort.[181]

Beck's presence in the last of hours of the lives of these neighbours may be explained in two ways. First of all, he may have visited them because neighbours in the early-modern period often played an important role in the last rites at death. They were, for instance, responsible for confirming the actual death, for carrying the coffin and for ringing the bells at the funeral.[182] Secondly, as a schoolmaster, Beck may have also had certain responsibilities at the moment of death. According to Schotel, it was either a schoolmaster or a *ziekentrooster* who was called to the bedside of the dying in order to comfort them.[183]

Although Beck attended funerals of people he hardly knew as a chaperone, at other times, he would refrain from attending the funeral of someone he was close to even though he was aware that this was inconsiderate.[184] In November, the wife of his *compeer* Matthijs Muller gave birth to twins. Unfortunately, one of them died soon after birth and was buried a few days later. Beck had intended to go to the funeral and was already on his way when he realised he would probably arrive late. Thus, he decided to return to school and to apologise to Muller in the evening. But it seems that he ended up being the one who missed out because when his uncle had returned from the same funeral that afternoon he was, according to Beck, "rather tipsy".[185]

That funerals could lead to an abuse of alcohol was not uncommon. After the funeral of Crispijn van den Queeborn's father-in-law, Beck himself got "relatively drunk".[186] One might think that this was because the death of this man was not that sad of an occasion since he – and this was a rather exceptional event in the summer 1624 – had died of old age.[187] However, the offering of wine and even meals after funerals was a long-standing tradition. According to Van Alkemade, it derived from the habit of providing friends and family who had come from out of town to pay their last respects with a meal in order to "in an admissible way temper and divert their sadness".[188] As one might expect, this was not appreciated by government officials who tried to outlaw this practice through legislation.[189]

So, all in all, sickness and death prompted several forms of gift exchange. People offered their support to the sick by comforting them, and by praying with them. The next of kin could count on relatives who would attend funerals, offer condolences and write poems in praise of the deceased. Funeral attendees were reciprocated for their support through the offering of wine or other alcoholic drinks.

Other Gifts

What David Beck's diary shows is that the most important gift in terms of quantity was hospitality. Hospitality was exchanged on a daily basis and every type of occasion from christenings to funerals and from carnival to the *kermis* had its shows of hospitality. Still, this was not the only type of gift that Beck and his friends, relatives and professional contacts were exchanging. Occasionally they offered other types of gifts as well. Unlike hospitality, these offerings were more likely to be connected to a specific occasion or a specific network. Rites of passage, for instance, were the only occasion at which David Beck and his family would offer material gifts. Even though gift exchange in contemporary society is largely associated with material objects as gifts, the offering of objects was quite uncommon in the seventeenth century. These objects were usually related to very specific occasions, of which there were only a few in the course of a lifetime. As a matter of fact, in the entire diary there is only one instance in which Beck mentions that an object was offered as a gift. This is when an uncle passed by Beck's house to drop off a present on behalf of his daughter Geertruyt for Beck's daughter Roeltje.[190] Geertruyt van Overschie was the cousin of his late wife and was Roeltje's godmother. This gift consisted of a silver cup and was offered to Roeltje as a belated christening gift. As shall be discussed later, this offering of a (silver) christening gift, or *pillegift*, was a common practice in seventeenth-century Holland. It was considered a proper gift from a godmother to her godchildren among all the social classes.

Even though objects may not have been the most common gift exchanged during David Beck's life, it is important to realise that objects received as gifts were quite significant in other respects. Since objects were offered largely during rites of passage such as christenings and weddings, which were, and still are, significant events, these objects were laden with meaning. Their symbolic meaning was obviously connected to the ritual event and referred to the passage from one stage of life to the next, but the symbolic significance of these objects did not necessarily prevent the recipients from appreciating their monetary value as well. As will be discussed in part II, the symbolic meaning and monetary value of these objects probably complemented each other.

Practical and emotional support

The number of material gifts mentioned in David Beck's diary may be slightly disappointing, but there are plenty of examples of offerings of support. The types of support that Beck described in his diary are mainly practical and emotional support. Financial support between family members must have been a widespread phenomenon in the early-modern period, but this type of support is not mentioned in his diary because Beck probably would have noted any money lent or borrowed in his account book.[191] As shall be shown in part III, the autobiography of Herman Verbeeck includes several references to the practical and financial support he received from his relatives. In fact, his whole autobiography can be read as a means of coming to terms with the unfortunate turns his life took and his glossing over the support he received from his relatives.

Even though Beck's diary does not refer to financial support, he does offer some insights on how he and his circle helped each other in their daily lives. Beck assisted several family members and close friends by writing letters and seeking intermediaries for those who needed a hand. Not only was he asked to put in a good word with the tailor on the occasion of Breckerfelt's wedding, Beck also mediated for others. He used both his skills as a writer and his good contacts in The Hague to do so.

When his cousin Mannes sought a position as an apothecary in the army, David went to great lengths to plead his case. The first mention of this type of support came during the *kermis* in May when Mannes spent a couple of days at Beck's house, and the two men inquired how Mannes should apply for the position.[192] In early June, Mannes spent a few more days at Beck's house "to promote his case".[193] During this visit, Beck wrote the neat copy of his official request to the States General.[194] He also asked his cousin Overschie, who was a medical doctor and an apothecary himself, to make a recommendation for Mannes.[195] Furthermore, he and Mannes visited some of the deputies of the States General to have them recommend Mannes for the job as well.[196] Eventually, it seems all these efforts were worth it, when Mannes secured the position.

In the meantime, Beck also assisted his cousin Pieter Beck from Amsterdam, when he needed to acquire passports for some relatives in Maastricht.[197] On 27 May, Beck went to see the Pieter Koenen, the clerk to the secretary of the stadholder, to request the passport. A month later, Beck picked up the passports and sent them to his cousin in Amsterdam.[198] A couple of days later, Beck received a letter from his cousin with some money to cover the expenses for the obtaining of the documents.[199]

The practical support one could offer naturally depended on one's skills and social contacts. Through his wife's family, Beck, for instance, had some relatively good contacts in The Hague who could help him or his friends out when needed. And since Beck was a particularly skilled writer – in the sense of the actual manual handwriting – he was often asked to write letters or other documents on the behalf of others.

These favours were returned whenever Beck needed the mediation of a person who one of his friends was acquainted with. This mediation could be offered spontaneously as well as upon request. It was the uncle of his friend Breckerfelt, for instance, who informed Beck that the schoolmaster at the French school in Arnhem had died, and offered to recommend him for the job.[200] This new position was why Beck left The Hague to live in Arnhem the following year.

But on other occasions, Beck also approached some of his contacts with the hope that they could mediate for him. This was the case when Beck was called up for duty in the civil guard in The Hague. The day after Beck had visited his brother Hendrik in Delft to celebrate the birth of his niece, he was called to the town hall by a messenger. When he arrived he was greeted by two of the burgomasters, Cassiopijn and Quartelaar, and the town secretary, Doublet, with whom Beck discussed the civil guard issue. Beck made it clear that he was not very eager to join, while they wanted Beck to join at all costs, whereupon he had to insist on postponing the decision for at least another day. In the end, they agreed to the postponement, and after leaving town hall, Beck immediately went to his cousin Clement Adriansz. van Overschie to beg him to use his contacts with burgomaster Quartelaar. Thereafter he went to his uncle Van Palesteijn to request that he "put in a good word" for him with both Quartelaar and Cassiopijn.[201] These two relatives were both members of the city council, and Beck hoped that they would be able to use their contacts with the burgomasters to let him of the hook.

In the evening, Beck also went round to the bailiff's house where he talked to his servant and asked him to recommend his case to his master. Beck was obviously very distressed, because after this visit to the bailiff, he again went to see cousin Van Overschie, to ask him whether he had already spoken to the burgomaster. This was unfortunately not the case, but he assured Beck that he would do so first thing in the morning. Beck then joined his mother-in-law for dinner, "being pancakes" as he noted despite his distress. The next morning brought relief at last; uncle Palesteijn came round to Beck's house to inform him that the result of the discussions he had had with the two burgomasters meant that they would not call him up for duty that year.[202]

This type of support was usually offered upon request and requesting favours was obviously not something Beck and his circle felt self-conscious about. In the course of this research, other examples will be offered that show that requesting favours was a common strategy in dealing with life's unfortunate events. It was not at all inappropriate to ask for help, but it is self-evident that who one could approach to ask for a favour largely depended on one's social position. Some people, for instance, could either ask the burgomasters directly for favours, whereas others could only approach a burgomaster indirectly through acquaintances.

Emotional support was not only offered to the sick and dying, as was shown earlier, but was something that could be offered to anyone in any kind of emotional turmoil. The plague brought so much distress to uncle Van Palesteijn that he asked for Beck, his mother-in-law and their friend Matthijs Muller to come round to his house to comfort him.[203] They all decided to have a few drinks to chase away "the melancholy a little". And after his tailor's wife died, Beck also spent an evening with him in order to raise his spirits.[204] The fact that Beck had just lost his wife himself may have made him more sensitive to the emotional needs of this new widower.

Attending funerals is also considered a type of emotional support in this study, as is the offering of funerary poetry and the writing of letters to the bereaving. Beck himself was highly honoured when a relatively well-known poet promised to write an epitaph upon the death of his wife, while he himself wrote poems on similar occasions .[205] These early-modern funerary poems and letters written upon the occasion of a death may appear rather rude and insensitive to the contemporary reader. The texts often advise the bereaved to be thankful for the death of their loved one, since there is no greater honour in life than to die and go to heaven. Even though this might suggest that early-modern individuals did not care about their fellow humans, this can more convincingly be explained in terms of the different mentality towards death during this period. This will be further discussed in the next chapter where funerary poetry and letters will be considered as a rite of passage gift. The meaning of these gifts will also be explored in greater depth.

Naturally, this system of offering and receiving support in times of need has a strong instrumental connotation attached to it. By receiving support one is obliged to return that support. In that sense, certain social relations could be used for personal gain, and purposes beyond the relationship itself. This obviously left room for the display of power for those in positions of offering support to a lot of different people and this most certainly happened, even to the extent that support may have been obvious corruption. However, offering support to friends and family in need was a natural and humane thing to do. On a subjective level, it was presumably also the obvious thing to do: it was just very normal to offer support to those in need. Even though objectively this system could be used as a strategy for augmenting one's social capital, it seems likely that those who were offering support were just offering support out of the kindness of their hearts and with a genuine interest in the well-being of their loved ones.

Intellectual and artistic gifts

Besides support offered in times of need, there were also some more playful gifts exchanged between Beck and his circle. There is, for instance, a striking amount of poetry exchanged within Beck's social network. Poems served as dinner invitations, were offered as wedding gifts and were exchanged by mail between Beck and his friends in Amsterdam.[206] As a matter of fact, intellectual and artistic gifts such as poems, books and drawings, were the third most common type of gift exchanged as noted in Beck's diary after hospitality and support. Needless to say, in this respect, that the gift exchange patterns as described in Beck's diary may not be representative of the Dutch population during this period. On the one hand, it was obvious that only those who could write, had the spare time and had an interest in the arts would write poetry themselves. On the other hand, however, the writing of poetry seems to have been a national hobby during this period of Dutch history. It seems that everybody who could write and had a certain interest – yet not necessarily the talent – wrote poetry. These poems were exchanged for fun, and were offered on special occasions such as weddings, funerals and – as noted above – on the occasional birthday.[207]

This barrage of poetry in Beck's case may be largely due to his ambitions as a poetic writer. He was certainly composing poetry for the sheer enjoyment of it, but also for another reason. It appears that Beck was seeking patronage. When one makes a thorough analysis of David Beck's diary, certain patterns emerge that show how Beck went about seeking patrons for his poetic works. The offering of poems to the nobleman Von Silbersteyn on New Year's Day was not meant only as a friendly gesture. Beck surely wished this honourable gentleman all the best for the New Year, but offering his poetry was also a means for getting this gentleman acquainted with Beck's poetic abilities. Beck obviously hoped this gesture might lead to the offer of a writing commission by this nobleman. His strategy apparently worked in this case, for Beck – as was shown earlier – later did receive some sort of payment from Von Silbersteyn, which was most likely offered to him for writing jobs Beck had performed for him. These probably did not involve the composition of poems; Beck also copied poems and official documents upon request. Unfortunately, his commissions were often somewhat less artistic than Beck would have hoped, and he ended up doing more copying than he probably would have liked.

Another acquaintance Beck was writing for was Christina Poppings. She lived in Amsterdam and occasionally wrote to Beck with the latest news, to send him copies of poems and to ask him to write her some poems.[208] Beck was commissioned to compose two poems in honour of her two nephews, but it is not clear on what occasion Christina would present these. Beck composed some verses straight away and sent them to Amsterdam along with a letter to Poppings herself.[209] Based on the fact that she sent him gossip stories and a copy of a poem one might consider Christina Poppings's relationship with Beck as more of a friend than as a patron. This seems unlikely, however, since Beck noted that she had not yet been informed of the death of his wife, which in the case of a good friend would have been rather insensitive considering that she had passed away over a month ago by this time. In that sense, the poems he composed for her were less likely gifts from Beck to Poppings, than gifts from Poppings to her nephews.

This was not an exceptional case. Beck was also asked to write other poems that would be later offered as a gift to a third party. When relatives had a wedding, one of Beck's uncles asked him to compose a poem for the newlyweds. This wedding poem would be copied by one of the young nephews of the couple "as though it was his own".[210] The young man would then read it aloud to them at the party, after which the written version would be offered to them as a gift.

Not only did Beck enjoy writing poetry, he enjoyed the arts in general. He regularly spent his evenings discussing the arts with his friend Herman Breckerfelt and the two friends also exchanged drawings and the like. Breckerfelt was actually a glass engraver and whenever he was commissioned to engrave something that needed a poem he would ask Beck to compose the requested poetry. This was done when one of Beck's relatives renovated his home, which would create a nice office for the cousin involved. The sister of this cousin thus ordered some engraved window-panes from Breckerfelt as a housewarming gift to add some cheer to her brother's new office. Breckerfelt in turn asked Beck to compose some poems that he could then engrave on these windows.

All in all, the offering of artistic gifts was quite common during this period. Whenever there was something to celebrate, poems would be composed for the occasion, and if one did not have a talent for poetry, one could always order a third party to write something nice. Furthermore, inscriptions and engravings on objects or glassware were very popular gifts. Gifts were usually custom-made for the recipients. They might include names, dates, and character descriptions or parables of proper behaviour. This resulted in a gift exchange system that was, especially when it came to occasions like weddings, highly personalised.

It should be pointed out, however, that occasional poetry also existed in a pre-printed version where only the names of the individuals involved and dates of the occasion needed to be added. Furthermore, there were also certain traditions and conventions within poetry that left less room for personal creativity than one might expect.[211] Nevertheless, even these cases involved at least some level of personalisation of the gift.

What makes the offering of Beck's poetic gifts so interesting is the fact that they so often seem to be on the verge of becoming something else. They were friendly tokens of affection, but they can also be interpreted as poetic adverts to obtain commissions. In chapter 3 Beck's strategic offering of poems to possible patrons will receive further scrutiny, as will the behaviour of some of the more important poets of that period like Hooft and Vondel. It is interesting to note that in the cases of these three poets, the exchange of poems, dedications and other gifts largely depended on their general position in society as well as their reputations as poets.

Food and drink

Food and drink as gifts here include all of those instances in which food or drink is delivered to another person as a gift and not offered as hospitality within the confines of one's own home. It could be, for instance, the wine or food that one would bring to a dinner party. Even though this did happen in Beck's case it was certainly not a habit to bring food, or anything else, when one was invited to dinner. The obligatory bottle of wine, box of chocolates or bunch of flowers that are nowadays the obvious dinner guest gift were certainly not in style in seventeenth-century Holland.[212]

As was shown earlier, Beck was occasionally offered game or poultry by relatives and on other occasions he received a fully prepared hotchpotch from his aunt. These kinds of foods – if not yet prepared – would usually be prepared as soon as possible and were commonly shared with others in a joint meal. Thus, the offering of food often led to the offering of hospitality. This was due to the fact that the food could not be kept for too long. It made sense to have it prepared and eaten on the earliest occasion.

There were also food gifts that were less practical and were more luxurious or decadent. Beck's children occasionally received candy from adults. The feast of *Sinterklaas* featured the tradition of offering food to children and this also applied to the Beck children. Both their uncle and their grandmother made sure they received their well-deserved *Sinterklaas* goodies. Beck himself brought his children cakes after visiting the *kermis* in Amsterdam. Many children were also spoiled by their godparents. Beck bought his godson David, the son of his brother Hendrik, a *tymp*, which is a type of sweet bread, on the occasion of New Year's.[213] Beck's own son Adrian received a bunch of grapes, which was then still a rather exotic fruit, from his godmother when she came to visit from Leiden.[214] Geertruyt Overschie, the godmother of Beck's daughter Roeltje, brought her two pounds of sugar within two months time, after the child had returned from the wet nurse to her fathers house.[215] It is unclear what the meaning of this gift of sugar was. It must have been an expensive gift, because sugar was not yet the staple it is now.[216] Since it was offered twice within a short period of time, and shortly after Roeltje left her wet nurse to live with her father, the sugar may have been a contribution to the household.[217]

When offered from adult to adult, these luxurious foods were mostly offered as reciprocation. Although it was a special case, David's brother Steven did at some point bring a bottle of wine to a dinner at his brother's house, which was finished by the three Beck brothers in no time.[218] Since Steven was probably living with his master Riccen, and spent a lot of time travelling with this master, he presumably did not have the opportunity to reciprocate hospitality offered to him by his brothers. He made up for that by occasionally bringing a bottle of nice wine for dinner.

The same might be true for Jaccomijntje, who was born out of wedlock from an affair Roeltje's father had with another woman. Interestingly enough, Jaccomijntje lived with Roeltje's mother, the wife of her two-timing father. Since she, like Steven, did not have her own household, she also did not have the opportunity to return hospitality she received from Beck and others. This explains why she also occasionally brought the Beck household gifts of food.[219]

Other than those instances when the offering of food and drink was a means to reciprocate received hospitality, food and drink were mostly offered on a spontaneous basis as a random act of kindness. However, Beck occasionally also offered food such as a rabbit upon request, which implies that, in these cases, they were not necessarily offered as a gift but the food or drinks were an order that may or may not later be settled in repayment.[220] These food and drink orders were not so much part of a gift exchange ritual as it was a normal routine. In an age when there were no department stores and shopping malls, people depended on their relatives to provide the necessary food, drink and clothing.[221]

Networks of Exchange

Family

The most important network of gift exchange in Beck's diary is the family network. This applied both to his own gift exchange behaviour and the exchanges between others he described. Most ritual occasions were celebrated within the family and daily gifts were mostly exchanged within the family network as well. Furthermore, an analysis of the gift types and the networks in which they were exchanged showed that the family was the most common network of exchange for all but two types of gifts, being poetry and money. Hospitality, support, food and drink, and objects were all most frequently exchanged within the family network, whilst gifts like poems and money were more frequently exchanged within Beck's professional network.

More than half of all of the exchanges that Beck described in his diary took place between family members. These contacts included both family members by blood and by law. The person that Beck actually received the most from was his mother-in-law, Anna van Overschie, whom he usually referred to as "mother" or "R. mother", the "R." referring to his late wife, Roeltje. He had meals at her house over ninety times in 1624, which is quite an impressive number. The fact that she had an inn may have facilitated the frequency, but it was not only convenience that brought Beck to her home so often. However, their gift-exchange relationship did seem to be the most imbalanced relationship described in Beck's diary. Whereas, Anna van Overschie offered her son-in-law a total of 106 gifts over that year, Beck only reciprocated her kindness 24 times. In order to grasp the nature of their arrangement, the relationship between David Beck and his mother-in-law will be explored further in part II.

The third most important individual (after Beck's friend Breck-erfelt) with whom Beck exchanged gifts was his brother Hendrik. Their exchanges during 1624 were not fully reciprocal, which could be explained by the fact that Hendrik was severely ill for a period of time. This meant that David offered him more support than would have been necessary under normal circumstances. The brothers exchanged basically everything except money; they frequently enjoyed each other's hospitality, they supported each other in times of need and they wrote the occasional poetic letter to each other.

The importance of family members is also revealed by the fact that of the top 20 individuals that David Beck himself exchanged gifts with most frequently, thirteen were members of his extended family. These included his mother-in-law, his brothers, his cousins and uncles of his deceased wife. The others were four friends, two patrons and his daughter's wet nurse.

Friends

The second most important gift-exchange network for David Beck was his network of friends, which was in fact not a separate network. Beck's friendship network consisted of single individuals that Beck would see individually, but the network was also integrated into the larger family network. As matter of fact, David Beck did not really have that many friends. Herman Breckerfelt actually accounted for the majority of the exchanges that took place within the friends network. Other individuals with whom Beck was friendly were his tailor Berent Zwidde and David de Moor. His relationship with the former evolved after the death of Zwidde's wife. Beck's relationship with De Moor is one that requires further scrutiny. Even though Beck used the rhetoric of friendship to refer to him, his behaviour with regards to De Moor seems to suggest that they were more likely patron and client than close friends.

The single individual with whom Beck spent the most time was Breckerfelt. The two friends spent many evenings having dinner, reading and singing psalms. But Breckerfelt was not merely a friend. He was also adopted into the larger family network. This meant that if Hendrik Beck threw a party, Breckerfelt was also invited, even if David himself did not attend. Whenever there was a festive occasion at Anna van Overschie's house, Breckerfelt was very welcome to join. After Breckerfelt got married, the same hospitality also applied to his wife. Occasionally her brother, who also lived in The Hague, was invited to a Beck family gathering as well.

Professional contacts

The manner in which David Beck maintained his professional relationships was different from his behaviour towards family and friends. Some of the people he hired to work for him, such as tailors and the wet nurse, received his hospitality. This hospitality did not have to be reciprocated since it was part of the professional relationship they maintained. Others, like the people Beck was in contact with in the hope of receiving writing commissions received poems from Beck, more than anything else. In fact, this was the only network in which hospitality was not the most important type of gift exchanged. The exchange patterns that existed between David Beck and his professional contacts will receive more attention in part III.

Children and other neglected contacts

Considering the fact that Beck's diary was supposed to be "a mirror of his life" for his children, it is striking to see how little attention his children receive in his notes. They were rarely mentioned. Beck did reflect on his son's progress in school on his birthday, but he doesn't even mention his daughter Sara's birthday, let alone reflect on her development. His daughter Roeltje was mentioned most often, but almost always in the context of the wet nurse. One thing Beck duly noted was when they were invited to dinner or to stay over at relatives, or when they were offered small gifts or candy. Beck only once mentions that he offered them a small gift himself, which was when he returned from the fair in Amsterdam.[222] One could certainly say that his children were not spoiled. Although, it might well be that he offered them occasional sweets and small gifts more often than he bothered to note in his diaries.

This general lack of attention on Beck's part also applies to the other members of his household. Even though he lived with his sister Diliane and must have been in contact with her on a daily basis, he certainly did not mention her every day. His brother Abraham comes up only when he has gotten himself into trouble again. The only time the household received any attention in Beck's diary was when they came into contact with the outside world through dinner invitations or offerings of gifts.

Another category of individuals who were also largely neglected were the women Beck came into contact with. It was not that he failed to mention them as such, but that the women in his environment were referred to as separate individuals only when there was no husband present. This meant that his mother-in-law, who was a widow, and Jaccomijntje, his sister-in-law who was not yet married, would always be referred to on their own account. Beck referred to his mother-in-law, as R. mother or mother, while Jaccomijntje was mentioned by her first name only.

By contrast, he would only seldom reveal the name of the wife at whose house he was having dinner when her husband would be hosting the event. Women who attended these dinners in the company of their husbands were referred to with the phrase "and his housewife". This is does not necessarily create a problem, but it does seem rather inconsiderate to only mention the host and not the hostess, especially since she was responsible for preparing the meal.

Another group of people one would expect to be more at the centre of attention in Beck's diary were his neighbours.[223] Whereas Davis argues that neighbourly generosity was one of the main categories of exchange in sixteenth-century France, Beck hardly mentions neighbourly exchange at all.[224] According to the secondary literature, neighbours were of vital importance in the early-modern period.[225] Although the diary shows that Beck was certainly on speaking terms with some of his neighbours, it does not attest to their great importance in his daily social life. This does not necessarily mean, however, they were of little importance to him.

The relative lack of contact with his neighbours might be explained by the fact that Beck had only moved to The Hague in 1618 and therewith was not yet adjusted to his new environment, but this does not seem like a very valid argument. It must have been possible to establish a relationship with one's neighbours over a period of five years. Although, as a newcomer, he might have been more apt to remain in contact with his own family and older friends rather than getting acquainted with his neighbours.[226]

It is also possible that we just don't read much about his neighbours because they were never expressly identified as neighbours and we are largely unaware of where the people he spent so much time with lived. Beck did offer one explicit reference to a neighbour, however, and, as a matter of fact, it seems his neighbours were more of *mortal* importance rather than of *vital* importance. When his neighbour's wife died, Beck was the first one called to the house and he was the one who went round to announce the sad news to rest of the neighbours and acquaintances.[227] This seems to coincide with observations by other historians who have claimed that neighbours played an important role in the rituals that surrounded death.[228]

Conclusion

What we can conclude based on this analysis of David Beck's diary is that hospitality was the most important gift in terms of frequency. It was literally offered on a daily basis, but was also of great importance during ritual occasions such as calendar feasts and rites of passage. Hospitality was the most common gift for all of these occasions and events. For almost all of the individuals Beck described in his diary, hospitality was both the type of gift they most often offered and received. Other types of gifts were far less common, but as we shall learn later, were significant for other reasons.

Furthermore, Beck's diary makes it clear that the gifts exchanged were largely offered within the circle of family members and close friends. In that sense, there was no real place for outsiders, as some foreigners occasionally complained. But, within the circle of family and friends, Beck and his environment were indiscriminate. When it came to offering hospitality to close friends and relatives, it was also evident that this hospitality would extend to close friends and their families as well. Moreover, one would naturally offer a drink to professional contacts who came to visit. This means that most of the exchanges took place as a means of maintaining existing relationships rather than establishing new ones.

In addition, the diary also shows that gift exchange in David Beck's life was not so much about big events and big gifts, but rather about the daily exchange of basic offerings of hospitality and support. These small offerings allowed Beck and his family and friends to maintain their relationships in a manner that was to them probably very obvious and that in general did not lead to trouble or doubts. Food, a bed, and support were just offered as a matter of course and Beck and his friends would generally not waste words on the affair. In that respect, David Beck's diary sufficiently shows that the exchange of gifts was indeed a phenomenon that was part of daily life.

Part II: Gifts and Meanings

A. Rites of Passage

As the diary of David Beck has shown, hospitality was quantitatively the most important gift in seventeenth-century Holland. This gift was commonly used to maintain social relations, both in the sense that it was offered most often and in the sense that it was offered on a daily basis. However, other gifts carried greater significance in qualitative terms. This is especially true of the gifts that were – next to a host's hospitality – presented on those occasions that celebrated or mourned life's significant events.[1] These were events like birth, marriage and death, but also academic promotions and other events that symbolised passages in one's life.

This type of event is generally referred to as a rite of passage, a term first introduced as a research subject by the French ethnologist Van Gennep.[2] A rite of passage is understood to refer to both the rituals related to life's important events and those related to the calendar. In this chapter, rites of passage are discussed solely in connection to ritual occasions in the course of a lifetime, because in terms of gift exchange, there is a significant difference between the two: calendar feasts are usually celebrated with the offering of hospitality (and the occasional food or small gifts), while life's passages are not only celebrated with hospitality but also commemorated by the offering of material objects.[3]

In this chapter a number of specific gifts are discussed that were connected to specific passages in life: weddings, christenings and death. For each of these occasions a specific (type of) gift is discussed in detail in order to investigate the possible meanings seventeenth-century individuals ascribed to gifts. The gifts themselves are taken as a source, but their meaning is further contextualised by the use of other sources from that period.

Marriage and Cooking Pots

Husband and wife

The idea that marriage is a cornerstone of society is a conviction that was very much part of the early-modern mentality.[4] As the popular writer Jacob Cats noted in his book "*Houwelick*", or "Marriage", the wedded state was a "groundstone of towns" and a "breeding ground for regents". Therewith the rest and unrest of households, God's church and the common interest of the country depended on the quality of its marriages.[5] According to Cats, it was therefore worthwhile to pay attention to how marriages "could commence properly" and how they could be "performed honourably".[6] This was, at the same time, his motivation for writing this work, which described the various stages in the life of women. In each of the chapters, a particular stage, be it Bride, Wife, Mother or Widow, was the focus as Cats described the behaviour considered appropriate for a woman in that particular phase of her life.[7] The work was written in the vernacular and its intended audience was upper-middle-class women. It was already a popular book in the early seventeenth century and remained influential until the 19th century.[8]

According to Cats, married life was honourable if both spouses were committed to the tasks required of married life. For the husbands, these tasks were threefold. First and foremost, the husband was obliged to take care of "the religion within his house", to render his household like "a small congregation of the Lord".[9] Furthermore, the husband should show perseverance and good governance in the maintenance of his household, and he should provide for it. Last but not least, the husband was to maintain a "hearty love" and "friendly courteousness" towards his wife. [10]

Whereas the husband's main task, as the provider of the household, was to a large extent outside the home, the housewife's tasks lay mostly inside the home.[11] She took care of the house in terms of cleaning and maintenance, she bore and raised the children – at least for the first few years – and she was responsible for preparing wholesome daily meals for both her husband and children. Moreover, she was to support her husband in any way she possibly could. Naturally, what Cats described was an ideal-typical situation; in practice for instance, a lot of families were unable to survive without the extra income brought in by the housewife.[12] Nevertheless, his work did offer good insight into what were then considered the norms of a successful marriage.

This emphasis on the mutual tasks and obligations of spouses within the institution of marriage does not leave a very romantic impression of early-modern married life. Add to that the general notion that marriages were contracts of mutual support between families rather than a loving relationship between husband and wife, and the idea of the arranged and therewith loveless and unhappy marriage is easily established.[13] However, the choice of partner in the Dutch Republic was usually left to the partners themselves. They had considerable liberty in meeting suitable partners and in courting a possible spouse before fixing an official engagement.[14] Therewith, the likelihood that two persons that would eventually marry could actually get along was rather enlarged. In that sense, the fact that the parents – after the announcement of the engagement – arranged the marriage settlement did not necessarily interfere with the affection that had already developed between the couple.

The correspondence between Pieter Corneliszoon Hooft and Leonora Bartolotti from their courting period, offers a good example of how both affection and other interests played an important role in the marriage. In the summer of 1627, after the death of his first wife Christina van Erp, Hooft was courting Leonora Hellemans, the widow of Jan Baptist Bartolotti, a wealthy Amsterdam merchant who had died in 1624. In one of his letters to her, Hooft tried to impress Leonora by offering her poems, which "fruit", as he called it, he "abused for the occasion of offering her some verbal proof as leaves and flowers of his devotion to her obedience".[15] Hooft imagined that the (conventional) mediocrity of his poems would not prevent her from at least enjoying them. He used this and other well-chosen words to charm his way into Leonora's heart, which leaves a very romantic impression indeed.

One can imagine that Leonora found it difficult to refuse his affections after Hooft's flattering words, but as it turned out, things were slightly more complicated than that. Most of these complications did not deal with the emotions involved, but rather with practicalities, as Leonora told Hooft: "You affect me so much, I wish I had the inclination to marry".[16] She had called Hooft "dear" a number of times, even after he had asked whether he had heard her correctly.

According to Van Tricht, who edited the publication of Hooft's correspondence, Leonora's reluctance was the result of complications of a material nature. Leonora Hellemans was the daughter of wealthy southern Netherlandish traders and she had married well to Bartolotti; she was a woman of fortune. During her marriage to Bartolotti and after his death, she had lived in Amsterdam, but in order to maintain her southern Netherlandish property, she had herself officially registered in Zevenbergen, a town that had been declared neutral by both the southern Archdukes and the States General of the Dutch Republic. This neutrality offered people who had fled the south an opportunity to manage their southern properties from a non-hostile residence. Thus many of them either lived there legally or physically. Leonora knew that if she married Hooft she be with a man who was serving a country hostile to the southern Netherlands. Therewith the marriage would probably also harm her property rights in the southern Netherlands.[17] This is why she was initially somewhat reluctant toward Hooft's charming efforts.

In her writings to Hooft, however, Leonora did not refer to the Zevenbergen issue. From Hooft's reaction to one of her letters, we learn that some of her doubts about marrying Hooft were of a religious nature. She was concerned that Hooft was not religious enough, to which Hooft responded: "religion is in the mind and not in the exterior".[18] Furthermore, she had also heard that Hooft's friends had religious convictions different from her, which she also considered disturbing. Besides, Hooft, his friends and Leonora also did not agree on matters of state. Hooft, however, claimed that she had been aware of these political and religious differences all along, and that this had not discouraged her from developing affections for him. Moreover, he claimed that this could not possibly be a reason not to marry him.[19]

To these reasonable arguments he added the fact that he was sick of love as a means of convincing her to marry him. He had had some problems with his leg, but it was his emotional turmoil that had brought him close to death, or so he claimed. It may have been true that Hooft had been severely ill, but it may also have been a rhetoric trick to persuade her into marriage.[20] He used other strategies as well. Hooft wrote a charming letter to Susanna Bartolotti, Leonora's daughter from her first marriage, in which he also referred to his ill health. He claimed that his doctor agreed that the fever caused by his leg injury was compounded by the melancholy of Leonora's refusal to see him.[21]

Leonora had by this time left for Zevenbergen to see her brother and sister-in-law. Presumably, she went to figure out the damage to her and her property if she were to marry a man serving the Dutch Republic.[22] This ultimately turned out to be not much of a problem, it seems, since Leonora and Hooft got married a few months later in November 1627. Caspar Barlaeus, Willem de Groot and Constantijn Huygens wrote poems for the occasion.[23] The Hooft-Hellemans alliance seems to have been a happy one. Hooft was a proper father to Leonora's daughters, Susanna and Constantia Bartolotti, and the couple had two more children together, Christina and Arnout Hellemans Hooft. It seems that the Hooft family had a pretty satisfying life together. Hooft's friends even commented on how lucky Hooft was with a wife that was so lively and entertaining and who enjoyed receiving Hooft's friends to their house. She was praised for her hospitable qualities.[24]

So was this a marriage of love, or of strategy? It is obvious that Leonora went to great lengths to protect her property rights and it seems that she may have refrained from marrying Hooft if it was going to result in her losing her property. Yet, it is also clear that affection played an important part in their relationship. Hooft even argued that because she had feelings for him, she should marry him regardless of the other circumstances. In fact, both love – or at least affection – and strategy were important features in the establishment of marital relationships. It was important for both partners to develop a certain level of affection towards each other before the actual ceremony took place, but it was also important that their capital be secured for the family and the next generation, especially if these generations were the results of earlier marriages.[25] In that sense, instrumental considerations did not necessarily interfere with the development of affection between the partners.

This not only applied to people who were free to choose their partners; even arranged marriages did not necessarily exclude feelings of mutual affection between the spouses.[26] Stadholder Willem Frederik van Nassau-Dietz, for instance, had promised his mother on her deathbed that he would marry a woman who would uphold the standards of the Van Nassau-Dietz family.[27] In his case, this meant that one of the daughters of Frederik Hendrik of Orange, stadholder of the provinces of Holland and Zeeland, would be the most suitable, since Frederik Hendrik was the most powerful man in the Dutch Republic at the time. In his efforts to have one of the princesses married off to him, Willem Frederik felt it was important for the princess to develop a certain affection for him. He thus devoted a lot of time to the princesses whenever he visited the court of Frederik Hendrik in The Hague. He had dinner with them, he tried to make conversation and, every once in a while, he would offer them a small gift.[28]

In order to increase his chances of being able to marry one of these girls, he also had to establish a relationship with their mother, Amalia van Solms-Braunfels. This took quite some effort, especially since Amalia and her husband, Frederik Hendrik, were still rather upset with Willem Frederik because he had taken the position of stadholder of the Northern provinces at the expense of Frederik Hendrik, who was eager for this position because this would allow him to become the stadholder general.[29]

However, initial hostilities notwithstanding, Willem Frederik did manage to establish a more or less friendly contact with Amalia. Their relationship became especially close after the death of Frederik Hendrik. One particular evening, Amalia even confided in Willem Frederik that she missed her late husband terribly, adding that "she had been so happy with him, that they had loved each other dearly and that SH [His Highness] had communicated everything to her".[30] "In *somma*: the happiest marriage in the world", Willem Frederik remarked at the time. Still, he went on to note that if their relationship was actually as happy as she claimed, Amalia's suffering over the loss of her husband must have been very painful. If Amalia had indeed expressed her sincere sentiments as to the loss of her husband, this would go to show that even an arranged marriage, which an alliance in those circles usually was, could actually be a happy marriage. Or to put it differently, the instrumental character of the alliance did not necessarily exclude the development of affectionate sentiments between the two spouses.

This does not mean that arranged marriages were never problematic. As Louise, the eldest daughter of Frederik Hendrik was said to have exclaimed: "Oh, if only I were either dead or a countrywoman for then I could pick someone whom I know, liked and loved."[31] Willem Frederik did occasionally complain in his diary about how unfair it was that he could not choose a wife who was totally to his liking. These heartfelt sentiments did not keep him from pursuing his mission of marrying one of the stadholder's daughters, however. Meanwhile, he had his physical needs taken care of by the occasional prostitute and one of his servants. This usually left him with a sense of unease, especially in the latter case, because he was always anxious about the possibility of this servant becoming pregnant by him, in which case it would be difficult to deny fatherhood.

Willem Frederik also developed a relationship of a more affectionate kind with a certain young woman, whom he refers to in his diary as Pycke.[32] She was the daughter of one of the regents who attended Willem Frederik's court in Leeuwarden. The feeling was obviously mutual, but it never led to a public or official relationship. They wrote letters and exchanged gifts, and they even entered a petting stage, but this ended abruptly when she was married off to another man.[33] Although Willem Frederik was rather sad about this turn of events, he did nothing within his power to prevent it. So, it seems that regardless of his despair at having to arrange a suitable marriage for himself, he saw no real opportunity to avoid it by actually marrying a woman he liked and loved.

In the end, Willem Frederik got what he wanted. In 1653, he married Albertine Agnes, Frederik Hendrik's second daughter. Even though he explicitly acknowledged in his diary that this was what he had "waited, worked and wished for", he did express his desire to be "content, peaceful and happy" with his wife.[34] In that sense, it seems that even though marriages in these circles were instruments of power and allegiance, it was still appreciated if they – at the same time – would lead to love, respect and joy for the partners involved.

Social and economic factors probably also played a role in the choice of spouse for those who were not rich and powerful. Yet also in these cases it did not mean that love, or at least lovingly behaviour, was not considered an important factor in the relationship between husband and wife. As Jacob Cats stressed in his book *Houwelick*, it was the task of both partners to avoid arguments and make an effort to live together in peace.[35] It was also considered good taste for the husband to praise his wife in public.[36] Furthermore, Cats considered it important for partners to accept each other's shortcomings and that criticism be expressed within the confines of one's own home and never in public.[37]

Again, what Cats described was ideal-typical behaviour, and not necessarily how marriages functioned in practice.

The norm of a loving marriage was, however, not just something prescribed in books. Other writers also expressed their appreciation for happy marriages. Constantijn Huygens, in the memoirs of his youth, stressed the fact that his parents had a "very happy" relationship.[38] David Beck, after noting in his diary that the housewife of a certain Jan Crabbens had died, noted that this couple "did not get along at all and had carried on badly", therewith implicitly subscribing to the standard of the loving marriage.[39] So it seems that even in the seventeenth century it was considered important to have a "good marriage", not only in the sense that it bring financial and social capital into the family, but also in the sense of the spouses respecting and loving each other. As Jacob Cats observed: [40]

> No ring, no feast, no crown, no flowers,
> But true love makes the bride.

Rituals of marriage

This may have been true, but the ritual of marriage – including the ring, the feast, the crown and the flowers – was very important indeed. The importance of the institute of marriage as such was reflected in the event that symbolised this transition to the married state, the wedding.[41] Unlike the period before, weddings in the seventeenth century were no longer a private matter between bride and groom but (semi-) public rituals that included first of all official public announcements of the intended marriage and secondly the wedding itself, to which family and friends were invited to witness the transition.

As we mentioned earlier, Dutch youngsters enjoyed relative freedom when it came to finding a suitable spouse. Once the young man, after a period of courting, received a confirmation from his intended bride that she was willing to marry him, the engagement was announced to the families.[42] These families would then join together one evening to discuss the wedding contract. These contracts prescribed what the partners would bring to the marriage, and what would remain in the hands of the family after the death of one of the spouses. According to Hieronymus

Sweerts, in his satire *The Ten Joys of Marriage*, these wedding contract discussions were bound to cause trouble.[43] According to Sweerts, it was obvious that the parents of both the bride and the groom would be unwilling to offer what the other party was expecting for their child.[44] It also seems that the speed with which the dowries were paid by the respective families after the marriage, was something that often left room for improvement. Cats criticised parents for not paying their dowries immediately and especially urged the fathers of grooms to pay what they had promised.[45]

After the wedding contract was settled, the families and future bride and groom would join for a drink to celebrate their engagement. This was the beginning of a rather demanding period for both the bride and groom and their closest relatives, for once the marriage contract was signed, the wedding festivities began to be arranged. This meant many tasks as well as a reasonable amount of stress. First of all, guests had to be invited to the wedding banquet. This was usually done in person when the guest lived nearby, or otherwise a letter of invitation was written to the invitee. This in itself was not so problematic, but what often led to arguments between the spouses' families was the question of whom to invite.[46] Another problem involved the table arrangements; it was important to not insult guests by assigning them a less honourable place at the table than they were convinced they were due.[47] This led Sweerts to suggest that if the bride and groom had been able to foresee these problems, they would have never gone through with the marriage in the first place.[48]

Another issue of particular concern was the wedding attire. The bride and groom usually had a completely new outfit made for this occasion. Considering that textile prices were rather high, this must have been quite a costly event. It was no wonder that Herman Breckerfelt called on his friend David Beck for assistance when he got engaged.[49] After the wedding the clothes would be reused for other special occasions such as other weddings and funerals.

The actual wedding was celebrated by offering a dinner to the invited guests.[50] Naturally, this dinner had to also be arranged in advance and this was a task of considerable importance. The guests were offered food and drink, which for a large part had to be ordered and prepared beforehand. Dutch patricians considered wedding banquets occasions of great distinction, especially those upper-class burghers who could afford to show off. As revealed by various ordinances from that period, municipal governments made an effort to impede the wedding extravagances and splendour of the well-to-do, but presumably to no avail.[51] The fines for having too many guests at the wedding banquet or serving food considered too luxurious, such as sugar works, never quite had the desired effect. These fines were just added onto the total wedding costs. Another problem officials tried to deal with through ordinances was the extended wedding feasts which could last a couple of days. It was ordained that weddings were to last no longer than two days. Whether people actually abided these laws remains unclear.

Not only government officials, but also moralists like Jacob Cats appealed to young couples not to celebrate their weddings too lavishly. He compared weddings to a market where people show off their wares.[52] Cats argued that the couple was better off just throwing a party for close friends and relatives and saving their money to buy furniture and kitchen utensils. He especially objected to the idea that young couples were spending huge amounts of money on huge amounts of guests they did not even know personally.[53] These were usually people invited by the couples' parents. The correspondence of Hooft shows that many of the guests invited to the wedding of his second wife's daughters were indeed invited by Hooft, and were actually *his* friends.[54]

Other unexpected guests at weddings were vagrants, at least in the countryside.[55] They presumably just showed up whenever there was a feast to enjoy the free food and drink. Van Alkemade and Schelling offer several examples of by-laws enacted to prevent vagrants from attending weddings they had not been invited to. It is unclear how common this practice was, but at least their descriptions show that this problem did exist.[56]

However, most guests at weddings were invited officially and were thus welcome at the party. The invitations were sent to family and friends of the bride and groom, the new couple's neighbours, and those invited by the couple's parents. Naturally, it was an honour to have important people attend, but this was not necessarily the only reasoning behind the invitations. Most invitees were invited based on their relationship with the couple or their relatives.

These weddings involved several types of reciprocation.[57] First, there was a certain amount of reciprocation at the event itself, or the morning after. These consisted of gifts that guests brought the newlyweds. These could be artistic gifts like poetry written especially for the occasion or material objects. These objects often involved artistry as well. Engraved objects, or objects with inscriptions that served as wedding gifts can still be found in many museum collections. They were very popular during this period and would often include the date, the names of the newlyweds, or the new life they were about to embark on. In other words, the gifts were highly appropriate for the occasion. However, the bride and groom also received household things, like kitchen utensils and the like, but since these were so ordinary they rarely left a trace in history.

Another means of reciprocating bridal hospitality was by inviting the couple to dinner not long after the wedding. Whereas the wedding banquet was normally offered by the parents of the bride, this reciprocal dinner was expected to be offered by the parents of the groom. They were supposed to throw what was called a *wederbruiloft*, or counter-wedding.[58] This counter-wedding was customary and often as sumptuous as the original wedding itself.

Other guests could also invite the couple and their parents over for dinner to show their appreciation for the attentions they received during the wedding. Furthermore, the couple could also be invited by people who had not been able to go to the wedding celebrations because they lived too far away. Visiting these people involved the necessary travel and, even though these trips were not yet called that way, it was not uncommon for newly weds to take a little honeymoon, or *speelreisje*. The trip was supposed to be fun, but also allowed the partners to introduce each other to those relatives who had been unable to attend the wedding.[59]

Weddings and gifts

Besides hospitality that was offered to the guests on the occasion of the wedding, marriage also included other types of gift exchange. First, there was, of course, the offering of the wedding ring that the groom traditionally gave to his bride. Cats noted that this ring was not just a piece of jewellery, but also a "*zielepand*" or "pawn of the soul". He detested the new fashion of wearing the ring on any other finger but the ring finger.[60] Another gift from the groom to the bride was a necklace on one of the days of the actual wedding. Even though this was an old tradition, Cats objected to the fact that these gifts became more and more costly. He preferred the bride and groom to consider the more symbolic meaning of the gemstones that were set in the piece of jewellery and therefore added a list of symbolic or rather moralistic meanings of gemstones, such as diamonds, rubies, coral, amethyst and sapphire.[61]

Accepting these gifts meant the bride had no other option but to come up with a "counter gift", as Cats put it. According to him, this reciprocation usually consisted of a set of linen.[62] As a matter of fact, women spent a large part of their maiden life preparing this linen "uitzet" or trousseau. It even seems that linen was actually the only thing the trousseau consisted off. Their linen was an issue of great honour for women in this period. It was supposed to look neat and clean, and any holes or stains could ruin a housewife's reputation. The linen was put away in big, expensive drawers and it is no wonder, considering the importance of the material, that women in seventeenth century paintings and prints were depicted holding their linens and putting them away in big drawers.[63]

There are several references that note that other utensils or furniture needed to establish a household were usually acquired by the couple, or specifically the bride, the day after the wedding. This is why Cats preferred the couple to not spend too much money on the actual wedding feast. Similarly, Roemer Visscher in one of his emblems urged young couples – in a more metaphorical manner – to refrain from "buying cool wine" until they had properly settled into their homes with all the necessary accoutrements. When all of that was completed and when they had finally saved up enough money, they could afford a little foolishness such as drinking.[64]

Sweerts described the purchase of household utensils and furniture as the second joy of marriage. In his example, the newlywed wife is so excited about this event that she can hardly sleep.[65] She ends up buying the most luxurious and costly things, which the husband is afraid he will not be able to afford. Sweerts satirically reminded the husband to refrain from any comments on his bride's behaviour, because her life as a married woman would be hard enough as it was spending all his money.

As mentioned earlier, the guests of the newlywed couple also offered gifts to the couple. Unfortunately, little is known about these gifts.[66] However, these might have included both artistic gifts like poems and objects like household utensils.[67] Other popular wedding presents were utensils with engravings or inscriptions on them.[68] Hooft, for instance, asked Tesselschade Roemers Visscher to engrave a glass for the wedding of Jacob Pergens and Leonora Bartolotti, the sister-in-law of his second wife. The engraved objects came in many shapes and sizes, from cups to fire clocks, from plates to pitchers, and they could be made of materials such as glass, earthenware or silver.[69] It is, however, very difficult to find actual references of the offering of gifts by guests to bride and groom in sources such as diaries and letters.

Occasionally the gifts themselves are mentioned in the recipient's thank-you note, but it is almost never clear how the gift was offered on the actual event. Hooft, for example, thanked his dear friend Tesselschade Roemers Visscher for the "breast of jet" that the latter had offered his second wife, Leonora Hellemans, on the occasion of their wedding.[70] Hooft also wrote several letters to friends and other acquaintances to thank them for the wonderful poems he had received.[71] The letters and poems the couple had received from their friend Barlaeus were supposedly of such exquisite quality that they had Hooft "tingling with immense joy".[72]

So, even though these sources made it clear that wedding gifts were actually offered by guests to the newlyweds, not much more can be gleaned from these egodocuments. Obviously, in the case of wedding poetry, there are still a great number of these occasional poems, both from famous poets such as the likes of Hooft, Vondel and Barlaeus, and from more obscure poets. Yet very little information can be retrieved through egodocuments as to the actual material objects that were offered as wedding gifts.

Other sources like probate inventories are also not very useful in this respect. They occasionally do include descriptions of objects that were presumably wedding gifts, such as plates with a date and two family arms on them, but these references are not very revealing, since they lack other reference points. They are singular examples that are difficult to interpret in a broader framework. Besides, these objects that are mentioned for their peculiar character rather than their ordinariness. There is, however, one incident mentioned in a probate inventory in which three students of the University of Leiden, who were sharing a house before, were splitting their inventory because they had finished their studies and were leaving Leiden. All of the household effects were divided among the three students except for one kettle, which was to go to their servant because he was getting married.[73] Nevertheless, this is just an incident that can only serve to point out that kitchen utensils were considered appropriate wedding gifts, also from master to servant.

In that respect, it is more fruitful to take actual material objects that functioned as wedding gifts as a starting point. Naturally, these do not necessarily tell the whole story of gift exchange from guests to newlyweds, but at least they can function as an example of what type of gifts were considered appropriate, and it leaves an opportunity to establish what the possible meaning of these gifts was in the broader context of Dutch society in the seventeenth century.[74]

Cooking pots as wedding gifts

There is one type of object that, in every sense of the word, is appropriate for this occasion. It is a collection of cooking pots from Schermereiland, an area north of Amsterdam that includes the small villages of Graft, De Rijp and Noordeinde.[75] Spread over different museums and private collections, there are a total of 39 of these cooking pots, which all share the same features.[76] They are all three-legged cooking pots, with one or two handles and sometimes a spout, made out of red earthenware, decorated with *slib,* a thin white clay, and glazed with a metal glaze. The pots are decorated with figurative as well as non-figurative drawings and occasionally some texts as well. The texts include Biblical quotations as well female names, and dates.

The objects are themselves not very exceptional. Their shape is typical for earthenware as well as metal cooking pots from that period.[77] The three legs made it possible to place the pot in the fireplace which allowed the fire to heat up the pot and its contents evenly. The ears allowed the pot to be hung from a chimney crook in the fireplace and the spout was useful for pouring out any excess liquids. As a kitchen utensil, the cooking pot was an ordinary object found in every seventeenth-century household. A large number of the meals were prepared in a cooking pot and these meals were generally referred to as *potspijzen,* or 'foodstuffs from a pot'.[78] The Dutch culinary mainstay *hutspot,* or hotchpotch, refers to the object it was traditionally prepared in.

The fact that these pots were decorated is also not exceptional. The decoration of objects was an old tradition, but seems to have been especially popular in the seventeenth century. Glass and tin were often engraved, and earthenware was decorated with *slib*.[79] Objects were decorated with both depictions of scenes and with pieces of text. In general, the textual decorations on objects from this period consisted of proverbs, allegorical texts, mythological and of course Biblical references.[80]

However, a number of these cooking pots are actually decorated in a way that is quite extraordinary. They are decorated with female names and dates and on some of these pots the line "and her beloved" is added. Decorations of this type can be found on some other earthenware objects, such as pitchers, but are never seen on any object that is not earthenware.[81] This fact makes the otherwise rather common cooking pots instantly more interesting while at the same time presenting the historian with a number of quandaries. Why are these pots decorated in this manner? What was their function? What meaning did seventeenth-century inhabitants in Graft and De Rijp ascribe to these homely utensils that made it worthwhile to decorate them in such a fashion? And what did these objects have to do with weddings, if anything at all?

To begin with the last point, the names and dates on the pots do suggest that these pots may have been linked to special occasions in the lives of the mentioned women. Presumably these were their engagements or weddings, especially since they included the phrase "and her beloved" in some instances. The most obvious way to find out which occasion these objects played a role in is to check the names and dates in the archives of these villages.[82] This reveals that the dates on these pots referred to wedding dates for the women mentioned on the objects. It is thus likely that these cooking pots functioned as wedding gifts. This leads to the question of who offered this gift to whom, and for what reason.

The central figure regarding these cooking pots is obviously the bride, it is after all her name that appears on the objects. Yet the bride herself would probably not buy a pot with such an inscription and the same holds true for the bridegroom. They would both not buy an object that refers to the husband as 'her beloved'. It therefore seems likely that the guests offered these objects as wedding gifts to the couple, and especially to the bride. It was, after all, her task to assemble a fully equipped household as soon as possible after the wedding, and the guests contributed to this by giving her basic household utensils. A cooking pot, then, was an appropriate gift, because it was a common utensil in every household. The interesting thing about these cooking pots is that they were never actually used for cooking. None of these pots, however, have any traces of fire, or any other indications of use.

Yet this doesn't mean they were useless. These pots were not used as household utensils, but rather as decorative objects. They were placed on drawers, mantelpieces or on consoles for everyone to see. According to proto-ethnologist Le Francq van Berkhey, who wrote an ethnological study on the Dutch in the eighteenth-century, the people of the northern part of Holland were especially keen on these earthenware decorations and even preferred these to paintings or prints.[83] Other objects made of Delft blue or the more expensive China were also used for decoration, but, unlike China, red earthenware was not at all valuable. The significance of these cooking pots therefore presumably did not lay in their monetary value, nor in their use as a status symbol, but rather in the symbolic meaning or meanings that were ascribed to them by seventeenth-century onlookers in general, and those from the Schermereiland in particular.

What then were the meanings that were ascribed to the cooking pot in seventeenth-century Holland? Since these pots were all found on Schermereiland, it would be interesting to interpret them within their local cultural context. The problem with the villages of Graft and De Rijp is, however, that even though their seventeenth-century social history has been fully described by Dutch historian Van Deursen, little is known about their cultural history. A cultural history of these villages is difficult if not impossible to write because of a lack of suitable sources, therefore the interpretation of the meaning of the cooking pot in Graft and De Rijp depends on a larger cultural context, which, in this case, is seventeenth-century Holland. It is not that this context literally refers to the meaning of the objects in this period, but at least it can offer an idea of what meanings these objects were generally associated with. This associative context consists of sources such as Biblical texts, emblem books, literature, paintings and prints. In the case of the earthenware cooking pots, several features can be distinguished that may have carried meaning for seventeenth-century onlookers, among these are the material these objects are made of, their shape and their function.

Red earthenware was not a material that was associated with luxury, but rather with the basic necessities of everyday life. It was used for making a range of objects, such as plates, bowls, pitchers, cooking pots and fire covers. As such, earthenware objects were present in every Dutch household. In probate inventories, these earthenware kitchen utensils are commonly referred to as "*eenighe aarden rommeling*", or "some earthenware junk", which indicates that the value of these objects should not be overrated.[84] This also explains why in some inventories earthenware is not even mentioned at all, especially not in the inventories of the well-to-do: earthenware was so worthless that it was literally not even worth mentioning.

Earthenware was, nevertheless, a material with a strong symbolic value that was not only the result of its lack of economic value but especially of its fragility. Several Dutch authors have used this aspect to teach their readers moral lessons. Johannes Luyken, for instance, was the author of a very popular emblem book who used a number of trades as metaphors for life and its lessons.[85] These emblems depicted various trades, each with a motto and a rhyme that was to function as an explanatory text.[86] His depiction of the potter was accompanied by the motto "Carry in thy barrel of earth, a treasure of greater worth". [87] This emblem suggested – by referring to Jeremy 18: 1-10 – that the human body was no more than an earthenware casing that was only useful in this life, whereas in the afterlife the spiritual contents of this casing would be of much greater importance. Man would therefore be wise to pay more attention to his inner life as an investment in the future. In that sense, earthenware was associated with the fragility of both the human body and human life.

Earthenware cooking pots did not only carry meaning on basis of the material they were made of, but also their shape.[88] Johannes Luyken also used cooking pots as a vehicle for getting across his spiritual messages. In his emblem book *Het leerzaam huisraad*, or "the instructive furniture", Luyken used ordinary utensils as symbols of morals and one of his examples was the cooking pot.[89] He complained – this time with reference to John 6: 27 – that although the pot may cook the daily meal in order to feed the body and fulfil one's earthly needs, most people should take better care of their spiritual lives and the daily food of their soul instead.

Luyken was not the only one to refer to the human body as a vessel, Jacob Cats did exactly the same in his writings and emblem books. However, in his case, the pots or vessels were not necessarily associated with the human body in general, but rather with the female body. In his *Houwelick*, Cats even tried to explain that even though women were seen by many as the "weaker vessels", this did not mean that they did not deserve to be treated with honour.[90]

This association of women with the image of the weaker pot or vessel can also be found in Roemer Visscher's emblem book *Sinnepoppen*.[91] One of his prints shows a metal and earthenware cooking pot that are floating down a river. The explanatory text makes clear that the male pot, which was made of metal, has requested the female earthenware pot to join him in his float. The earthenware pot wisely refuses, for she is convinced that with the first current they will bump into each other and since she is made out of weaker material she will be the one to break. This short story was used by Roemer Visscher as a metaphor for marriages between man of high social stature and women of lower social stature. These marriages were bound to run into trouble, and when they did the women would suffer most severely. Therefore those in their courting stage were recommended to always consider the "wisdom of the earthenware pot".

Still, this association of women with pots was not always so spiritually or morally sound. Especially Cats produced several emblems in which the cooking pot referred to female sexuality. The fact that even in these cases the emblems were also filled with some moral advice does not exclude that they included quite a few sexually connoted puns as well. One of these was entitled "An open pot or open pit, a dog lightly sticks his muzzle in it".[92] The print in the foreground shows a dog licking a pot that is lying in the fireplace. The background shows a servant who is being told off by her mistress. The latter tells her servant in the explanatory text that an open pot is likely to bring shame and mockery upon the cook. Or to put it in other words: if the maid behaves too liberally, men are bound to abuse this and she is likely to bring disgrace to herself and the family she is working for.[93] The daughter of the house is in the end of the poem kindly requested to keep her pot covered, as if not to bring the same shame to the family as the maid has already brought.[94]

Unlike sexual activity before marriage, procreation within marriage was highly esteemed and even considered one of the main purposes of wedlock. In Sweerts's "joys of marriage" the young wife turned into a state of panic when she was not pregnant as soon as she hoped or expected to be. She claimed that she needed "to have a child or else she would loose her senses" and abused her husband by calling him names such as "Dry John" and "Seldom Comer".[95] Whereas Sweerts obviously represented the ironic or satiric view on married life, seventeenth-century genre paintings usually offered an ideal-typical view.[96]

Several paintings have survived that depict and idealise motherhood and it is striking how many of these also show earthenware cooking pots.[97] This depiction of cooking pots is partly due to the setting in which mothers are usually depicted. Since the wife and mother was responsible for taking care of the household, cooking the daily meals, and raising the children, she was frequently depicted in the kitchen, with a child on her lap, in front of the fireplace.[98] In that sense it seems obvious that – due to its function – a cooking pot would also appear. It is after all a kitchen utensil that was commonly used to prepare meals above the fire. However, there is more to the connection between cooking pots and motherhood. Earthenware cooking pots were in the Dutch cultural context of the seventeenth century not only appreciated for their function as a kitchen utensil but also associated with the human body, especially the female body, and with female sexuality.

As such earthenware cooking pots through their shape, function and the material they were made of held reference to the typical female tasks within marriage: taking care of the household, preparing meals and providing the family with progeny. Therewith the cooking pot became a symbol for the (house-) wife, which also made it into a suitable wedding gift from guests to bride.[99] By offering the cooking pot as a gift the guests emphasized the female's new stage in life. She was no longer the daughter of her father, residing in his house and falling under his jurisdiction, instead she was now the wife of her husband, which brought new tasks and responsibilities. This passage from one stage to the next was symbolised by the offering of an object that within that particular cultural context was associated with the female tasks within marriage. In that sense the value of these objects lay in their symbolic meanings, rather than their economic worth.

Birth and Christening Gifts

The Christening, Christening Witnesses and "Pillegiften"

Like weddings, the christening of a newborn child was an important social event in the early-modern period. The baptismal ceremony was a ritual by which the child would become both a member of the church and of the civic community.[100] Christenings
would take place as soon as possible after the child's birth, which
meant that the mother would not attend. Attendees included the
father, the christening witnesses, and the women that had assisted
with the delivery.[101] Even though it was not obligatory, most parents would request others to stand as a witness for the child. Within the baptismal ceremony, these godparents had several tasks.
One of the godparents was to "raise" the child to the font. The
godparents had to answer the ritual questions of the minister on
behalf of their godchild and one of the godparents was to give the
child its name. This was normally not a matter of choice for the
godparents, but rather a matter that was decided upon by the parents themselves.[102]

However, Constantijn Huygens suggests in his autobiography
that the godparents were free to choose the name of the godchild
and would normally name it after themselves. Yet his own godparent, Justinus van Nassau, had not found it necessary or appropriate to have the child named after him.[103] He therefore left the
choice to Constantijn's parents who decided to call him Constanti-
nus. This lead Constantijn to believe that even though he was not
named after his noble godfather as such, his parents at least used
Justinus's name for inspiration for they both did share the same
"ending".[104] Still, unlike what Huygens suggests, children were
generally named after close relatives and not after their godparents. [105]

David's new niece was named Sara after her late paternal grandmother. Sara Beck was christened on the 9th of April and had her
maternal grandmother Anneke Pieters and her uncle Steven Beck,
David's younger brother, as her godparents.[106] So she was in fact
not named after her godparents. David's nephew, on the other
hand, did have the honour of being named after his godfather:
the young David was christened in April in the year 1621 and his
godparents were David Beck, Pieter Beck, Judith Pieters and

Pietertje Aelbrechts.[107] This naming of a child after a godparent was, however, the exception rather than the rule among David Beck's circles. The christening records in The Hague, Delft and Rotterdam show that among David Beck's relatives and friends only few godchildren were named after their godparent.[108] A child was actually more likely to be named after some other relative like, for instance, the father, the grandfather, or of a sibling that had died prematurely, than to be named after its godparents.[109]

Young David's christening was rather exceptional in another sense as well. He had four godparents to witness the christening, while among his social circle only one in six children experienced the same privilege. At most christenings only two witnesses would be present, a godfather and a godmother, while some ceremonies included three witnesses. In the latter case the baby girls usually had two godmothers and one godfather while for the boys it was the other way around. Although it was more common to have four christening witnesses in the case of boys, the choice of having this large number of witnesses seems to have been taken at random. The number was not necessarily reserved for the first born child within a family, nor is there any indication that this was a practice that either died down or became fashionable later.[110]

In general, David Beck and his circle of family and friends preferred to have kinsmen as christening witnesses for their children. A vast majority of the godparents was either linked to the child by blood or by marriage. Hendrik Beck, for instance had a total of fourteen godparents for his five children and only one of them was not a relative.[111] Guillaume Willemsz du Rieu stood as a godparent for Hendrik's son Stephan in 1627.[112] Like Hendrik, Guillaume was a schoolmaster in Delft, which might suggest.that Hendrik chose him as a godparent in order to ensure his son's future as schoolmaster. [113]

The upper class Huygens-family reveals a rather different pattern in the choice of christening witnesses for their children. Christiaan Huygens was secretary to the stadholder of Holland, and with that position his social network consisted of relations of a totally different order than those of David and Hendrik Beck. Maurits Huygens, the eldest son of Christiaan and his wife Susanna Hoefnagels, was named after stadholder Maurits, who stood as a witness at his christening. The other two godparents were the Council of State and Maria of Orange and Nassau.[114] Constantijn, the second son of the Huygens family, had the Council of the province of Brabant, Justus van Nassau, and the city of Breda as god-parents. The provincial council was represented by three of its members: Nicolaas Bruyninck, Andries Kessels and Lodewijck Meganck. The city of Breda was represented by Agnes van Haghe, the wife of one of the burgomasters of Breda. It is clear Christiaan Huygens preferred government and city officials to stand as wit-nesses for his two sons, rather than choosing next of kin as god-parents.

Constantijn noted in his autobiography that it was common practice to have two male and one female godparent.[115] This was obviously not necessarily the case for the likes of David Beck, but also at the christenings of Constantijn's sisters the parents opted for another possibility. Constantijn's four sisters each had two christening witnesses, a man and a woman. Of these eight god-parents six were relatives of Christiaan Huygens and his wife. Only the eldest daughter Elizabeth and the youngest, Constantia, had officials as their christening witnesses.

However, being a godparent involved more than just being a witness at the christening in church, it also involved a ritual of gift exchange. Godparents were expected to offer their godchil-dren an appropriate gift. Therewith the christening was also an important event in terms of gift exchange. Through the ritual of baptism the child was made part of a larger religious community and through the offering of a gift the godparents symbolically linked the child to the larger social community. This *pillegift*, or christening gift, was the first offering the child received from the outside world and it was thus of great symbolic importance as a tie-sign.

In some cases the christening was actually not so much a cause for offering a gift as it was cause for the promise of a gift.[116] God-parents on the eventful day would declare what they intended to offer the child as a *pillegift*, but the actual gift itself would not be offered until there was some indication that the child stood a good chance of surviving infancy.[117] In the case of David Beck's daugh-ter Roeltje, this meant that godmother Geertruyt did not present her gift until Roeltje was nine months old. On 9 August Geer-truyt's father passed by to deliver the gift on her behalf.[118]

The offering of silver or gilded objects as *pillegiften* seems to have been common practice in Holland during this period.[119] Pro-bate inventories mention silver and gilded christening gifts ran-ging from spoons to sugar boxes and from cups to mustard pots.[120] When Hooft became a godparent, he sent two silver candlesticks to his godchild and in the accompanying letter he expressed his wish that the candlesticks "would inspire a divine flame" in the child.[121] Although this symbolic meaning was probably much appreciated by the parents of the child, there are some indications that these gifts were not only appreciated for their symbolic significance but also for their the monetary value.[122] They are actually the only type of gifts that are consequently referred to as such in probate inventories using phrases like "one covered gilded cup, with arms, being *pillegiften*" or "two silver bowls with two silver spoons, given to the orphan as *pillegiften*".[123] In other cases one might suspect that certain objects were presented as, for example, a wedding present, but this was hardly ever duly noted as such.

Father Christiaan Huygens did not only keep notes on the christenings of his six children, indicating who served as godparents, but he also made sure to mention what gifts were offered and, most importantly, what the value of these gifts was. His eldest son Maurits, for some reason, received only one gift, offered to him by the Council of State. It consisted of "a big gilded cup with money in it" that was valued at a total of three hundred guilders.[124] The total value of the gifts for Constantijn Huygens was five hundred guilders. He received gifts from all three of his christening witnesses: a gilded cup with lid, one small gilded cup with lid, and a gilded dish "without lid".[125] The sisters Elizabeth, Geertruyt and Catharina each received either silver cups or silver plates from both their godparents. Constantia was the odd one out; she received no gifts at all.[126] Or at least her father did not note any gifts in her case.

Supposedly the value of the gifts was not indicated by the givers, but was calculated by Huygens himself. He estimated the quality of the material of each individual object and assessed what this material would cost per ounce. The gilded cup with cover offered to Constantijn by the Council of Brabant, for instance, was valued at two hundred guilders "if calculated at 5 guilders per ounce". The small gilded cup offered by Justinus van Nassau was worth only sixty gilders, because it was smaller and presumably made of lower quality material. Huygens figured it was worth only four guilders per ounce.[127]

Even though Christiaan Huygens evidently attached economic value to the gifts offered to his children at their christenings, his son Constantijn, who was to follow in his father's footsteps as a secretary to the stadholder, addressed a different side of the matter. In his autobiography he wrote: "The gifts by which the christening witnesses, conform the practice at these occasions, showed their affection, do not need to be mentioned here. For this was by no means the reason why my parents asked such noble witnesses."[128] The practice of noting the value of the *pillegift* and the statement that the value of these gifts was actually not important seem to be in contradiction with each other, yet this is not necessarily true.

It seems that in practice the choice of godparents and the value of the gift were both very important. Godparents during this period did not just have a symbolic function in the life of the child, but they were supposed to help support the child during its life. They were to look after its general wellbeing and ensure that the child attained its due position in society.[129] Considering the privileged position of the Huygens family in Dutch society it seems only natural that Christiaan would ask such "noble" witnesses, because he was surrounded by people of rank and social status. By the same token David and Hendrik Beck will have asked "noble" witnesses as well. In their case this did not necessarily mean noble in the aristocratic sense, but at least those who could be expected to be magnanimous and paragons of proper behaviour. In that sense, the choice of godparents was not motivated by the actual value of the gifts that they might offer, but rather by the reputation the future godparent had in his or her social network.

Nevertheless, this does not mean that the gifts as such were unimportant, because they were and for more than one reason. They may have been signs of affection with some symbolic and moral meaning, as well as a sign of the child's membership of a certain social network, but they also functioned as a form of insurance for the child. If the godchild would one day become an orphan, through the christening gift it at least possessed some object of value which could be put to some use.[130] This is also why these gifts were specifically mentioned in inventories. Notaries did not necessarily mention what the object was worth, but, in order to ensure that each child could claim its own "insurance" when needed, they would always indicate to which of the children it belonged. It was of course not appropriate to talk about these matters in public. Godparents were chosen on, as Constantijn Huygens put it, the basis of their "noble" standards, not because of the valuable presents they might offer. But privately, of course, it did not hurt to keep account of their value.

Hence, unlike the cooking pots that were offered as wedding gifts to brides on the Schermereiland, the importance of the christening gifts was partly their monetary value. This did not exclude their being appreciated as tokens of affection, or for the religious meaning they represented, but when worse came to worse it was the economic value that would be put to use. Beside which, the monetary value of the objects was also a measure of the esteem in which the child's family was held.

Nevertheless, godparents did not only offer their godchildren presents of permanent value. They were also supposed to offer their godchildren guidance and support in times of need. Moreover, it seems that during their lives godchildren also received small gifts of food from their godparents. As was shown earlier, Roeltje Beck not only received a silver christening gift of her godmother in her first year. Geertruyt also dropped by in The Hague twice that year to check up on the small infant and on both occasions she offered the child a pound of sugar.[131]

Death and Support through Poetic Letters

As with weddings, poems were considered appropriate offerings whenever a friend or acquaintance lost a loved one.[132] Naturally sympathies for the bereaved could also be expressed through plain letters, as was done upon the passing of Christiaan Huygens, who died on 7 February 1624 and was buried a few days later, of which events David Beck made notes in his diary.[133] Huygens's mother, Susanna Hoefnagels, in the meantime wrote a letter to her son Constantijn, who was in London at the time, to express her heartfelt appreciation for all the condolence letters she and the Huygens family received after the demise of their husband and father. In these letters, as she revealed to Constantijn, his father's outstanding character and qualities were highly praised, which of course did his grieving wife a lot of good.[134] Constantijn himself received a condolence letter from his friend Pieter Corneliszoon Hooft. This letter did not comment on his fathers qualities, but focused on the sadness over the loss of Huygens senior provoked. As Hooft put it:[135]

Your sadness hurts me, I had almost said your loss is my suffering. But considering nothing is lost unless it's owned, it can really not be called loss to relinquish what is lent to us under condition that it can be recalled at any time.

Although Hooft's words seem rather harsh, this was in fact a conventional way of showing support for the bereaved. Huygens himself also expressed his sentiments over the loss of loved ones in more or less the same terms.

When Constantijn was still an adolescent one of his younger sisters, Elizabeth, died at the age of fourteen.[136] He commented on this event in the autobiography he wrote of his youth.[137] What he specifically remembered about this period was his parents' extreme sadness which he considered quite inappropriate. He acknowledged the bereavement as such, but thought his parents could have been more considerate to the fact that their loss did not amount to much in light of the fact that their beloved daughter had now joined the Lord in heaven, and had therewith found her appropriate place. He thought his parents were in fact doing an injustice to the "Almighty and Highest God ... now that He prematurely claimed the blessed part that He had entrusted to the mortal remains".[138] The same applied when he wrote a poem on the death of his neighbours young daughter. Presumably the child's mother had been very distraught, for Huygens urged her to calm down and abide by the will of God because her daughter would be better off in the hereafter.[139]

This seems a highly insensitive line of reasoning, but it was in fact the general discourse regarding the mourning of loved ones during this period. Strong emotions over the loss of a loved one were generally denied the bereaved, because they were to bear their fate and trust in God who had now taken their beloved and had given them their deserved place in heaven. However, this discourse does not necessarily imply that people were in fact insensitive to the loss of their children, husbands and siblings. Huygens's parents, for instance, commemorated the death of their young daughter every year.

On the other hand, Constantijn does leave the impression that the death of his sister did not affect him all that much. He mentioned writing some poems in several languages on the occasion of her death, which made his father burst out into tears whenever he read them. Of course, it was in itself a nice gesture that he had written these poems in honour of his sister, but in his autobiography, after telling the reader of his sister's death, he went on to comment that he had kept these poems for posterity. Not as a way of commemorating his deceased sister, but as a means of showing his descendants his language and writing skills at an early age.[140]

Nevertheless, these poems were generally written to honour the deceased and to offer comfort and support to the bereaved. They could take on several shapes and forms. First there were the poetic letters that the friends Pieter Corneliszoon Hooft, Tesselschade Roemers Visscher and Constantijn Huygens exchanged when one of them was confronted with the loss of a loved one. These will be discussed shortly.[141]

Another type of poetry that coincided with death was of course funerary poetry. It was quite common to write funerary poems on the occasion of the death of some great figure. These poems could be read at the actual funeral, which, especially when the author was an established poet, added lustre to the whole event bcause of the honour it bestowed on the whole affair.[142] Yet the fact that the poem in itself would express the exquisite qualities of the demised will also have brought relief and support to the family.

Sometimes these honorary poems were offered to the bereaved after the funeral had already taken place, as was the case with David Beck and Daniel de Kempenaer. David was very pleased when De Kempenaer promised him he would compose a poem in honour of his late wife, as many other poetic friends had also promised.[143] David himself spent the larger part of the year writing a lamentation on the death of his wife.

Occasionally, this combination of poetry and death could turn out slightly morbid, if it wasn't that quite yet. Sometimes honorary epitaphs were written before the person to whom it was directed had actually died. Constantijn Huygens for instance composed "an epitaph in anticipation" for Peter de Vooijs.[144] This offering of funerary poems before one's actual demise was considered a great honour, although it somehow also leaves the impression of tempting the gods. A character like Vondel even found it within himself – in his old age – to write an epitaph upon his own death. His had quite a nice pun in it. In Dutch it said:[145]

Hier leit Vondel, zonder rouw
Hij is gestorven van de kouw

Here lies Vondel, but don't mourn
For the cold made him forlorn.

This joke referred to the medical convictions of that period, which involved the idea that as people grew older they became colder due to a re-balance of "humours" in their body. Vondel lived to be 92 and had obviously felt very cold towards the end.

However, in most cases the epitaphs were composed in honour of the death and most of these were rather traditional. Both Hooft and Vondel wrote a funerary poem on the occasion of the death of Pieter van Veen, a lawyer and artist from Alkmaar. The poets commented on Pieter's qualities as a lawyer and artist and complimented him on his amiable sociability. The only difference in terms of the content between these two poems was the order in which Van Veen's qualities were discussed.[146]

Poetic support among friends: Hooft, Tesselschade and Huygens

Poetic letters were a proper means of showing support from a distance.[147] Hooft, Tesselschade and Huygens did not attend the funerals of their friend's beloved, but instead offered them support by sending them their condolences and words of comfort. To contemporary ears these words of comfort might sometimes sound slightly harsh, while in fact they were part of the seventeenth-century convention that one should accept the will of God and that life on earth was just fleeting.

In the same year that Constantijn Huygens lost his father, his friend Pieter Corneliszoon Hooft lost his wife, Christina van Erp.[148] Tesselschade had heard of Hooft's loss and wrote him a letter in which she claimed that the earth had been unworthy of hosting Christina for such a long time, since she was worthy of a place in heaven. It had also come to her ears that Hooft had been inconsolable over the loss of his wife. This did not live up to the expectations Tesselschade had of her cultured friend. She told him in her letter that she felt for his loss, but could not believe, that he, who was so wise and knowledgeable, could not find it within himself to accept the death of his wife. She thought he would have found solace in his wisdom.[149]

Hooft responded by observing that even though wise men prescribed that "what can be lost should be loved light-heartedly and that what is lost should be lost without sadness", he had not even managed to live up to the first command, let alone the second:[150]

> [He] who had done nothing but look for needles and nails to fix what he loved to his heart, how could it be torn from him without incurable tears?

He claimed he wasn't looking to mourning, but grief knew where to find him anyway, and mentioned that he had never been sad over the loss of worldly goods, but had also been overwhelmed by the earlier death of his children. He added to that that even wise men like Seneca had not always found it within themselves to follow their own prescriptions of not mourning over the loss of what is loved. These words reveal that although there was a requirement for sadness to be carried stoically, this sometimes interfered with the very real and strong emotions one was experiencing. Or to put it in other words, the norm of accepting fate with grace was in practice hard to live up to; people could not help but mourn over the loss of their loved ones. Hooft's words also imply that affection was indeed very important in the relationship Hooft had to his wife and his children.

These words of condolence in some cases were rather belated as a result of the loss for words. This was especially true after the death of Allard and Tadea Crombalck, the husband and daughter of Tesselschade Roemers Visscher. Her husband and daughter had died the same day within hours of one another, which even in the seventeenth century was considered a dramatic loss. While Tesselschade was mourning the demise of her beloved, her friends Hooft and Huygens were bickering over the question of who would offer her his condolences first. They were so affected by her tragedy that they were afraid that they would not be able to find the right words to comfort her.

Hooft informed Huygens about these sad events in a letter. He had received a letter from Tesselschade in which she had informed him of the tragedy. Her little girl had been only nine years old and had been suffering from small pox. It was customary in that region for parents who lost a child to offer cookies to the children in the neighbourhood. Tadea had asked her mother to serve these cookies while she was still there to witness it and so they had. Four hours later the child had died. According to Hooft the child's father had loved her so much that his (physical) pain over losing her was enormous. The doctor had tried to better his condition by feeding him some potion, but this had only made things worse. He started throwing up blood and bled to death. Both the husband and the daughter were buried the day before Hooft received Tesselschade's letter.[151]

In his letter Hooft requested that Huygens send Tesselschade a letter of condolence. Huygens wrote back that he had already heard of the deaths of Tadea and Crombalck via an acquaintance who was travelling from Alkmaar, where Tesselschade lived, to The Hague. This news, however, was rather belated, which he regretted because he thought it would have been appropriate for him and Hooft to have attended the funeral since he considered this to be "one of the most normal duties of friendship".[152] As far as writing to Tesselschade was concerned, he figured it would be better if Hooft could do the honours first because Huygens simply was not capable of finding the right words. Before either of them could actually write Tesselschade, she had already written a letter to Hooft, in which she expressed her grief, which she "carried with weeping soul and grieving spirit yet with dry eyes".[153] Upon receiving this letter Hooft could naturally no longer postpone his response. He sent her a letter in which he offered his apologies for not writing earlier and showed his admiration for her bravery with which she carried her loss. He admitted that there was a lot he could learn from the way she dealt with her bereavement.[154]

Huygens had in the meantime also lived up to expectations. He had composed a poem that he offered to Tesselschade via Hooft, who only handed it over to her after he had convinced himself that she would be strong enough to handle Huygens's poetic words and after realising that it might be "a potion to her heart" to know that others honoured her so much that they would take her fate to heart.[155]

These letters reveal that emotions regarding spouses, children and friends were nothing extraordinary in seventeenth-century Holland. People mourned over the loss of loved ones, even though the words they used to express their feelings were not necessarily the words that would be used in contemporary society. It was a convention not to become besieged by grief and this was mirrored in the letters and poems people sent to offer support to friends. Yet even though this was a convention, it was obviously not easy to just let go of these strong emotions and accept fate. Tesselschade apparently managed to remain strong, for which she was complimented by her friends, but Hooft had clearly wallowed in his emotions.

However, there are examples of condolence letters that take both the conventions and the emotions into account. Especially the letter that Tesselschade sent upon the death of Huygens wife, Susanna van Baerle, is one of classic beauty. Constantijn Huygens was in fact not half as insensitive as he has thus far been pictured. His writings may give the impression that he was a man devoid of emotions, but as a matter of fact he did experience his share of grief during his life.

Constantijn Huygens married the affluent and beautiful Susanna van Baerle in 1627. This was an alliance that the Huygens family had long wished for. When Huygens was in London in 1624, his sisters wrote Constantijn several times about the efforts they had made to establish a relationship between his elder brother Maurits and Susanna. Much to their disappointment their attempts failed, but the fact that their brother Constantijn married the girl eventually must have brought his sisters some pleasure. This was not only an alliance that the Huygens family had longed for, the marriage itself was generally regarded as a happy one. When Susanna died in 1637, soon after the birth of her daughter, Huygens was overwhelmed by grief.

As could be expected, Tesselschade offered him a poetic letter to express her sympathies. The letter was actually addressed to Hooft (as was Huygens letter to *her* after the death of her husband and daughter), who was asked to pass it on to their mutual friend. Tesselschade in this letter stuck to the rule of advising that the bereaved let go of their grief and be grateful for the fate of their loved ones, but at the same time she acknowledged Huygens's loss by insisting that he should focus on writing poetry as a way of dealing with his sadness. Her advice to him was that he should both trust his words to paper, and trust this paper to give him comfort so that his inner pain could be expressed in words. According to Tesselschade Huygens should "record his suffering, so he won't have to remember."[156]

Afterwards both Huygens and Hooft expressed their admiration for Tesselschade's ability to address the issue in such a conventional and, at the same time, original manner. It seems Huygens took his friend's advice at heart. Some months later he wrote a poem upon the death of *Sterre*, or little star, his nickname for his wife.[157] Years later, in 1681, Huygens wrote a poem which expressed his appreciation for the wise words Tesselschade had once offered him.[158] He admitted that he still missed his wife, but that Tesselschade's suggestion that he trust his sadness to paper had helped him deal with his bereavement.

This shows that, even though they occasionally come across as harsh, these supportive letters actually meant a lot to the bereaved. Friends would reprimand each other for not carrying their loss in the conventional stoic manner, but this was just a norm that they were aware was sometimes impossible to live up to. They all experienced grief and they all realised that this brought suffering to the extent that it could not always be carried with the prescribed stoic dignity. This is what made Tesselschade's words so wise; she acknowledged Huygens's pain, while at the same time offering him a suggestion of how to deal with it in a dignified manner.

Interestingly enough, it is the discourse on bereavement in letters and the like that historians have interpreted as a sign that early-modern individuals were not emotionally attached to their spouses and children. People were to accept their fate with dignity and should not let themselves be overwhelmed by emotions. What the letters by Hooft, Huygens and Tesselschade show, is that while this was a discursive norm, it was something that could not always be lived up to. People experienced pain over losing a loved one, but they were just expected to express it very discreetly.

Conclusion

The gifts that were offered upon the occasion of rites of passage are clearly of a slightly different character than the gifts that were exchanged on a day to day basis. The gifts that accompanied life's significant events were themselves also significant. They carried meaning in different ways. The earthenware cooking pots show that gifts could carry symbolic meaning and thus have symbolic value. They were worthless in monetary terms, but they implicitly referred to the next stage in the life of the young bride. Christening gifts, on the other hand, were not devoid of symbolic meaning as such, but were especially significant because of the monetary value they represented. This was not only because this monetary value could be used in every day life, but it was also a means of measuring the esteem in which the child and therewith his or her family were held. The supportive and sometimes poetic letters were significant in the sense that they offered support to the bereaved. The recipient could find comfort in the idea that others had gone through the trouble of commemorating the loss of their beloved in a letter, but moreover could also find comfort in the words eloquent friends offered.

Both the cooking pots and the christening gifts held a strong reference to the ritual event to which they were connected. They referred to the new stage in life that the recipient was entering; the pot referred to the female tasks within marriage, while the christening gift acknowledged the young child as a member of the Christian community. In that sense, the gifts were important in the larger community in which the recipient functioned; they had a more or less public character. Since these objects were so strongly related to these rituals and were of a public character, the offering of these gifts was, to a certain extent, a social obligation. Those guests who were expected to participate in the ritual by offering these gifts could not refrain from doing so. This would be considered as disgraceful in their social circles, but it could also bring shame upon the donor within the larger community.

The letters exchanged after the death of relatives of a friend were of a slightly different nature. They were offered from one individual or one household to the next and did not necessarily play a role in the larger community of which the giver and the recipient were both members. These letters, however, were naturally very important in the maintenance of the relationship between the giver and the recipient. Not offering condolences in person or through a letter to relatives, friends and acquaintances who had lost their loved one would be inconsiderate on a personal level, but would not necessarily have consequences within the larger community.

Nevertheless, it is important to realise that even though these ritual gifts could carry strong symbolic, monetary, or emotional meaning, gift exchange in seventeenth-century Holland consisted of a lot more than just gifts that were offered on the occasion of a rite of passage. In quantitative terms these gifts were not very significant at all. They would only be offered upon occasion, in contrast to hospitality, which would surely be offered on these occasions but on any other type of occasion as well. Hospitality was a gift that was literally offered on a daily basis and thus was of great importance in the system of gift exchange. It is largely through the offering of hospitality that relationships were maintained.

B. Hospitality

Spontaneous events, personal incentives and social obligations

The gifts offered on the occasion of rites of passage were of great symbolic, economic and emotional value. The gift of hospitality, on the other hand, had a quite different character. Hospitality had a less explicit significance and was of a temporary nature. Whereas objects such as cooking pots and christening gifts could be displayed in the home and be kept for generations, and funerary poetry could be reread whenever the occasion called for it, hospitality disappeared the moment the party was over.

It is interesting to think that while material gifts are the permanent reminder of a relationship, one might say that hospitality *is* the relationship. A relationship consists largely of the contact that exists between two – or more – individuals, and in the daily life of individuals this contact was and still is for a large part maintained through hospitality. Naturally, there are other means to be in contact, by corresponding for instance, but in general one might say that the offering of daily hospitality is the most vital gift in the establishment and maintenance of social relations. However, since hospitality hardly leaves a trace in history only relatively little is known about hospitality in the early-modern period. This is particularly true for hospitality among burghers. Even Felicity Heal, who has written a very interesting book on hospitality in early-modern England, acknowledges that little can be said about practices of hospitality among the common folk, due to a sheer lack of sources.[159] It is precisely this gap that the diary of David Beck fills.

As the chapter on David Beck showed, hospitality was by far the most important gift that was exchanged in the social environment of this seventeenth-century schoolmaster. Not only was it the most common gift offered and received, but it was also the gift type that was offered upon any kind of occasion. As a matter of custom, it played an important role in the festivities that surrounded the ritual calendar. As a matter of social obligation it was an important element in the rituals that surrounded life's important events such as birth, marriage and death. Yet as a matter of course it was exchanged on an daily basis, whenever relatives, friends or professional acquaintances were in contact with each other. The hospitality offered could be anything from a glass of wine or a meal to a place to sleep.[160]

The Organisation of Hospitality

Overall a distinction can be made as to the ways in which shared meals and dinner parties were organised. First, there were those meals that were spontaneously shared with others, as a matter of course, and for which no particular inducement was necessary. This was a regularly recurring phenomenon that could occur any day of the week and any time of the day. However, since these joint meals were so common they did not receive much attention in David Beck's diary. He never failed to mention whenever he had dinner with others, but it was especially these ordinary shared meals that seldom warrented further comments. Beck would just note that he had his "*portie*", or meal, at his mother-in-laws house, that he had "eaten" at a friend's house, or that he had had a friend "as a guest".[161] On some occasions he would add what he and his company had actually eaten and, if it had been really good, he would comment on the quality of the food or wine. Every once in a while, when a meal had turned out to be more enjoyable than expected this would be noted as well.

Besides the ordinary meals that Beck and his friends shared on an almost daily basis, they also organised joint dinners. This was the type of hospitality that was also offered spontaneously in the sense that the host was not necessarily socially required or obliged to organise the event, but ventured into it as a matter of personal choice. These events could be the result of occasions like calendar feasts, but any personal motivation for offering a dinner was quite acceptable as well. Hendrik Beck, for instance, seems to have really enjoyed organising dinner parties, given that he used every opportunity he had to offer dinner to a rather substantial number of guests. This he did with any type of calendar feast as well as spontaneously.[162] Unlike the ordinary exchanges of shared meals, these events did require some organisation in advance. The guests would usually be notified beforehand by word of mouth or written invitation.[163]

Other than the ordinary daily hospitality and the spontaneously organised dinner parties that were offered, there were also dinners that were the result of a social obligation to offer hospitality.[164] This was usually the case with rites of passage.[165] The birth of a child was normally followed by a number of dinners; both on the day of the birth itself as well as in the weeks to follow. Even though these were highly enjoyable events, they were not something that could be avoided by the new parents, or – in fact – the new father. The father of the new born child was socially required to share his joy about its birth with his and his wife's relatives. The same applied to weddings. These were preceded by some official dinners, were celebrated with a big feast and were followed by so-called counter-weddings, and all of these events did have a somewhat obligatory character. Funerals were customarily followed by the offering of drinks to the attendees, but offering a meal was also not out of the ordinary.[166]

The food and drink served during these ritual occasions were naturally more likely to be cause for concern than the food served on any ordinary day. Whereas guests on ordinary days were "to eat what the pot offers", as the Dutch expression goes, the hosts went to great lengths to offer exquisite foods on these ritual occasions. The quality of these ritual foods had to surpass the quality of the food served on a daily basis. Furthermore, there were certain events that also required that specific foodstuffs or drinks to be served. Not only was this a costly matter, but in some cases it also required the help of others. On the occasion of big wedding feasts it was not uncommon for the host to ask his friends and relatives to supply like game and poultry.[167] Whether the latter would offer the food as a gift to the host or whether the host would eventually pay for it, is not always clear. It is obvious, however, that it was not at all considered inappropriate to ask for these contributions.

Even though these ritual events had a largely obligatory character, it did not mean that they were not highly enjoyable nor did it imply that the hosts would actually consider not celebrating these events. Hospitality at these events as such went without saying, but it did involve a certain amount of social stress since the hosts had to live up to social expectations and, moreover, specific social standards. Issues of concern included the food and drink that were offered, and the number of guests that were to be invited. Furthermore, it was important for the host to receive his guests with the right amount of honour and respect, which also involved the correct placement of the guests around the dinner table.

Beck does not mention any problems concerning these issues, but through other authors it becomes clear that these were indeed delicate issues that might cause a great deal of trouble if they were not handled with care.[168] If the host did not live up to the standards of his social environment this could result in a serious loss of honour.[169] This is in itself not typical for the early-modern period alone. Contemporary society also has ritual occasions that call for the offering of hospitality from hosts to guests, and in contemporary society these events also bring both a degree of enjoyment and social anxiety. People today also feel a need to live up to social expectations whenever an important event in life presents itself.[170]

Discourses on Hospitality

As Heal has pointed out, attitudes towards hospitality are revealed by what people did and what they said.[171] Since what David Beck did in terms of hospitality has already been discussed in part I, the question here is how Beck and company perceived all these offerings of hospitality. In fact, one cannot really know how David Beck or his company experienced hospitality, but it is possible to at least look at what Beck said about it. Certain observations can indeed be made based on David Beck's diary. The way Beck described his encounters with hospitality does sometimes reveal something about how the gift of hospitality was supposed to be performed. Those happenings that were ordinary day to day events were likely to receive little attention, whereas the more exceptional cases would be discussed more extensively in his diary, be it in a positive or a negative way.

As stated earlier, Beck usually described day to day hospitality in neutral terms. Unless either the food or the company had been exceptional, he just casually mentioned having offered or having been offered a drink, a meal or a place to spend the night. What he did occasionally describe was the sorts of topics discussed over dinner or the other ways in which he and his companions spent their time. Beck and his company discussed news, poetry and the arts, or just had a chat, but could also enjoy other forms of entertainment, like singing psalms, reading together or making music.[172]

Of course, the discourses he had over dinner or whenever he paid a visit largely depended on the company. With his "poetic" friends Beck would usually discuss poetry and the arts in general. These individuals were taken up to his office, or *comptoir*, to admire Beck's art works.[173] Beck not only composed poetry, but was also a calligrapher and he enjoyed drawing the occasional picture. This was naturally the result of the general interest in the arts and dilettantism in the arts that characterised Beck's cultural environment in general, but what is interesting in Beck's case is that he seemed to aspire to be more than just a dilettante.[174] Showing potential patrons his artistic work, was a means of interesting them in his work. With the uncles of his late wife, who did not necessarily share Beck's interest in the arts, he was in the habit of talking about earthier topics. This included the latest news about war and politics, as well as infomation about the wellbeing of other relatives and the occasional talk of a miracle tree somewhere in Germany, for instance.[175]

In general, Beck was more likely to have conversations of a more personal nature with women. With them he would also exchange news, but this was usually news on private instead of political matters. He discussed how one or the other relative was doing, or would inquire about somebody's health. Furthermore, Beck was more prone to discussing personal matters such as the sense of bereavement he experienced after the loss of his wife, and later his attempts of making the acquaintance of a possible new partner, with women in his environment.[176] Although these topics were occasionally also discussed with some of his friends, such as the widower Berend Zwidde, his brother Hendrik, his friend Breckerfelt or his "*compeer*" Matthijs Muller, these issues were largely confined to the conversations Beck had with the women who played a role in his life.

In that respect, his mother-in-law was not only important in terms of serving him food on a regular basis, but also in listening to his sad stories. One of the most difficult days Beck had in the course of the year that followed his wife's death, was when he was clearing out her things and found some of the letters she had written to him when they were courting. This left Beck very emotional and that evening he went to find solace at his mother-in-law's house, which she naturally offered.[177] The same can be said for an occasion later that year, when Beck – through the offering of a poem – had sought contact with a possible new lady friend. She had refused his approach, which did not do his self-confidence a lot of good. As he mentioned himself, he was "looking for company to chase away the half heavy thoughts, as I was somewhat moved this evening". In this state of mind Beck went to his mother-in-law's house that evening in search of dinner and some comfort.[178] It might seem strange to the contemporary onlooker that David would share his misery with his mother-in-law, but in their case it is not so surprising. Anna van Overschie had just lost her daughter and David Beck had just lost his wife. Between the two of them they were doing everything to keep Beck's household going: they jointly paid for the baby Roeltje to be at the wet nurse and Anna took care of Beck's other children whenever this was necessary. Furthermore, they also spent a lot of time together. Beck often had dinner at her place and he would invite Anna whenever he was organising a dinner party at his house. So in fact, their relationship was very close during 1624.

All in all it becomes clear through Beck's descriptions that the exchange of hospitality in fact offered more than just a meal, a drink or a bed. It was a phenomenon that could bring merry company as well as the latest news and artistic inspiration as well as emotional solace. It was thus something that was, in most cases at least, highly enjoyable and in other cases quite comforting. As such, the offering and acceptance of hospitality also functioned as a means of strengthening existing social ties, and of feeding intimacy into social ties that had not yet fully developed as friendship. Offering and receiving hospitality – on an objective analytical level – was instrumental in the sense that it helped maintain social ties, while on a subjective level it just brought some enjoyable company.

Beck's diary not only describes the discourses he and his friends and relatives had while enjoying this hospitality, but it also reveals certain discourses on the phenomenon of hospitality as such. These may have been particular to David Beck but they also seem to have been characteristic for his social environment. Even though he mostly referred to the exchanges of hospitality in neutral terms, Beck did occasionally express a more judgmental side. Whenever he did pass judgement on the way he was received by his hosts it was usually in positive terms. He mentioned being "treated well", which could refer to the civility with which he was received as well as the quality of the food that had been offered to him, or to the fact that his host had "made good cheer".[179] Otherwise, he referred to the company as having been "sweet", "merry" or "delighted".[180]

Only seldom did Beck make any notes on bad experiences he had when offering or receiving hospitality. He did complain being "packed like a herring" when he and Breckerfelt had slept at his brother's house, but this should be interpreted more as a joke than as criticism of the way Hendrik had received them. Of course, the rather unfortunate Bilsen incident that was discussed earlier was a slightly disappointing experience, but it is worth considering that it is the only example of a "gift gone wrong" in a diary that describes over a thousand instances of gift exchange. In general, one could therefore claim that the hospitality that Beck and his social environment exchanged was both well offered and well received.

On the other hand, Beck does offer some hints of certain peculiarities of social behaviour. He did occasionally pay special attention in his notes to the circumstances under which certain social exchanges, like talks or meals, took place. These pertained to either the timing or the placement of the event. As to the latter, he might every once in a while note that he had had a talk at somebody's door, which, especially when he mentions how long this talk lasted, seems to imply that he was somewhat affronted by not being invited into the house for a drink.[181] But in most of these instances he did not find the master of the house at home. This means that the talk he had was with the maid of that particular household and she was probably not in a position to invite acquaintances of her master into the house for a drink.[182] In those cases, Beck's disappointment for not being invited in for a drink may well have derived from his actual thirst. On the other hand, he may simply have been impressed by the long conversation he had.

On other occasions he distinguishes between having had a meal "in front" or "at the back", the former one of these options being more honourable. "In front" in this case usually referred to Beck having had dinner in the front room of the inn of his mother-in-law, where the "Gentlemen of Gouda", who resided in the inn whenever there was a general assembly in The Hague, would dine as well.[183] It meant that Beck had dined in their company, which he considered an honour. In contrast to that he would sometimes also have dinner in the back, which was his mother-in-law's private quarters.[184] In these instances he would have dinner with his mother-in-law and members of her household, which included Jaccomijntje and one of the brothers of his late wife. However much he may have appreciated these relatives, it is quite clear that he preferred dining with the honourable gentlemen.[185]

Whereas Beck's notes on dinner placements and standing outside for talks can be interpreted as criticism, the departure times he mentioned usually indicated something positive. By stating how long or till what time he himself had stayed as a guest or his guests had stayed at his house, he emphasised the enjoyable character of the gathering.[186] He did not reveal these times in order to point out that some guests may have outstayed their welcomes, but rather to show how welcome the guests had obviously felt.

Another example of how Beck used terminology with a rather negative connotation to actually describe events that he experienced positively is by the way he uses formulas that refer to coercion whenever he received an honourable and spontaneous invitation. Whenever he was asked to have dinner with somebody he was not particularly close to but did feel honoured to be invited by, he usually stressed the fact that he was invited "par force", "on their strong request" or that he "had to stay as a guest".[187] Although these expressions, when taken literally, imply that he did not necessarily want to accept the forceful invitation it is clear through his further descriptions of these events that he was actually flattered by the invite and enjoyed being kept "against his will".

So, with the exception of a few incidents, the exchange of hospitality was a rather enjoyable social phenomenon. It was generally not overtly used as a means of establishing or maintaining social ties, but was a goal of having social ties as such. Beck and his family and friends obviously enjoyed each other's company: they had the occasional squabble, and they offered the occasional shoulder to cry on, but most of the time they were merely enjoying themselves.

Hospitality towards Professional Contacts: Tailors and Wet Nurses

Not only were meals offered to family and friends, there were circumstances where relative outsiders would also be offered this type of hospitality. This also applied to those professional contacts who were paid to perform chores within the household, and would enter the confines of one's home, like salters, peat-men, and tailors.[188]

Tailor Abraham Breckeveld van Cuijlenburg was ordered to make a suit for David's younger brother Abraham on Monday, 15 January.[189] He started work at Beck's house the next day, and returned there every day for a week to finish the suit. On these days he joined the Beck-household for dinner every evening.[190] On some of these evenings Beck would be present himself, but even if he was not, Abraham would be offered a meal in the company of sister Diliane and the Beck children. The meals offered to these professional contacts were a result of both convenience and custom: it was customary to provide tailors or other professional contacts, like the salter or the peat-carrier, who worked in the house, with a meal when they were around on mealtimes.[191]

On the other hand, there are also examples of individuals that are referred to by Beck as being professional contacts, while as a matter of fact a closer look at the actual relationship between Beck and that person is one that can be considered friendship, more than anything else. This is the case, for example, with Beck's other tailor Berend Zwidde. Soon after tailor Abraham Breckeveld had finished working on some clothing for David's younger brother, David Beck contracted Zwidde to make him "a French mourning cloak".[192] Unlike Breckeveld, tailor Zwidde did not work at Beck's house but in his own workshop and, in the days that followed, Beck visited him regularly to bring cloth, buttons, ribbons or tags. On some of these occasions, Zwidde offered him a drink or even a meal, which is just ordinary professional hospitality.[193] A little less than two weeks after ordering the garment, Beck noted in his diary that he was wearing his "new French mourning cloak" for its "first voyage" and expressed his wish that the Lord would have him wear it in good health.[194] Since this garment was finished, one might expect that this also implied that the contact between Beck and his tailor was over, but this was not the case. During the year, Zwidde and David Beck paid each other visits, which were sometimes accompanied by a drink of "anise water".[195] They also invited each other to dinner parties, which were usually very enjoyable. Beck talked of being "well-treated and merry" and of being "very sweet and merry" on these occasions, so it does seem that these two men appreciated each other's company.[196] In November, Zwidde organised a *harst* to which Beck was kindly invited as well. It turned out to be a very merry occasion.[197] In that sense, Berend Zwidde was not just Beck's tailor but also a friend.

Another special case with respect to the offering of hospitality to professional contacts was the wet nurse. She was hired after the death of his wife to take care of Beck's infant daughter Roeltje.[198] The wet nurse was obviously not a family member nor could she be considered a friend, but she was to a certain extent quite a central figure in David Beck's life in 1624. She was, after all, taking care of one of his children, and thus he visited her house on a regular basis. These facts notwithstanding, it is impossible to identify her: Beck never mentions her by her first name or her maiden name, nor does he ever reveal the name of her husband.

This is quite extraordinary. Most of the time Beck's male acquaintances were referred to by at least their last names and Beck would usually add their professions as well. The aforementioned Zwidde was both his tailor and friend, but would nevertheless always be referred to as "tailor Berend Zwidde". Whenever he mentioned women with a specific function he would describe them in the same manner. Women that he just saw as the partners of his male acquaintances were usually referred to by mentioning the husband first, and then adding to that "and his housewife".[199] So, the fact that the wet nurse is only designated as *de min*, or "the wet nurse", is quite striking. She cannot be identified other than by her professional task within the Beck household.

As a matter of fact, her entire position in David Beck's life and his social circle is quite exceptional. On the one hand, David Beck regularly visited her home to see his little girl and to pay her, which are obvious things to do. On the other hand, she was the only person with whom Beck had a relationship of a solely professional nature who was invited to dinners that were organised to celebrate calendar feasts. Normally, these events were only celebrated in the company of relatives and close friends, but the wet nurse was invited to have pancakes with the Beck's on the occasion of Carnival and joined the Beck household for a *kermis* meal.[200] Furthermore, the wet nurse also had lunch at Beck's house right before Christmas, by which time she was in fact not taking care of little Roeltje anymore.[201]

This suggests that even though she maintained a professional relationship with the Beck household, she was to a certain extent part of the household since she took care of one of its members. However, even though she was present both in the diary and as a guest at these dinner parties, the wet nurse, as mentioned above, remains anonymous and not only because her name is not revealed. Whenever Beck noted that he had visited her at home, he never mentions what they discussed, which is something that he duly noted whenever he visited other women like the aunts of his late wife. In that sense, her participation in these festive occasions seems dependent upon her function in the Beck household. Naturally, her professional relationship with Beck would not have excluded personal appreciation, but there is no hint of any personal involvement with or appreciation for the wet nurse in David Beck diaries.

Stadholders and Forced Hospitality

Beck sometimes offered hospitality to people, who visited for professional reasons. This offering of hospitality was a matter of custom and to Beck it was the obvious thing to do. In other cases, the offering of hospitality was the result of one's professional duties. Hooft for instance was obliged to offer hospitality to the stadholder on the occasion of his inspection of the stronghold Muiderslot. This brought quite a lot of stress, and it seems Hooft would have preferred not receiving the stadholder at all. However, this was obviously an occasion in which Hooft himself had no say: if the stadholder wanted to be received, Hooft had no other option but to receive him.

In general, one might say that Hooft's years at the Muiderslot were quite peaceful.[202] Even though Hooft, as the bailiff of Muiden, indeed had certain responsibilities concerning the defence of Amsterdam, there were hardly any threats to the stronghold during this period, which left Hooft time to concentrate on his writings and the entertainment of guests. One of the more exciting events that Hooft experienced in his capacity as bailiff was the intended visit of stadholder Frederik Hendrik to the castle of Muiden. He was informed on this visit only a few weeks in advance, which meant Hooft was under a lot of time pressure to organise an impressive reception for the stadholder.

Hooft's efforts to make the event a success can largely be read through his correspondence with Joost Baeck, who was married to the sister of his late wife. Joost Baeck lived in Amsterdam – as did Hooft in the wintertime – and was a regular correspondent of

Hooft's during the summers when he resided at the Muider castle. The brothers-in-law discussed everything from politics to the latest news on relatives, and from mutual visits to literature. Baeck was also the person Hooft would turn to whenever there were practicalities that needed to be taken care off. Baeck ordered wine for him, but would also deliver letters to others on Hooft's behalf. In this respect, it is not surprising that Hooft would turn to Baeck for support in the organisation of the reception of the stadholder.

One of the first favours Hooft asked Baeck in this context was for him to mediate between Hooft and Dirk Sweelinck, the organist of the Old Church in Amsterdam. Hooft would make "good cheer" if he could manage to have Sweelinck play at Muiden on the occasion of Frederik Hendrik's visit. Yet Hooft remained unsure whether Sweelinck could be persuaded. He therefore asked Baeck to put in a good word, but if Baeck thought his efforts were insufficient Hooft suggested that Baeck should ask some other influential friends to talk to the musician as well.[203]

Hooft also wondered whether the city of Amsterdam would reimburse some of the costs of the reception for the stadholder. Muiden was a small town near Amsterdam and was vital to its defence. The stronghold of Muiden was therefore largely maintained by the city of Amsterdam and Hooft expected that a visit by the stadholder would also be considered part of its maintenance costs. This was clearly not an issue in which Baeck had any say, but what Hooft did ask Baeck to do was to inquire what Hooft could expect from the city of Amsterdam. Furthermore, Baeck was going to ask influential friends to also have a gunner sent to Muiden on the occasion of the stadholder's visit.[204]

A couple of days later, Hooft sent Baeck another letter concerning the same issues. He once again asked Baeck whether the city of Amsterdam would reimburse the costs of the reception. In any case, Hooft figured the burgomasters of Amsterdam would grant him the gunner and would not refuse to have Sweelinck play at the castle of Muiden. He thus gave Baeck instructions that both the gunner and the musician were to arrive at Muiden one day in advance.[205]

Presumably the costs of the reception were reimbursed by the city council, for in another letter to Baeck, Hooft expressed his wish that even though "those of Muiden were not allowed" to pay the costs of the prince, they at least wanted to prove their good intentions. According to Hooft, this was done by "something exceptional" that at the same time would not be too costly. In that respect, Hooft thought of a wine he once had at the house of the father-in-law of one of their friends. This was a "*Vin Muschat*" that was so good one of the people present had remarked that "it was a wine not to drink but to eat and chew".[206] Hooft knew that the stadholder also had a taste for this type of wine since he had some of it sent to him from the cellars of the King of England every year. Yet Hooft was convinced that some of the muscat wine sold in Amsterdam was of a much better quality. He thus suggested that Baeck should buy some of this better quality wine in Amsterdam, adding that if the wine was too expensive he should buy a slightly smaller barrel.

Interestingly enough, it seems that Hooft considered the stadholder's visit as a costly nuisance more than anything else, and he obviously tried to spend as little on it as he possibly could. This might be better understood when one considers that the time and money invested in these events were enormous, which might not be an issue to honour an important guest, but the problem was that it was not a matter of choice. It was the right of the stadholder to be received at the castle of Muiden and it was Hooft's duty to fulfil his every wish. This is not to say that it was not an honour or a joy to receive the stadholder, but since it was a costly obligation it must also have been a burden to those with these obligations. Even though this party demanded a major effort on his part, there was no way to refuse without insulting the stadholder and without losing his reputation.

However, despite the strained character of the reception, Hooft did make an effort to get the prince all the best in terms of musicians and wine.[207] He again wrote a letter to Baeck with wine as its main topic. Hooft had heard of a certain other brand of wine for which he was willing to pay 120 or even 200 guilders per barrel, if Baeck could get his hands on it. If not, Hooft suggested Baeck to get someone's advice on another French wine that could possibly be served with some decency, because Hooft had heard that the stadholder did not drink Rhine wine unless he was forced to. Hooft was also looking for sugared fruits, but only the best quality, because all else would seem "like daily bread" to the stadholder and his entourage.[208]

Another problem was when Hooft was to expect his princely guests. The latest Hooft had heard was that Frederik Hendrik was in Wesel at that point, which according to Hooft, meant that it would take at least another five or six days for the party to arrive at Muiden. Yet Hooft could never be too sure, so he asked Baeck to inform him further. By the end of the letter, Hooft expressed his appreciation for Beck's hard work and assiduity in the whole matter by hoping he could reciprocate in due time with "some substantial services". He added that "the want to take this work, was to follow God".[209] This suggests that both Hooft and Baeck saw the efforts they made for Frederik Hendrik's visit to Muiden as something unavoidable. This was partly the result of their world view, where to serve the stadholder was indeed a means of obeying God. But on a more practical level, it was out of the question to insult the Republic's most powerful man by receiving him without the honours he was due. The fact that Baeck assisted Hooft was for a large part self-evident: as brothers-in-law and friends this was part of the general solidarity expected. At the same time, this did not prevent Hooft from expressing his appreciation for his brother-in-law's efforts.

As it turned out, Hooft's expectations on when the prince would arrive had indeed been correct. On the evening of 18 September, Constantijn Huygens, secretary to the stadholder and friend of Hooft, informed him that the stadholder would arrive the next day to have his lunch in Naarden and that he would inspect Muiden in the "*achternoen*", or afternoon. Huygens expressed his regret that he had not been able to inform Hooft earlier, but the situation had been rather hectic in the prince's entourage since he changed plans constantly. In this latest plan, Frederik Hendrik had also decided to leave for The Hague straight from Weesp, another small town in the area, without passing through the nearby city of Amsterdam. This was problematic since the stadholder wanted to speak to one of the burgomasters of Amsterdam who now needed to be ordered to Muiden the following day. Huygens kindly requested Hooft to do the honours.[210]

A letter dated the same day as the one from Huygens, was sent from Hooft to Baeck. In this letter it is obvious that Hooft was not yet aware that the honourable visitor would arrive the next day. The letter once again dealt with the sweet wine that Baeck was supposed to have ordered, but which he obviously hadn't succeeded in procuring yet. Hooft was "at the end of his hope", especially since he would receive "little thanks" if he only served the stadholder ordinary Rhine wine. Besides that, he discussed the fish to be served, which he himself would arrange, and sugared exotic fruits, which he asked Baeck to arrange. Furthermore, he wrote to Baeck that he had heard somewhere that the stadholder was spending the night in Amersfoort that evening and that he would arrive in Muiden the next morning, but this seemed quite unlikely to Hooft. He was sure that if the stadholder arrived in Muiden the next day he would have heard already. Nevertheless, he asked Baeck to inform him as soon as there was any news.[211]

Obviously the rumours were correct. The stadholder was visiting Naarden, Muiden and Weesp the next day, which must have come as quite a shock to Hooft once he received the news from Huygens. Another hurried letter was sent to Baeck: Hooft needed Baeck to inform the burgomasters about the fact that the stadholder would have lunch in Naarden that day and furthermore that he needed to know whether the musician and gunner could come as soon as possible. Naturally, there was also more mentions of wine.[212] Still another letter followed: Hooft had received word that the cooks in Naarden were already preparing a meal for the prince. This left the representatives in Muiden with nothing to do other than order some wine. Baeck was to send the wine to Naarden by return courier.[213]

The stadholder's visit turned out to be slightly disappointing for Hooft, who described the whole event in a letter to Baeck the day after the visit. He explained why the visit was such a surprise, even though he had known of the prince's intentions for a couple of weeks. The stadholder had not made his mind up as to when to visit these towns until the very last moment. As a result, Hooft only heard of the arrival of the prince a day ahead of time through Huygens's letter , which was a lot later due to the fact that the courier had gotten himself drunk, as he himself explained to Hooft.[214]

The visit itself was very short and hectic, and as it turned out, the stadholder did not inspect the castle of Muiden at all. While Hooft had expected the stadholder to also have a meal at the castle in Muiden, the stadholder only had his midday meal in Naarden and slept in Weesp that evening. This made Hooft's efforts rather purposeless. The famous Sweelinck, for instance, had shown up at the castle to play for the stadholder after all, which turned out to be unnecessary and left him with nothing to do but to tune Hooft's house organ, since he could not return to Amsterdam until the next day.

Moreover it seemed that Hooft could have refrained from bothering so much about the wine. Although it arrived on time, it was hardly consumed since the stadholder and his men had had too much beer earlier. Hooft was now stuck with a huge quantity of wine, which he would keep for himself. He would pay the wine merchant for it, once Baeck had bargained a fair price and had informed Hooft how long the wine would keep. In order to thank Baeck for all his troubles, Hooft sent him some of Tacitus's work "as a plaster for the blisters" he obtained from his efforts in helping Hooft.[215]

Naturally, this gift did not fully reciprocate Baeck efforts, but this was not the aim. With the gift of Tacitus, Hooft wished to show his appreciation for Baeck's efforts and symbolically assure him that he was much obliged in both senses of the word. Obliged in the sense that he was grateful for all that Baeck had done, but also in the sense that he was obliged to support his friend whenever he needed help. Surely Baeck had not helped his friend with the intention of making him feel obliged to him. To him it was just self-evident that he would help his friend and relative out, as Hooft would do for him.

Only in a letter to his friend and secretary to the stadholder Constantijn Huygens does it finally become clear what Hooft had actually arranged in honour of the stadholder. Not only had he invited the organist and the gunner for entertainment, but a number of actors to perform some plays during dinner. Moreover, Hooft had invited his friends Tesselschade Roemers Visscher and Francisca Duarte, who were among the most talented female singers of their generation, to sing for the stadholder. Furthermore, Hooft had intended to decorate the entire dining hall with flowers and leafage. There was even some talk of having different live fish – bream, carp, pike and bass – as decorations.[216] In this same letter, Hooft expressed his disappointment about the unsatisfactory visit of both the stadholder and Huygens with the following words:

> Like a pregnant woman, who puts her mouth on a glass of tasty wine that is thrown into pieces against her teeth, or an Alchemist, whose seven-year work and the bottom dregs of a groundless hope explode around his ears, so I stood bashed on the head at the swift passage of his royal serenity and your honour, seeing

the joy I anticipated in the honour of your presence disappointed.[217]

Hooft's expressive capacity is striking, and even somewhat over the top perhaps. Was he really that disappointed? Of course, one can never be sure. In that respect, it is interesting to note the way Hooft expresses his feelings of disappointment. He uses two evocative metaphors that are not necessarily realistic, but that fit nicely into the literary style of private correspondence of the Dutch cultural elite of that period. This was in fact a private letter to Huygens, which also included an invitation to Huygens and his wife Susanna van Baerle to visit the castle at Muiden, as a means of offering comfort to their disappointed friend. Since these two men were friends it seems quite likely that they regretted not having had the opportunity to have an evening with good food, nice wine, inspiring entertainment and interesting conversation.

It is unsure whether the same can be said about Hooft having missed the company of the stadholder. His intended visit to the castle of Muiden had been forced upon Hooft and even though it was an honour to receive and entertain the stadholder, it also brought the necessary obligations in terms of money and efforts. Yet since Hooft had already made all of the preparations it seems quite likely that it was in fact a great disappointment to him that the stadholder had passed the *Muiderslot* by, as well as a great waste of time and money.

In his reaction to Hooft's metaphoric letter, Huygens expressed his wish that he had known about Hooft's plans for the reception of the stadholder earlier because it would have been easy to persuade the stadholder to have his afternoon walk in Weesp and his evening entertainment at the castle in Muiden, instead of the other way around. Huygens did confess that he and Wijts, the other secretary to the stadholder, had presumed that Hooft would organise such a grand reception, but since they hadn't had proof they were unable to convince the stadholder to alter his plans.[218]

This seems to be an implicit criticism from Huygens: they both could have been spared the disappointment if Hooft had informed Huygens better. Huygens further expressed his regret that the extended visit had not happened, by referring to Hooft's metaphor of the alchemist. He himself was also not free of "seven years worth of bottom dregs". Huygens was, however, comforted by the idea that Hooft was still willing to receive him and his wife at the castle, but insisted that Hooft and his wife visit him in The Hague first.[219] Hooft accepted this invitation gracefully.[220]

Hospitality and Reciprocity

As was shown earlier, the offering of a *foy* was a means of reciprocating hospitality, but naturally there were other ways in which hospitality was reciprocated. Within the circle of family and friends it was obvious that the guest would reciprocate any hospitality offered by the host at the earliest opportunity. Naturally, when the hospitality was the result of a spontaneous event, like a spontaneous invitation to dinner, it was not always clear when the reciprocation would occur. It was not as if the terms of reciprocation were ever explicitly stated. Still, there was a mutual understanding that this would eventually occur. In fact, a quantitative analysis of David Beck's diary shows that it actually did.

In most cases, the exchange of hospitality from one person to the next was quite balanced. The few exceptions are Beck's mother-in-law and Breckerfelt. Why Breckerfelt would have received so much more from Beck than he offered, is unclear. For the first few months of the year it would have made sense, since Breckerfelt was still a bachelor then and even though Beck, as a widow, was a single man himself, at least he had someone in the house to prepare his meals for him. These meals were easily shared with a friend. However, after Breckerfelt's marriage this pattern did not change.

That Beck's mother-in-law offered many more meals than he returned can actually be explained by the fact that she kept an inn, which made it easy for her to have him as a guest on a regular basis. Besides which, even though she might have offered him more in quantitative terms, it seems that Beck did live up to reciprocal expectations in qualitative terms. Whereas she often let him share a meal that she had prepared for her guests anyway, Beck was more likely to invite her for special dinner parties during calendar feasts.[221] Moreover, it took Beck almost the entire year to write a lamentation on the death of his wife, which included several different poems. When he finally finished this lamentation, his mother-in-law was the first to receive a neat copy, which was for him probably the most suitable way of expressing his appreciation.[222] She had indeed been very supportive and

Beck expressed his gratitude by offering her a poetic work that he had worked on for a very long time and that referred to someone they had both been very close to. With this gift he offered "mother" something which in quantity did not measure up to all she had offered him, but at least in quality showed her how much he was indebted to her. In that sense, Beck and his friends did not require reciprocations of gifts of equal form and value.

This was different for the hospitality during the festive summer season, when the towns in Holland took turns celebrating their annual fair. It was clear to all participants that any hospitality offered by one host in one town, would be returned whenever he or she visited the fair in another town. It was not something that would be explicitly stated, but it was obvious to the parties involved. This was the sort of reciprocation that worked from one individual to the next and obviously involved the same type of gift.

The exchange of gifts that surrounded rites of passage was of a different character. Since births, weddings and funerals did not necessarily have a clear temporal pattern, like calendar feasts, and were in general not events that individuals could actually orchestrate themselves, like offering daily meals or organising dinner parties, these could only be celebrated upon occurrence. This obviously hindered patterns of reciprocity, for it was impossible for the individual to maintain a balance of reciprocity.[223]

Furthermore, these ritual occasions were not only lacking in reciprocity by nature, but also in the way these ritual events were performed. It was not like guests at these events didn't contribute. At a birth it was clear that the christening witnesses would offer the new born child a gift. While at weddings, the guests offered the newlyweds presents and poems, and at funerals the attendants offered support to the bereaved. Moreover, guests were occasionally requested to provide some food prior to the event.[224] Yet these gifts, in quantitative terms, could never equal the amount of money the hosts spent on hospitality, food and drink at these events. The total value of hospitality offered at weddings would be greater than the total value of the gifts offered by the guests. At christenings, only the godparents would offer gifts, whilst there were indeed more people that enjoyed the hospitality that was offered on these occasions. Moreover, the amount of emotional support and honour that funeral attendants brought the bereaved is impossible to measure at all. The strong qualitative or symbolic nature of the gifts offered made up for this.

Gifts presented by guests at these occasions were usually not meant for those who offered the hospitality. As a matter of fact, the hosts at these events hardly ever received gifts. Christening gifts, for instance, were for the godchild and not the parents. While weddings were normally offered by the parents of the bride, they did not receive the gifts. Wedding gifts were meant as contributions to the new household that the bride and groom were about to establish.

This supposed lack of reciprocity within the rituals that surrounded life's important events was the result of the special character of these ritual exchanges. The terms of exchange within these rites of passage were totally different from that of any other exchange occasions. Whereas other exchanges took place between individuals or households, ritual events were occasions for exchange between a community and its members. These communities might entail an extended family, a neighbourhood or a borough, or a professional guild. Gifts exchanged therewith did not have to be reciprocal on an individual level, but within the whole of the community there was general, yet largely implicit, awareness that certain occasions called for the offering of hospitality from the community members central to the occasion to the rest of the community. Members of the community would offer the community as a whole hospitality on occasions as such births, weddings and funerals and would this would be reciprocated whenever another member of the community celebrated a birth or a marriage, or mourned death.

This also explains why the offering of hospitality on such occasions was not a matter of personal choice but a social obligation. In order to remain a respected member of the community, any member of this community had to follow the rules that surrounded these rituals. A refusal to follow these rules could discredit not only the hosts of these events, but more importantly, also the people for which the celebration was intended. A refusal or inability to follow the rules of the ritual implied a bad start within the community for a newborn child and a newlywed couple, and a bad end for the deceased. This did not only have consequences for the child, the couple or the deceased, but brought dishonour to their family. Naturally, this principle of indirect loss or gain of honour did make the system of long term reciprocity within the community all the more effective.

However, it should be made clear that this analysis of how the system of gift exchange within the community functioned did not necessarily coincide with the way in which individuals perceived these exchanges. Fathers of little babies were certainly proud of their progeny and the same was probably true for parents of daughters that were married off to respectable men. Moreover, this analysis of the functioning of a system of gift exchange does not exclude the notion that those who lost loved ones experienced feelings of sincere bereavement.

Conclusion

In this chapter, the gift of hospitality was discussed in greater detail. It showed how hospitality was organised and how it was perceived. In general, one can say that the offering of hospitality was not just a means to an end – the maintenance of social ties – but also an end in itself. Both the offering and receiving of hospitality would in the majority of cases bring pleasure and enjoyment. The reciprocal offering of hospitality brought company on an almost daily basis. It offered an opportunity to discuss a variety of topics from politics to the arts, to be merry, or to just be comfortable and relax.

Even though there are certain clear patterns of reciprocal behaviour that can be determined from David Beck's diary, this does not mean that this was an issue that overly concerned Beck and his circle. Hospitality and other gifts were offered as a matter of course, a matter of custom or a matter of social obligation and also returned as a matter of course, a matter of custom or a matter of social obligation. The reciprocal nature of exchange was not something David Beck dwelled upon in his diary, which of course does not mean that it was not an important issue to him. But there are at least no clear signs in Beck's diary that it was, and there are no other reasons to assume that it might have been. It therefore seems hard to believe that Beck meant his diary to be an account book of his social contacts.

Part III: Terms and Conditions of Exchange

Gifts in relationships

In the first chapter, it was made clear that gift exchange took place within several different types of social networks. Gifts were exchanged within the family, between friends, and also with people who someone would be in contact with for professional reasons. There are some general patterns that can be ascertained for these different networks: The family played a more important role in life's important events and were therewith more likely to receive material objects, friends received hospitality on a day-to-day basis and during calendar feasts, and the gifts that professional contacts received depended on their profession. Nevertheless, the way gifts were dealt with within these different relationships obviously depended on the individual relationships. In this chapter, a number of these individual relationships are discussed. By looking closely at these relationships it becomes clear how gift exchange functioned within certain relationships and what the terms and conditions were under which gifts were exchanged between certain individuals. Furthermore, this close reading shows what the conventional discourse was for seventeenth-century individuals whilst dealing with the exchange of gifts.

Brotherly Exchange

Herman and Pieter Verbeeck

One example of a relationship in which the offering of gifts played an important role is that of Herman and Pieter Verbeeck. According to the Herman Verbeeck's autobiography, these two brothers could not get along at all. They argued and fought constantly. As far as Herman was concerned, it was all Pieter's fault while he was just the poor victim of these terrible situations, or at least that is the impression that Herman leaves in his autobiography.

The negative feelings between these two brothers as it is described in the autobiography were partly the result of the generally pessimistic view of life that prevails in Verbeeck's writings. The egodocument can be characterised as a strikingly negative account of the strikingly unfortunate life of a strikingly grumpy man. This is a matter of discourse more than anything else: Verbeeck chose to represent himself in this way. His autobiography uses the Book of Job metaphor as a means of showing that he carried life's burden with Christian devotion. Yet this writing strategy also helps position him as a victim of life's unfortunate incidents, as opposed to his brother who was always lucky in life. This offers him the opportunity to claim that his brother had never done much to support Herman. In fact, Verbeeck makes a strong connection between the unfortunate course his life had taken and the generosity, or lack of generosity, he received from his social environment.

Even the early years of his youth were generally unhappy and – according to Herman – things did not take a turn for the better in the years that followed.

The first part of the autobiography reveals how the two Verbeeck boys were prepared for their future trades. His elder brother was predestined to become a tradesman in Archangel, while Herman was to take over his father's furrier shop.[1] This was a course of events that Herman was not too pleased with, because as could be expected in his case, he preferred being a tradesman himself. But since it was considered bad for competition that both brothers become tradesmen, Herman lost out. He regarded the shop as a heavy burden and claimed that "while my brother was exalted, I remained a slave".[2] However, he did not want to go against his father's wishes so he bore "the very heavy cross on this innocent body".[3]

In fact, as can be understood from his autobiography, this heavy cross actually gave him the most joyful time of his life as well. Part of his training included an apprenticeship in France with one of his relatives and it was during this period that Herman seemed to be the happiest. As he put it, "a hundred years of fun in Holland could not compete with one year of fun in France".[4] His happiness was the result of the way he was received by his master and his wife. When he arrived, only the wife was home. Unluckily, she did recognise Herman as their new apprentice and had left him to sleep in the barn. But when her husband returned home, Herman was received with the greatest respect and was offered the best of foods and was even paid quite generously. This led to his remarking that he felt more like a family member than a servant, which in fact was true.[5] His reference to the generous hospitality he received in France shows that Herman's happiness was closely linked to the generosity he received from others.

Unfortunately, this period in France did not last as long as it might have. Herman's father fell ill and Herman went home to say his farewells and take over the business. His return trip was a small disaster. Instead of taking a vessel from France to the southern Dutch province of Zeeland, Herman ended up on a ship bound for England.[6] Eventually, Verbeeck did manage to get back to Amsterdam safely and this just began a new chapter of trouble with his brother.

Back in Amsterdam, Pieter and Herman fell in love with the same woman and much to Herman's disgust, his brother abused the fact that Herman was at home sick to make his move. It was this abuse, not the fact that his brother had stolen her heart, that left Herman so sad. However, he did believe that if these two people loved each other they should be allowed to get married and Herman was obviously not the only one who thought along these lines. One of his aunts even asked him what the most suitable moment would be to offer the future couple their wedding gifts.[7] She could have saved herself the trouble, for as it turned out, his brother did not have any intentions of actually marrying the girl, which must have brought some disgrace to the Verbeeck family.

Things improved slightly for Herman when he met Clara Molenaer. He was quite infatuated by her as it was, but the fact that her father owned a business without having any male heirs presumably added to the attraction. Although their feelings were mutual, Herman was still afraid that he wouldn't be able to convince her to marry him, because he did not have "the style to keep her in honour".[8] By this he meant that he was afraid he lacked the financial means to offer her the sort of life she deserved. Interestingly enough, his relatives thought just the opposite; that she was not good enough for the Verbeeck family.

However, luckily enough, Clara's father died during this period, which certainly enhanced Herman's chances of marrying her.

Herman and Clara in fact got engaged and Herman was very sa-
tisfied to be part of the Molenaer family, especially since mother
Molenaer had promised Herman that she would teach him anything he needed to know about the business.[9] As Catholics, Herman and Clara got married in the church as well as in the town
hall. The wedding dinner was offered by her mother and, as Herman put it, their guests "were received in honour".[10]

After the wedding, Herman and his new wife went on their
"*speelreisje*", or honeymoon. This was not so much intended as a
possibility for the newlyweds to have some romantic time together, but as a means of introducing the new spouses to family
members around the country. Even though these *speelreisjes* do not
live up to contemporary standards of romance, they were indeed
very enjoyable. Herman commented that he and his wife were "received in honour" and "treated with eagerness", which shows that
the hospitality extended on these occasions was important, but the
way it was extended was essential to Verbeeck.[11]

Unfortunately, as usual, something went wrong; Herman was
summoned because his mother was ill. This was unlucky indeed
for Herman and Clara had just arrived at the home of one of their
cousins who was about to "show a lot of friendship".[12] The end of
their *speelreisje* was, according to his autobiography, also the end of
any joy Clara and Herman had in their lives. Despite the fact that
Herman described his alliance with Clara Molenaers as perfectly
agreeable, what they experienced during their marriage was nothing but misery. As Herman put it:

> Marriage is not necessarily fun as it is, but even when you do
> manage to live in peace with your wife, there are always other
> people that are ready to spoil it.[13]

In his case, his marital bliss was largely spoiled by his own relatives, or so he claimed. This began when Herman and Clara returned from their short-lived honeymoon. They heard some gossip that they were unsuitable for each other because of their social
status. According to his relatives, Herman could have done a lot
better for himself than marrying one of the Molenaer girls.

In general, unequal marriages were not approved of during this
period.[14] It was considered bad taste for men and women to marry
people that were not their equal in status, property or age, as was
shown through the emblem by Roemer Visscher which included a

metal and an earthenware cooking pot. It was believed that un-equal status would result in serious problems within the marriage and was therefore strongly discouraged. This sense of inappropri-ateness towards unequal marriages does seem to be an early mod-ern strategy to keep loss of social capital at bay, but in contempo-rary society there is also a strong preference for marriage alliances between social equals.[15] Even though this is not revealed so much via the general discourse on marriage, it certainly shows in mar-riage patterns.

Naturally, Herman was not pleased when he heard his family had been talking about him and his wife behind his back and he confronted his relatives on the issue. They obviously felt bad; not necessarily about the gossip as such, but about the fact that Her-man had heard about it. They offered Herman and Clara a diaper basket as a peace token, which was a very suitable gift since by then Clara was pregnant with their first child.[16]

Shortly thereafter, Herman ran into financial troubles, and as usual his own relatives were reluctant to help him out. Thus he turned to his mother-in-law who offered to remit some of his debts with her.[17] Later on, his relatives decided to help him out after all, but only after it was agreed not to make any of it public for it would have certainly resulted in a loss of Herman's hon-our.[18] However, since Herman's reputation might influence that of the Verbeeck family in general it was also in their best interest to be discreet.[19] In fact, it was only after seeing Herman's account books, that his relatives decided to help him out and only on the condition that he would offer them collateral so that he "could re-main in his honour". Herman complained in his autobiography that it was hard for him to "be eating food from somebody else's hand", but there was no other option because he "who has noth-ing, can do nothing but live off what is given to him".[20]

Nevertheless, it is difficult to avoid thinking that Herman brought some of his misery upon himself. It seems he did not manage his business or his finances very well, and that he was living beyond his means. When his son was born, for instance, he decided to bring in a wet nurse even though this was quite expen-sive.[21] He mentioned that his family had strongly opposed, which implies that a wet nurse was probably not a necessity but a luxury, because if it had been a necessity, clearly his family would not have opposed to it so strongly.[22] What must have struck the family as an even greater waste of money was the fact that Herman, his wife, and their baby son ended up having to join the wet nurse in the province of Friesland for a period of time, because she had certain legal matters to attend to.[23]

As a matter of fact, the next piece of gossip that came to Herman's ears was that his wife was a *nuf*, or a prim gal, with a talent for keeping up appearances and a keen eye for wasting other people's money. Herman was really hurt by these vile accusations, which he claimed were totally unfounded, and he defended the honour of both his wife and mother-in-law by describing the latter's virtues in particular as a person who had always been extremely supportive of him and his household.[24]

What is interesting is how Herman defended his mother-in-law by employing the terminology of gift exchange. It seems that Herman was trying to get back at his family by pointing out that others had always been more supportive of him than his own family. Others had generously offered their hospitality and others had offered him practical and financial support in times of need. His family only offered him a diaper basket because they felt guilty for gossiping about him and his wife, and they only offered financial support under certain conditions. Here Herman was implying that his own family had not only failed him, but had also failed to fulfil their familial duties, which was obviously not very honourable.

Herman further criticised his relatives by comparing them to a certain Mr. Benning, who had also offered Herman and his household support in times of need. Herman spoke very highly of this benefactor "because worthy is the man, who gives his treasures and knows nothing of it". To which he added, "he who opens his cash, and comes and gives with spite" will not be rewarded by God, for "God wants a pure gift", which according to Herman was surely not something that his family had been offering him.[25] Since Herman mentioned several times that he lived of giving, it must have made a great difference to him whether these gifts were pure gifts, or gifts that needed to be repaid either in the sense of family obedience or in the sense of the actual repayment of loans.

What Herman really despised about his family is that they kept on complaining about their own situation, even though they were becoming richer and richer.[26] This was especially hurtful to him because he was not only getting poorer and poorer, but, more importantly, he was also losing his reputation. As he himself stated:

"Before it was monsieur Verbeeck, but now [I] am barely called Herman, so has my honour been stripped away."[27] In seventeenth-century Holland, only people who were less respected, like servants, were called by their first names. Hence, by mentioning that he was being referred to by his first name, Herman was stressing the fact that his environment had less respect for him due to his financial situation.[28]

He also claimed to be the outsider amongst his mother's offspring; "three are great in honour and the fourth seems disowned".[29] As a matter of fact, the only person who really cared about him and his household, according to Herman, was his mother-in-law who helped Herman whenever she could. This help involved buying his household meat and peat in wintertime, as well as offering them a roof over their heads when they could no longer afford the rent.[30]

Herman was, again, particularly disappointed in his brother when the latter refused to help him with his debts with the excuse that he could not give to Herman what belonged to his children.[31] Herman made a real fuss and even started crying after which his brother felt obliged and offered him some money anyway, but then Herman declined arguing that his brother should keep whatever he said belonged to his children. As it turned out, his brother arranged to take care of Herman's rent with the landlord. Even though his "honour was saved" by this arrangement, Herman did not show much gratitude for his brother's gesture.[32]

When later on, the Verbeeck's ran into financial trouble again, Herman was upset with his brother for not offering them any help even though he visited them regularly and, according to Herman, must have noticed on these occasions that they were again going through rough times. Herman stubbornly resolved not to confront his brother on the issue, but ended up talking about his troubles with his sister in tears, who then went to their brother to ask for help on his behalf. The brother again visited Herman at his house to offer him the fair amount of twenty guilders, but Herman thought that considering his extremely bad financial state twenty guilders would not do him a lot of good anyway and he decided to refuse his brother's gift.

On another occasion, what Herman had regarded as a gift turned out to be a loan instead. Herman had received money from his relatives to improve his situation with the conviction that it was a gift, but soon afterwards he was called to his brother's office who forced him to sign an I-owe-you. His brother simply took the money Herman owed from his inheritance, which once again convinced Herman that his brother was not at all concerned about his well-being and was only concerned about his own interests.[33]

Still, his brother was not the only person who disappointed Herman. Another relative, described in the autobiography on several occasions as a stingy person because she failed to offer what Herman thought he was entitled to, was his sister-in-law Maria Molenaer. Both his sisters-in-law were lay sisters and still lived with their mother, which also meant that they lived with Herman and his family for a large part of the time. The elder sister, Bartha, was generous like her mother, at least according to Herman. But the younger sister thought that the Molenaer family had done more than enough for Herman and his family, and that it was about time that he began taking care of his own business.[34] This was, of course, an opinion that Herman disagreed with. In his mind, his bad financial situation was a matter of fate, and not necessarily something he could influence.

However, living off others at a certain point also annoyed Herman himself. He claimed that even if someone had offered him his own weight in gold he could no longer accept the gift, since he preferred a life of sobriety and tranquillity.[35] He wrote that from then onwards he would not accept the help or support of any relatives, but would in the future only count on the grace of God. His wife, however, was not convinced that this would in any way solve their problems and insisted that Herman not depend solely on the grace of God but also on a certain Mrs. Schut who was in the position to help Herman get another job.[36] Mrs. Schut did in fact manage to get Herman another position, which yet again did not help solve his financial troubles. By the end of the autobiography, Herman was once again lamenting how unfairly his brother was "enjoying roast meat" and drinking "clear wine", while he was eating "dry bread" and drinking nothing but water "in his misery".[37]

The question remains, however, why he felt the need to complain so vigorously and why he felt he needed to present himself the way he did in his autobiography, for in the end the impression he left of himself was in many respects the one of the grand loser. It seems that by writing this autobiography he tried to come to terms with, as well as defend the unfortunate route his life had taken. According to his writings this was not due to his own failure. He tried to show that he indeed had done the utmost to provide for his family, which was intended to make clear that he himself was certainly not to blame. Furthermore, Herman claimed that his life was the result of God's will. In that respect he partly accepted his circumstances in the conviction that this was the way that God had chosen for him. Yet on the other hand he made a very clear case of blaming his own failure in life on the failure of others to help him out the way they should have had. His relatives and his brother especially had failed to fulfil their familial and Christian duties towards him.

In his writing, he used several strategies to make his self-image seem more convincing. First, he judged certain people explicitly; they were either good or evil based on the amount of support they offered during the course of Herman's life. His sister Geertruid, his mother-in-law, his elder sister-in-law and all the intercessors who helped him out were highly esteemed for their efforts and their generosity. But anyone who refused to go through the same trouble was judged unworthy, not only as a friend or relative of Herman, but also as a Christian in general. This applies in particular his elder brother Pieter.

His brother's image is further brought to disgrace by the way in which Herman reveals some of his moral dispositions. Naturally, the fact that his elder brother became a trader and Herman did not, was something beyond their own power, as was the fact that Pieter earned so much more money than Herman. So these were not necessarily things he could actually blame on his brother. Still, other incidents were clearly used by Herman to paint a negative picture of his brother. Herman described these in his autobiography as a means to show that even though his brother had been more successful in life, it had been Herman who had always had the moral right on his side. It was Herman who had good intentions with the girl that both brothers had fallen in love with, while his brother went around disgracing the family through his contact with her. It was Herman who was obliged to live a life of sobriety and simplicity who was willing to suffer for a loftier end, while his brother led a life of luxury. It was Herman who suffered financial problems because his brother loaned him money rather than offering it as a gift, as every real brother and Christian would have done. This very negative portrait of his brother allowed Herman to avoid taking personal responsibility for the way his life had turned out.

He explained all this quite explicitly, but occasionally he would also use more indirect methods to cast aspersions on a person's honour. On several occasions, he emphasised how he had always been happy with his wife, with his supportive mother-in-law and with the Molenaer family. Although there is no reason to assume he did not love his wife, or did not appreciate his mother-in-law, he also had no other choice but to claim so. He had in fact become connected to the Molenaers without his relatives' approval and he was unwilling to admit that this might have been a mistake. He preferred painting a perfect image of this family as another way of showing that he had done nothing wrong and that it was his family who had done him wrong by not approving the alliance.

Naturally one cannot judge whether his family had actually done him wrong. Herman said they did, but his brother Pieter would probably say the opposite. It does appear that Pieter and the Verbeeck family in general would be intend on helping out their needy brother.[38] This may have been motivated by a warm interest for their sibling's well-being as well as by a general interest in the family's reputation, for naturally Herman's success in life also affected the image of the Verbeeck's in general.[39] But since the latter was the case, it was quite unlikely that their gift could ever be a pure gift, as Herman wished for them to offer him.

It could never be a pure gift, because it would be offered with certain expectations of return, not necessarily in terms of monetary repayment so much as a certain type of behaviour.[40] For them to offer Herman financial support, he had to adjust his behaviour and expenditures to please the Verbeeck's. He was expected to live in a style that would not dishonour the family, but not so extravagantly that it would lead to financial problems. But whether it was bad luck or just bad bookkeeping, this was obviously not something that Herman was very good at. It seems that he lived off his mother-in-law for a large part of his adult life, for which he justifiably showed his gratitude, but his family would have preferred him to earn his own way, which, despite some attempts, he was not very eager to do. In that sense, it does not seem so strange that his family refused to support him at a certain point.

The life story of Herman Verbeeck reveals that the offering of gifts, in the sense of support, can in fact be used as a type of social leverage. His family was only willing to offer Herman support if he, in return, would live a life, marry a wife and get the type of job they expected him to. The fact that he failed to fulfil their expectations was enough reason for them to withhold support. This seems rather harsh, but is in effect a natural feature of gift exchange, especially when it comes to the offering of gifts for which no reciprocation – in terms of gifts – can be expected in return. This is generally the case in situations in which there is a power imbalance between the giver and the recipient, such as parent-child relations, poor relief and other types of charity.[41] In most of these cases the expectation of return does not consist of a counter gift but the expectation of good behaviour. Naturally, this only applies on the objective level, because subjectively the giver will not necessarily make these expectations explicit.[42]

David and Hendrik Beck

The bond between the brothers Beck had a somewhat different character than the one between the Verbeeck brothers. Solidarity between David and Hendrik was a matter of course, and was claimed whenever circumstances called for it. When at a certain point, Beck's brother Hendrik fell ill, David was informed about his brother's ill health via a letter from Eva, his sister-in-law.[43] Upon receiving this worrisome news, both David and his friend Herman Breckerfelt hastily departed for Delft. They found Hendrik feeling slightly better because he had had himself purged, but he still felt too weak to leave his bed. Beck thus took it upon himself to mind Hendrik's school that afternoon. After that, he visited some relatives in Delft to inform them of Hendrik's condition. In the evening, David and Breckerfelt ate some stewed pears with the sick man and moved his bed to the back chamber where there was a fire blazing. They left him there that evening feeling relatively well.

The next day they received the news that Hendrik was feeling better. However, he again requested that David take care of his school that day. Beck naturally agreed, and arranged that his brother Steven would in turn take care of David's school. Although the bleeding did do Hendrik a lot of good, he felt worse the day after. His wife Eva sent Beck another letter to the effect that her husband had lain with "a deadly fever" for hours and requested that somebody come to take care of his school once again. This time Breckerfelt did the honours. He went to Delft, took care of the school, and returned to The Hague the same day to inform the Becks that Hendrik was still feeling very weak. Hendrik had asked whether either David or Steven could mind the school again the next morning, which Steven did.[44]

The day after, the children in Beck's school had the afternoon off, which offered him the opportunity to visit his sick brother. Hendrik had just seen the doctor, who told him he was suffering from tertian fever and that he would probably suffer another attack that same night. But when David arrived the next morning to take care of his brother's school, much to his surprise he found Hendrik there. He had survived the night without any further fevers. David noted he was very pleased, even though it meant he had come to Delft for nothing. He returned to The Hague straight away to work at his own school.[45] His brother was soon fully recovered and this was celebrated with a Shrovetide dinner.[46]

Thus, the Beck brothers, David and Steven, and their friend Breckerfelt clearly considered offering support to Hendrik as the obvious thing to do. It was offered as a matter of course, even if – in Beck's case – this meant having to find somebody to mind his own school. This was never a problem, however, and the three of them helped Hendrik out whenever they could. Obviously, it was also not a problem for Hendrik's wife Eva to ask for this support. She on two occasions requested their help in a letter and both times they came to her assistance without delay or strings attached.

Not only had Hendrik received practical support during his illness, he was also visited by many people who wanted to offer him emotional support.[47] These visitors consisted of his in-laws from Rotterdam, as well as relatives from The Hague. This implies that travelling a couple of hours to sympathise with the suffering was nothing out of the ordinary. Even if someone was unable to directly attend to the sick himself, his progress or lack of it was followed with great interest by those who could regularly check up on him personally. In that sense, Hendrik's illness was not just something that concerned him and his household, but something that involved all the relatives and friends to varying degrees. His offer to have people over for dinner to celebrate his return to health, may have been a way of reciprocating and showing gratitude for their support. However, whenever other relatives or friends fell ill, Hendrik was quite likely to offer his support as well and certainly not only because he felt he had to repay these people, but also out of a genuine concern for the well-being of his friends and relatives.

When one compares the Verbeeck and Beck cases, it becomes fairly obvious that the terms of exchange within these two brotherly relationships were very different. On the one hand, there were the two Verbeek brothers who were at perpetual odds, and among whom the offering of gifts was based on certain preconditions and certain considerations for the family's reputation. On the other hand, there were these two brothers who offered each other support as a matter of course, without any strings attached. This shows that gifts played a variety of roles depending on the relationship. As a matter of fact, the various patterns of gift-exchange behaviour were the result of the quite different character of the relationships between the sets of brothers.

The Beck brothers obviously got along fine. They enjoyed each other's company, had the same interests in poetry and the arts, had fun together and were willing to help each other. Moreover, they were equals in terms of age and social status, and even had the same vocation. Since their relationship was one of mutual respect and affection, the gifts they offered each other could be offered unconditionally and with sympathy. The one did not expect the other to change his behaviour because of a gift received, and in that sense they were never disappointed by the other. The only thing they – implicitly – expected was reciprocation for the gifts they offered whenever there was an opportunity or a need. This was not problematic: Their relationship included the trust that the other would do for him that he would do for the other.[48] Therefore conditions of return did not have to be stated explicitly.

This was different for the Verbeeck brothers. They did not get along at all, did not seem to respect each other and there was not a lot of love lost between the two. Herman was envious of his elder brother's success, while Pieter was probably disappointed in how Herman lived his life. Pieter wished the best for his brother, both for his brother's sake and his own. Since Herman was unsuccessful, this probably also resulted in loss of reputation for the whole family. In that respect, it was in both their interests for Herman to have a better life. Pieter was willing to support him, but only if he could be ensured that his efforts would actually improve Herman's circumstances. This is why he committed Herman to certain conditions whenever he offered his support. The general affection and trust that existed between the Beck brothers was lacking in the Verbeeck's case. The result was that the terms of exchange between the two brothers had to be constantly and explicitly reiterated.

Friendly Exchange

True friends: David Beck and Herman Breckerfelt

As was discussed in the prologue, several authors have suggested that friendship in the early modern period was of an instrumental character.[49] People maintained friendships to achieve certain goals, and affection was not necessarily an important feature of early modern friendship bonds. The idea of affectionate or "true" friendship some say only developed in the eighteenth century.[50] This, however, seems highly unlikely. Clearly friendship sometimes served certain instrumental purposes (as it continues to do in contemporary society), but this does not mean that relationships didn't also involve mutual appreciation and respect, and even affection. The difference between early modern friendship and friendship in the modern sense of the word may well be the discourse on friendship. Whereas, friendship is nowadays referred to in terms of affection, these affectionate terms were not always part of the seventeenth-century's references to friends.

In any case, friendship in the seventeenth century was often highly enjoyable as well as useful. A good example of this is the relationship between David Beck and Herman Breckerfelt. One might even say they were friends in the modern sense of the word, even though there are several clues that suggest the opposite. Beck, for example, never refers to Herman Breckerfelt as his friend and he does not refer to their relationship as a friendship. Breckerfelt is mentioned very often in David Beck's diary , but always as "Breckerfelt" or "Herman Breckerfelt". The one exception is when Beck writes a riddle in his diary which refers to Herman Breckerfelt as "our Herman".[51]

However, these instances do not exclude the possibility that these two men were actually good friends. The fact that Beck always uses Breckerfelt's last name, for instance, suggests several things. First, it suggests that Breckerfelt is close enough not to have to be referred to by his occupation, secondly it shows that

Beck respected him enough not to refer to him by his first name. Besides, the fact that their relationship was not referred to as a friendship does not mean anything. The relationship was not specified by Beck in any terms; he just noted what he did with his friend, but never analysed what their relationship meant.

It is strange, however, that Beck did not learn beforehand about Breckerfelt's intentions to marry Jenneke Arents. Beck was clearly surprised when he found out that his friend had left The Hague to travel with her to Arnhem to become engaged to her. Furthermore, Beck was obviously not invited to the wedding and, other than a poetic letter, did not offer them any gifts on the occasion. Thus the friendly nature of their relationship is not revealed by how Beck referred to Breckerfelt or their relationship, and is also not always obvious in his actions towards his supposed friend.

Still, as far as the wedding is concerned, the wedding might only have been celebrated in Arnhem with Jenneke's relatives and some close friends from the Arnhem area and that other friends and relatives, who lived farther away, were visited after the wedding, as was usually done during *speelreisjes*. In fact, after the newlyweds returned to The Hague, Beck rushed to Breckerfelt's house to congratulate the new couple.[52]

Furthermore, there are several reasons to assume that they were good friends. When considering the various features that constitute friendship, there are several that were of importance within their relationship. The two friends spent a lot of time together and clearly enjoyed each other's company. They saw each other on an almost daily basis, sometimes just for a chat, but they also shared a lot of meals together, both daily meals and meals on more festive occasions. The regular meals were spent discussing current events or singing psalms, and after dinner Beck would sometimes read Breckerfelt from one of his books.

Even though Beck never commented on the nature of his relationship with Breckerfelt, he did occasionally mention how enjoyable these get-togethers had been. Sometimes he noted that they had laughed a lot, while other times he observed how a party had been merry. This suggests that being around family and friends was indeed fun, and Breckerfelt was one of the friends that obviously added to the merrymaking, otherwise Beck's relatives would not have invited him whenever they threw a party.

Not only did Beck and Breckerfelt spend a lot of time together, they also shared certain interests. They both had a keen interest in the arts. Both of them were keen on drawing and enjoyed showing each other the result of their efforts. Beck also read Breckerfelt some of the poetry he had composed. Furthermore, they called on each other in times of need, like for instance when Breckerfelt needed to have a set of clothes made for his wedding.

There is another fact that suggests the two men were good friends. When Beck moved to Arnhem in 1625, Breckerfelt and Jenneke followed shortly thereafter and they obviously remained in close contact.[53] Beck stood as a christening witness to one of Breckerfelt's children and another child was even named after David Beck after he died.[54] The relationship between Breckerfelt and the extended Beck family also remained intact through subsequent generations: one of Breckerfelt's sons married one of Hendrik Beck's daughters.[55]

Still, whereas David Beck and Herman Breckerfelt were indeed close friends even though Beck never referred to their relationship as such, in other instances it was the other way around. In those cases, the actual relationship is different from the language by which the relationship is referred to.

Demanding Friends: Pieter Corneliszoon Hooft and Giacomo Badovere

In contrast to the Beck and Breckerfelt's relationship , which was friendship even though it was not discussed in those terms, the relationship between Hooft and Badovere was one that was expressed in friendly terms, but was anything but. As it turns out, Dorothea, with whom we commenced this book, was not the only person to appear impudent in seventeenth-century correspondence. Badovere, with whom Hooft exchanged letters from 1601 to 1611, was also quite straightforward in his request of services. He was also rather explicit in what he would offer Hooft as a gift in return for his services and all of this while the rhetoric of his letters was one of affection and humility.

Giacomo Badovere was the son of a Calvinist who had fled Venice to live in France. He served as a diplomat under Catharine of Bourbon-Navarre, the sister of Henry IV, and would later serve under Henry IV.[56] He and Hooft had met in Italy when the latter was visiting there on his Grand Tour.[57] After travelling together for a couple of days, the two men struck up a friendship that would continue in letters after Hooft's return to Holland.

The first surviving letter from Badovere to Hooft is dated 14 June 1601 and was a reaction to a letter Hooft had sent him to inform him of his safe return. Badovere was happy to hear that, but also expressed his disappointment in not hearing anything from Hooft earlier. Other than that the major part of Badovere's letter consisted of requests for information, requests for further information on topics that Hooft had already informed him about plus book requests, both for himself and a merchant acquaintance of his.[58]

Even though Badovere made an striking number of requests in this letter, its content is not necessarily inappropriate as such. Naturally a lot of information in the early modern period was exchanged via letters and it was not out of the ordinary to ask for certain information outright. The same is true for book requests, or anything else for that matter.[59] Corresponding was not just a sympathetic means of staying in contact with relatives and friends, it was also a means of communicating information. As was shown earlier, the birth of a child was communicated to relatives in other towns by mail.[60] News was spread over the continent, and even to other continents, by mail and entire political and religious discussions were argued through letters. So, the exchange of and request for information in letters was not at all unusual.

Correspondence was also a means for getting certain practicalities of seventeenth-century life arranged. This was not only true for Hooft's correspondence, but also for letters between Maria van Reigersberch, the wife of Hugo Grotius, and her brothers Nicolas and Johan. Their correspondence reveals recurring themes such as the fancy fabrics and hats they were ordering her to buy for them in Paris.[61] This correspondence revealed that Nicolas was not requesting these materials as a gift; he only asked Maria to order them on his behalf and he would later repay her.[62]

In that respect, the bold request for goods was not intended as a means of soliciting gifts. The requests were requests for goods (and not for gifts) that would at a certain point be paid back in cash or in kind. Still, this system of acquiring certain goods did involve a certain amount of benevolence on the part of the person approached. He or she would have to offer at least some time and often other efforts in order to fulfil the request. In these cases, the implicit mutual understanding was that the effort would be repaid on another occasion, either by fulfilling a request from the other party or by offering a gift to express one's gratitude for the efforts made earlier. Even though this was hardly ever explicitly stated, there was a sense among both the parties that their relation was of a reciprocal nature and that whenever one fulfilled a request, the other could be expected to return the favour. This was quite normal.

Yet, when one of the parties involved did not abide by these un-written rules, it could mean the end of their correspondence and presumably even their relationship. This seems to have been the case with Badovere and Hooft. The letters that followed were similar in character to Badovere's first one: seemingly very "normal", but with the nagging feeling that Badovere was not exactly playing by the rules. Badovere asked Hooft to tell him more about a certain religious sect and gave him further instructions on certain books that he liked to receive from Hooft.[63] What is striking about his letters is not necessarily the fact that he had so many requests or that he was so insistent about the requests being filled. What is striking, however, is how little he offers Hooft in return for his services. This would usually go unnoticed if it weren't for his own remarks that he was going to offer Hooft something in return, but that eventually there was always some excuse why it didn't happen. He claims, for instance, that "also I will send you what you have requested by courier or even something better, which I would have done with this sending if it weren't for the rush I was in".[64]

This in itself might have been a reasonable excuse, because Badovere may indeed have been a very busy man, but the character of the letter slowly changed toward the end. Badovere used the usual farewell routine of kissing Hooft's hand, blessing him and wishing him well, before he posed a last request to Hooft. It stated: "Would you be so kind as to find out whether Dominicus Baudius is in your country, he used to study in Utrecht, and would you secretly keep track of what he is doing or what he is planning to do, secrecy and tact are necessary".[65] Compared to his earlier requests for fabrics, books, rabbits and wine this was a very unusual one indeed. What Badovere had asked Hooft to do was keep an eye on Baudius and pass along any information to Badovere. In short, Badovere was asking Hooft to spy for him.

It only became clear in his next letter, dated 8 January 1603, why he had asked Hooft to do so. Baudius would later that year become a professor at the University of Leiden and he was as famous for his beautiful Latin poetry, as he was notorious for his terrible drinking habits and financial problems.[66] As it turned out, Badovere had lent a fairly large sum of money to Baudius, who had never bothered to repay him. Badovere was politely asking Hooft whether he had a good strategy for retrieving this debt. Badovere claimed that he and Baudius used to be good friends and he now hoped that Hooft, via his friendly contact with Baudius, could mediate in getting Baudius to pay him back, because he supposedly was in great need for it. Badovere added that he was not going to confront Baudius himself until he heard back from Hooft. Although Badovere also asked Hooft to pick up some nice liquor that his skipper supposedly had, it seems Hooft's role was generally changing from being a friend and a provider of goods and information into being a collector of debts on Badovere's behalf.[67]

In another letter, Badovere thanked Hooft for his efforts in finding out more about Baudius's situation, so it does appear that Hooft had agreed to at least be of some help to Badovere. The latter stressed that this should not lead to too much trouble for Hooft, because his claim on Baudius' money was so clear that he would get it anyway. If this had been the case, it seems strange that he would make such a secretive effort to discover whether repayment was a possibility.[68] In any case, Badovere was very appreciative of Hooft's efforts, for by the end of the letter he stated that he would send Hooft some volumes of French poetry if only he knew whether Hooft actually liked French poetry.

This is another example of Badovere's insincerity in his exchanges with Hooft. He asked for certain favours – which to a certain extent is normal – and explicitly claimed that he was willing to reciprocate Hooft's benevolence, but eventually he never ended up doing it. The strange thing about this behaviour is that one would normally not *express* intentions of reciprocation, but that one would in fact offer something in return. Badovere's claim that he did not know whether Hooft appreciated French poetry seems invalid. He must have known that Hooft read French, because this was quite normal in those circles and some of their past letters were actually written in French.[69] Furthermore, even if Badovere was not aware that Hooft was composing poetry himself, he might have guessed that Hooft probably had at least a passive interest in poetry as would any other man of his stature in Europe at this time. Besides which, it seems unlikely that Hooft would have refused such a gift. Badovere's hesitance to send the poetry seems to have been a matter of unwillingness more than anything else.

In another letter, it becomes clear that Hooft did actually make an effort to mediate between Badovere and Baudius. Hooft had requested Badovere for more information on what the debt actually consisted of, and he had advised Badovere on how best to resolve the issue. Hooft's suggestion was that Baudius would repay as much as he could every year, because he was obviously not capable of paying the entire debt in one payment. Badovere agreed to this and left Hooft to deal with the rest of the details. This was probably not to Hooft's liking, for it seems by now he preferred to have as little to do with his "friend" as possible. This is revealed in a remark made by Badovere in this same letter. He claimed that he would write Hooft more often, except for the fact that "I to my annoyance and sadness read from your silence that the letters to you are not delivered loyally".[70] Although it was not all that uncommon in this period for letters not to arrive at the intended address, it seems more likely that Hooft's silence was caused by his annoyance with Badovere's inappropriate behaviour. He was growing less keen on corresponding with Badovere.

This is quite understandable because mediating between Badovere and Baudius must have been rather tedious, especially since Baudius obviously could not repay Badovere in full. Baudius had written Badovere to tell him he barely had enough to survive on, and that – unless he married someone rich – saving money to repay Badovere was pretty much out of the question. Badovere then ordered Hooft to tell Baudius that if he did manage to marry into money that Baudius would have to repay him from the dowry he would gain through his marriage.[71] He ended this demand with the remark that in the following letter he would discuss more agreeable topics, but it is unlikely that this happened.

In the meantime, Hooft was now corresponding with Baudius. The latter explained that even though Badovere's demands for repayment were valid, it was fairly unlikely he would every fully be able to repay him. Any legal action on Badovere's part would not be worth it since it would only "ruin my fortune, without any advantage to his own".[72] Baudius explained to Hooft that his poverty was partly due to the illness of his late wife, which had cost him a lot of money, plus that he had trusted the wrong advisers on where to invest his money. He was, however, involved in a lawsuit that would eventually get him some of this money back, but this was going to take a while, especially since "the other party uses all possible excuses it can think of to slow down the process".[73]

The last word on this issue is a letter Hooft sent to Baudius.[74] Here Hooft explicitly stated that he did not appreciate the pressure Badovere placed upon him to get involved in this issue. Hooft would have preferred not bothering Baudius because of "the affection and reverence I keep for your grant qualities", if it were not for the fact that he was ashamed to do so "due to the old friendship" between Badovere and himself and the "reasonableness of his request". Thus he asked Baudius kindly to read Badovere's letter that was included with his own, which again explained Badovere's claims, and suggested Baudius try to repay him.[75]

Thereafter, Hooft did not waste too many words on the issue, since he was well aware that Baudius was in no situation to be able to meet Badovere's demands. He obviously felt awkward having to pressure Baudius on this issue even further. Hooft did what was expected of him based on his relationship with Badovere and he did it with obvious reluctance so as not to offend Baudius. Hooft's letter to Baudius was the last that mentioned this issue, and the correspondence between Hooft and Badovere ended.[76]

What made this such a strange relationship? The contents of the first letters were still what might be expected from two cultured men. They exchanged information, niceties and used the standard formalities to do so. This is probably also what Hooft expected from his relationship with Badovere; two well-educated men with similar interests in the arts and politics corresponding in style. However, at a certain point the character of the correspondence and the relationship changed. When Badovere asked Hooft to mediate in the Baudius affair, he was not very subtle in his demands. Even early on in their correspondence, Badovere's intentions seemed to be of a more instrumental nature. He was continuously pressuring Hooft to do his errands for him, and he used gifts that he promised to give to Hooft as an incentive, while in fact there was no actual gift ever offered.

This makes their relationship problematic in two ways. First, the explicitness of exchange is usually not a sign of a healthy relationship. In most relationships that function well the exchange of gifts is not discussed, but comes as a matter of course, like in the case of David Beck and his brother. One might ask for a gift, like for instance support, but the reciprocation or the terms of exchange are normally not explicitly negotiated, even though there is an implicit expectation that the offering will be repaid at a certain point in time. The fact that Pieter Verbeeck needed to state the terms under which he would offer his brother financial support did not necessarily make him a bad person, as his brother Herman claimed, but does serve as an indication that there was something wrong in their relationship. The same holds true for Badovere and Hooft. Their correspondence could have been a perfectly "normal" correspondence if it were not for the fact that the former made the terms of exchange within their relationship so explicit.

This is related to the second issue in these explicit relationships. What the explicitness makes clear is that relationships in which terms of exchange are explicitly stated are in fact of an instrumental nature. Badovere was, as it turns out, not at all interested in maintaining a friendly correspondence, instead there were things he needed from Hooft and he was willing to repay him in the form of gifts such as books of French poetry.

The Verbeeck brothers had also come to the point where their brotherly relationship was not longer central to their contact but the exchange of financial support for good behaviour. This is different from the relationships David Beck maintained with his brother Hendrik and Breckerfelt. The relationship as such was central to their contact and the exchange of gifts was not the goal of maintaining the relationship but only a natural result of the fact that this relationship existed. The gifts in these relationships were offered as a matter of course and the terms of exchange did not need to be stated explicitly. The exchange of gifts within these relationships was dealt with implicitly: it literally went without saying.

Professional Exchange

Master and Servant: P.C. Hooft and Aeltje de Lange

In that respect, it is usually a bad sign when people discussed their gift exchange behaviour explicitly. This was also the case when Hooft was corresponding with Aeltje de Lange. She was Hooft's former servant, but something had obviously gone wrong in their relationship after Aeltje had left the Hooft household. These problems were for a large part discussed in terms of exchange.

The relationship between master and servants was one of a professional nature; it involved the offering of services, which was rewarded by payment, but it involved more than that.[77] Servants were not only employees, but also members of the household.[78] This sometimes made their positions slightly awkward, because as members of the household they could also contribute or do damage to the honour and reputation of the family.[79] Next to their wages, servants were also to a certain extent repaid for their efforts by the offering of gifts from their masters.[80] Obviously, the relationship between master and servant was one of power, with the master being powerful and the servant being powerless, yet by being part of the household and therewith of influence to its reputation, the servant certainly had a means of control.

The letter that P.C. Hooft sent to his former servant was very remarkable in this respect. Hooft presumably was not in the habit of corresponding with his (former) servants, but he wrote one letter to Aeltje de Lange that was very revealing with regard to their relationship as master and servant and the importance of gifts therein. Aeltje had left the Hooft household to get married to a man that Hooft did not approve of. Her intended husband was broke and did not have a job, and if only Hooft could have been convinced of his good intentions he would not have objected to the alliance, but, according to Hooft, the man was basically untrustworthy. However, despite the fact that her master clearly objected, Aeltje married this man and the marriage turned out to be a very unhappy one. This would not have been a problem in itself, for her marriage was her own responsibility. But after some time, it became clear to Hooft that his former servant was spreading rumours to the effect that he had encouraged her to marry this man. This upset Hooft to the extent that he felt the need to write her a letter to set the matter straight.[81]

After initial references to her unfortunate marriage and the way in which it had come about, Hooft acknowledged that she had always cordially and faithfully served him and his family. Yet he went on to stress that she had always earned "honest board and wages" as a reward for that.[82] Furthermore he eagerly pointed out to her, that he had not only offered her what he owed her as a master, but had also given her much more than that in terms of gifts. She had been given many honours "both in money and in clothes" and he even put aside two hundred guilders for her to have a "free wedding", which he claimed was more than her own parents had ever done for her.[83] He mentioned that her friends had "always been welcome and well-treated" and he had even gone through the trouble of finding her brother a job aboard a ship. He went on to state that "all these benefactions notwithstanding", she was slandering him behind his back to her friends, "to Adriaen Cornelisse in letters and to me in my face with your letter and every time I speak to you". Therewith, he claimed she was "repaying good with evil".[84] Even though Hooft was obviously very upset, he presented himself in the letter as being noble enough to not respond in kind to the evil she had done to him. He offered her all the help she might need to improve her situation, but he did stress that he expected more thankfulness in return than she had shown thus far.

It is interesting to note in this respect that he expected more loyalty from her not just as a matter of general courtesy, but in particular because he had always been so generous to her. Even though it is not likely that he had explicitly told her when he offered her these gifts that what he expected in return was loyalty, now that it had come to a dispute, Hooft explicitly used the rhetoric of the gift to make his point to her. He stressed the fact that he not only offered her board and wages but on top of that gifts such as clothing and hospitality for her and her friends, which he implied should have made her even more loyal to his household than she should have been under normal circumstances. The fact that he had offered her all these gifts made his expectations as to her gratitude and loyalty very high, and she had clearly disappointed him in that respect.

Nevertheless, he was worried about the unfortunate situation in which his former servant found herself and offered to help her in any way he could. This was not only a means of offering lip service to his disloyal servant, because it seems he really did intend to help her out. There is no evidence of this in the correspondence that followed shortly after this incident, but some eight years later Hooft wrote a letter to his brother-in-law Joost Baeck in which he thanked him for "the cares and friendship" the latter had shown to Aeltje.[85] This implies that Hooft, in the long run, definitely did care for his servant's well-being, even though she had disappointed him with her ungrateful behaviour.

What this story reveals is how the offering of gifts can function as a means of obligation or displaying power. Hooft offered his servant things like clothing and money for her wedding, which she was obviously incapable of reciprocating, at least in the sense of returning the same type of gifts to him. She most likely did not have the means to ever fully recompense what she had received from him. This was, however, not expected of her. What was expected of her was loyalty to her master. She was to speak well of him and his family and she was to behave in a manner that would not bring disgrace upon his household. On the one hand, the offering of these gifts to his servant can be seen as a very powerful tool for Hooft with which he could ensure his servant's loyalty. On the other hand, it cannot be ignored that he indeed may have had her best interests at heart, both by offering her these gifts and receiving her family into his house, as well as by advising against her intended marriage. Other masters were also known to have been very protective of their servants, not only by warning them against evil as did the lady in the emblem by Cats, but also by taking their sides in disputes. Stadholder Willem Frederik actually describes in his diary how a certain Rink Burmania ordered one of his guests to leave his house because she had gravely insulted his servant. To stress the importance of such an action, Willem Frederik added that the guest was in fact the niece of the master of the house, which indicated that Burmania actually chose to defend his servant over his family.[86]

Furthermore, the relationship that existed between Hooft and Aeltje was in fact also beneficial to her. Not only did she have a job with the Hooft family, but it also brought extra benefits in terms of gifts comprised of money, clothes, and mediation whenever a family member needed a job. In that sense, even though this was in many respects a relationship in which the balance of power was generally in favour of the master, the relationship as such could be considered a "win-win" situation. Moreover, the one powerful tool that Aeltje obviously had on her side was the fact that she could actually do Hooft and his family great harm by discrediting them in public.

David Beck and David de Moor: True friends or patron and client?

Whereas Beck's friendship with Herman Breckerfelt was in his diary never discussed in terms of friendship, in some cases Beck did use the discourse of friendship when in fact there was more to the relationship than mere friendship. David de Moor is one of the few people in David Beck's diaries who is actually referred to in terms of friendship, while in fact he also served as his patron.[87]

The manner in which Beck maintained contact through the exchange of gifts with possible patrons was rather different from the patterns of exchange within his circle of family and friends. Within this more or less professional network the exchange of hospitality was of lesser importance than it was within the network of family and friends. This was partly due to the fact that most of his possible patrons resided in Amsterdam, which obviously made it impossible to visit one another on a daily basis.

In general, the contact between Beck and these individuals was maintained by the exchange of letters, an exchange that was by nature reciprocal. It was not uncommon for these letters to be accompanied by poems or copies of poems. These were offered partly out of a general interest in poetry, but, whenever Beck sent a copy of his own poetry it was also used as a means of establishing a patronage relationship. However, when Beck sent patrons the work they had commissioned, they often rewarded him by offering a book or some money. This was a gesture that he would not reciprocate.

Schoolmaster David Beck was a great lover of the arts in general, but had a special interest in poetry. He was quite an active poet in his spare time and had several contacts that shared this interest. Beck's brother Hendrik also enjoyed composing poetry and the exchange of poetic letters was quite common between the two brothers. Still Beck was not just writing poetry for enjoyment's sake: he was also searching for patrons for his writings. Naturally he hoped that they would be able to honour him with poetry commissions, but what he frequently ended up working on was just copying work.

As we saw earlier, in early 1624, Beck had sent a copy of his laudatory poems to a Bohemian nobleman named Silber von Silbersteyn. These were sent to him as a New Year's gift, but it was obvious that Beck wanted to be reciprocated for his generosity in one way or another, which ultimately happened when the nobleman threw his farewell dinner.[88] When Beck was about to depart, the nobleman offered him two rijksdaalders, which suggested that Beck was being rewarded for the laudatory poems or that these had enticed the nobleman to have Beck do the occasional writing chore for him. It is not clear what these jobs actually consisted of, but it is likely that these included orders to copy official documents or other writings, or commissions to actually write poetry.[89] This is the sort of work he also occasionally did for other people, such as the earlier-mentioned Christina Poppings.[90]

Another contact of David Beck's who occasionally commissioned him, was Jacob Hendriks, to whom David referred as "my old acquaintance". On 22 January, Beck sent Hendriks in Amsterdam six of his printed poems to offer to his friends. This was probably a sort of catalogue of his work that was used to induce these friends to order poetry from David Beck. It appears that he succeeded; in June Beck received a request from Jacob Hendriks to write nine texts. It took Beck three days to finish and he sent them off to Amsterdam on 27 June.[91] A little over a week later, Beck received a book from Jacob Hendrik, "which he had bought especially for me".[92]

So it turns out that Beck offered his poems to possible patrons in order to focus their attention on his talents as a poet, or at least as a copier, and some of them would repay his services by offering him copies of poems, books or small amounts of money. This seems to have been rather common in the literary circles of the Dutch Republic in the seventeenth-century.[93] The same patterns of behaviour can also be found among great poets like Hooft and Vondel, who also sought patronage and who were also rewarded for some of their work, which will be discussed later.

What is described in these examples is not necessarily clear-cut economic behaviour, nor pure gift exchange. The modern beholder might think of these gifts as disguised payment.[94] He might suggest that by speaking about these offerings as gifts the donor was trying to disguise the fact that, in reality, he was just paying the other for received products and services. Yet it is exactly this fact that these offerings were referred to as gifts that make them so interesting. An analysis of these gift-exchange patterns suggests that the counter-gifts the patrons offered were in fact payments, while in the discourse of the seventeenth century and in the minds of the seventeenth-century individual, the poems offered by patron-seeking poets were indeed gifts.

The relationship between a certain David de Moor and David Beck offers a good example of how Beck sought patronage, at least when one takes a closer look at the patterns of exchange instead of the discourse that is used to describe their relationship. In fact, a first reading of Beck's encounter with David de Moor suggests that David Beck had found a new best friend, but there was more to this encounter than met the eye.

Beck was first introduced to David de Moor on 27 May by a mutual friend. David de Moor was a rather affluent bookkeeper from Amsterdam who was visiting The Hague with this friend, as they passed by Beck's house for a chat. They talked about literature, religion and the arts, after which the three men attended church together. After this first introduction David de Moor and David Beck did not see each other until 30 August, when De Moor was once again visiting The Hague and on this occasion brought his brother Bernhard to Beck's house to see the drawings and poems he kept in his office. After this, the two David's started corresponding and when Beck was in Amsterdam a couple of weeks later he made sure to visit De Moor at his house. They looked at his poetry and Beck was invited to have breakfast with the family.[95] David Beck and David de Moor seemed to be becoming rather friendly with each other. They both shared their interest in the arts and poetry and they both adhered to the same faith. One might say that they were becoming friends in the true – affectionate – sense of the word.

Then in October councillor Adrian Pauw asked Beck to copy some official documents for him. The amount of work involved was rather substantial. Beck calculated that it would take at least one month to get all the copying done and he seemed rather pleased with that idea. Beck was all the more content since David de Moor had recommended him for the job.[96] In November Beck received another letter from David de Moor which included a number of copies of poems by Anna Roemers Visscher and the request by De Moor to copy some of his own poems for him. This copying took Beck quite some time, and when he did finally send the poems to De Moor he made sure to include a catalogue of his poetry.[97] Unlike what is described above, this behaviour suggests that De Moor and Beck were patron and client rather than good friends. Through the mediation of David de Moor Beck was in fact being offered certain copying jobs and he was also asked to perform certain jobs for De Moor himself.

But then again, by the end of the year David Beck wrote a poem for David de Moor, which was entitled "To our friendship". The poem was dedicated to "the artful, learned, distinguished, pious and devout gentleman David de Moor, my devoted and wished for friend and namesake". The poem started with the line "equal seeks equal" and it expressed Beck's appreciation of their friendship and their unity in "morals and preferences".[98] One might claim that this rhetoric of friendship is also a means of disguising the true intentions of the relationship, especially since Beck is using such formal terms to address his friend. However, just because this type of terminology sounds insincere to contemporary ears does not mean that it was considered insincere in its day. It was by cultural convention that people were to address their family, friends and other acquaintances with this woolly language, just as contemporary relationships are supposed to be referred to in terms of affection and love.

Furthermore, even though the pattern of patronage seeking is quite clear, it seems a bit odd to disclaim Beck's own intentions and feelings within this relationship. According to his poem he appreciated his friend highly – and not just because of the occasional job – and his offering of a poem was – subjectively – a sympathetic way of showing this appreciation. In this way, he objectively maintained his friendship with his new friend. The fact that this same friend at times also played an instrumental role in Beck's life does not exclude that the mutual appreciation of these two individuals may in fact have been sincere. As a matter of fact, this might serve as a good example of how appreciation for a person could coincide with this person's instrumentality in obtaining a certain goal.

Why would someone like David de Moor have himself "abused" like this? The fact of the matter is that he probably did not feel abused. He may have been quite convinced of Beck's qualities as a poet, he had after all familiarised himself with Beck's work on several occasions, and would therefore not have felt it was too much trouble to put the occasional good word in for Beck whenever he could. Furthermore, he may have been quite honoured by the fact that Beck had dedicated such a kind poem to him, which would also have added to his social status. The role of being both a patron and a friend to David Beck may have suited David de Moor very well.

Stadholderly patronage: Vondel, Hooft and Frederik Hendrik

This system of patronage was widespread in seventeenth-century Holland. It worked both ways: patrons could commission works of art and reward their clients with a gift afterwards, and clients could spontaneously offer works of art to possible patrons in the expectation that they would eventually be rewarded for it. One way of offering these type of gifts, in this case books and poems, was by dedicating the works of art to the intended patron, which can be considered a gift in itself.[99] These dedications were partly a great honour, but could also have a slightly compulsory edge to them because it was expected that the dedication would be rewarded with a gift. The author was therefore required to obtain permission to dedicate his work of art to the intended patron. As was mentioned earlier, the gifts offered by patrons were always on the verge of being payments.[100]

When Hooft finished his Nederlandsche Historiën, he used his contact with Constantijn Huygens, secretary to the stadholder, to obtain permission to dedicate this work to Frederik Hendrik. Eventually, he received permission and through the mediation of Huygens he received his reward.[101] It consisted of a silver ewer and a wash basin.[102] Hooft in turn wrote a letter to the stadholder to thank him for his generosity.[103] This exchange of honours can be retrieved both through the correspondence of P.C. Hooft and through the biography that Geerard Brandt wrote shortly after Hooft's death.

The interesting thing is that the same biographer, Geerard Brandt, also wrote a biography of Joost van den Vondel soon after his death. Both of these biographies were reissued in 1932 by Leendertz.[104] He pointed out in his introduction that the biographies that Brandt wrote of both Vondel and Hooft were not up to modern standards of objectivity. As Leendertz noted, what Brandt set out to do was not necessarily just describe the lives of the two authors, but rather to stress their qualities as writers and poets. To this effect, only those events and facts that were actually important to their writings were described. This included descriptions of their patrons, their literary networks and the gifts they received for their work. So even though these biographies are no paragons of objectivity (and then again what biographies are), they are actually very useful in light of this research.

A comparison of these two biographies shows that even though both do describe some of the gifts they received for their dedications and their work in general, the gifts Vondel received are grouped together in one paragraph. Furthermore, in Vondel's case, a lot more gifts are described than in Hooft's case, while in fact Brandt's motivation for describing Vondel's gifts at all was to show how undervalued he was by his contemporaries in terms of them being willing to reward him for his efforts. This is probably the result of the difference in social status and class between the two authors. Whereas Hooft was a patrician and did not have to depend on his writing to survive, Vondel – even though he owned a shop – did not have a secure income until after he was seventy years old.

Even though Brandt acknowledged that the stadholder was known for his mildness towards artists, he made sure to mention that Vondel in fact never received any rewards for the works he wrote in honour of the stadholder.[105] Vondel wrote laudatory poems on the stadholder's victories and wrote many popular plays, which the stadholder was said to have enjoyed. Still, Vondel was never offered any stadholderly gifts for his writings, because this would have brought the stadholder into a very awkward position. Vondel's religious and political ideas were controversial and on several occasions he had severely insulted some of the stadholder's political allies. This had made it impossible for the stadholder to reward Vondel for his writings. As Brandt put it, in order to avoid disfavouring himself, the stadholder could not do Vondel a favour.[106]

Vondel was generally not very lucky when it came to finding suitable patrons. Although he was even in his own time known as one of the most important poets and writers in the Dutch Republic he never managed to find a Maecenas who was willing to provide him with the financial support he deserved. This was largely due to the fact that Vondel was such a controversial figure. His religious preferences – he became a Catholic in the course of his life – were not necessarily approved of by the people on whom he most depended for support and he had made numerous enemies with his polemical essays.

As Brandt described it, Vondel did receive the occasional reward for his writings and dedications, but in the end these gifts did not amount to much. "The praise for his poetry was his only reward", or so his biographer observed.[107] This did not mean that he did not receive any gifts at all, but just that he received a lot less than could be expected for a poet of his reputation. The largest gift Vondel ever received for his work was a gold chain with a medal from Christina of Sweden. The chain was worth five hundred guilders and was offered to him as a thank you for the laudatory poem he had written in her honour.[108] He received a silver cup and dish from the Council of Amsterdam on the occasion of the inauguration of the new town hall.[109] Furthermore, he received "a bowl with a lit and a spoon or something like that" from the admiralty as a reward for the poem Vondel had written to honour one of their buildings. Even though he may never have been rewarded by the stadholder himself, he did receive a gift from his wife, Amalia van Solms. It was a gold medal, which was offered to Vondel for the wedding poem he wrote on the occasion of the wedding of her daughter, Henriette Catharina, to the Count of Anhalt. According to Brandt, among the memorable gifts Vondel received were an *aam* of Rhine wine and a "guilded silver cup".[110] So it seems Vondel did not do so badly after all.

However, the offering of gifts in the realm of patrons could take a turn for the worse. Brandt, for instance, describes an anecdote, which is quite telling in terms of the deeper meaning of this type of gifts. At a certain point, Vondel was offered a sum of money by a certain "religious elector" which was so embarrassingly low that Brandt refused to positively identify the giver. Brandt thought a sixteen guilder gift to the likes of a great poet was in fact an insult and not a gift.

On another occasion, Vondel received a painting from the archbishop of Mechlin. It was an altarpiece that was sent to him as a thank you for the fact that he had dedicated his *Altaargeheimnissen* to this archbishop. At first, Vondel was rather pleased with the painting and he even thought of sending the archbishop a poetic letter to thank him for his generosity. But when an art connoisseur informed him that it was not the masterpiece Vondel had assumed it was, but in fact a rather feeble copy, Vondel was infuriated and wanted the piece out of his sight immediately. He sent it to his sister in Hoorn, as not to be confronted with the "spiteful remembrance of this poor repayment" ever again.[111]

This goes to show that the value of the gift offered was supposed to be in accordance to the actual reputation of the recipient. If it did not, the offering became cause for insult rather than gratitude. That is also why, in some cases, Brandt is aware of the actual value of the silver or gilded objects that were offered. The value, as we saw in the case of pillegiften, was not only important because the monetary value in itself could be put to use at some point in time, but also because the monetary value expressed (or was a measurement of) the actual esteem in which the recipient, or in the case of christening gifts the family, was held. Dorothea van Dorp, for instance, wrote a letter to Huygens in which she expressed her pride because her brother had received a chain worth eight hundred guilders from the admiralty, "which is a great honour to him".[112]

Other than silver objects and chains, medals of gold and silver also functioned as gifts. These were offered to professors at universities to honour them and to express appreciation for services rendered.[113] Although these gifts to the modern beholder seem to be more like payments than gifts, it is important to note that individuals in the seventeenth-century did actually refer to them in terms of gifts. Maria van Reigersberch, for example, in one letter to her husband Hugo de Groot explicitly refers to the fact that he had given her orders to "offer four chains as gifts".[114]

The explicitness of this gift system was in general not considered offending. In fact, when it came to the honorary medals and chains that for instance admirals received for bravery it was not uncommon for them to bargain about the actual weight of their gifts.[115] Even though this would – in rational choice theory terms – be a good indication that these admirals were defending their self-interests, it was not necessarily self-interest in the purely economical sense. They were, in fact, bargaining for their honour, more than the value of the gift. It would be unlikely for them to put the actual worth of the object to use, but it would make sense for them to make the gift as "worthy" as possible.

This system of patronage did not work out that well for Vondel. He was then – and still is – considered the greatest poet of the Dutch Golden Age, but according to his biographer, this fame was not reflected in the gifts he received. Firstly, he did not get the sheer number of rewards one might expect for a poet of his stature; secondly, the gifts were in certain instances of an embarrassing quality and turned out to be insults rather than rewards. This is to a certain extent the result of Vondel's personality. He was a controversial figure, which probably made potential patrons less eager to be associated with him. In that respect, patronage was not just about the quality of the work that the client produced, but also about his behaviour. It was not attractive to be associated with an author who wrote the most beautiful pieces but was likely to damage the reputation of his patron by his bad behaviour.

Literary Exchange

Hooft, Huygens and their literary friends

"I am no writer".[116] With these words, P.C. Hooft in 1609 started off his letter to the famous professor Daniel Heinsius and he added a laudatory poem which he hoped would be printed in the reprint of Heinsius's play *Auriacus, sive libertas suecia*. Hooft expressed his wish that his poem would encourage a friendship with Heinsius, which was something that he "had wished for a long time".[117] Even though Hooft in 1609 did not yet think of himself as a writer, or pretended not to as a matter of modesty, the written word played an important role in his life. He enjoyed reading and writing. Not only did he write the many letters that function as a source for this research, but he also wrote poetry, plays and historical works.

This was in itself not exceptional; many of the literate in the Dutch Republic of that period had a great interest in reading and writing, and many of them were not just writing letters but also poetry and plays and others kept diaries or wrote autobiographies. One could characterise the Dutch Republic at that time as one with a strong literary culture, which required that one at least be able to read and write to participate, but which was also open to people from different walks of life.[118]

This literary activity was not necessarily meant as a means of acquiring an income, nor to grant fortune and fame on the level of status. In the first half of the seventeenth-century, creative writing was not yet a profession. Although authors might be rewarded with gifts for their work, most of them were not dependent on their writing for their incomes.[119] For most people, writing was an intellectual challenge and an enjoyable pastime. Still, there were those that did manage to have their works published and some who (occasionally) received rewards for their writings.[120]

Naturally, one's literary fame and success depended for a large part on talent, but also to a great extent, on contacts. These contacts came in many shapes and forms. One needed a circle of literary friends to at least have written texts read by others and have an opportunity to discuss and improve them. But these literary friends might also be vital to the promotion of one's work to a larger public and in recommending it to a patron or publisher. If one was lucky, one might even have the opportunity of dedicating a work to an important person, which might result in a material or financial reward from the person who had received the dedication.[121]

Gifts played an important role in the maintenance of these literary networks. Poems and books were offered as gifts to friends as a token of affection, but also to attract the attention of the recipient to the literary talents of the author. Some renowned authors could offer their support to literary talents by providing recommendations and introductions.[122] Furthermore, dedications can be considered as artistic gifts that were to be reciprocated with material gifts.

Books as gifts and books as loan

As mentioned earlier, books could function as gifts in relationships that did not have a literary character, but were of a solely friendly and affectionate nature. Anna Roemers Visscher, for instance, sent one of her father's *Sinnepoppen* to Christina van Erp, P.C. Hooft's first wife. Christina and her husband intended to stay at the castle of Muiden over the winter, and Anna thought the book might entertain Christina when "autumn time is hindering the sweet walks" and "the chilly wind and the drizzling rain require you to stay at home".[123]

This book was a collection of emblems, consisting of pictures, mottos and explanatory texts, written and compiled by Roemer Visscher. These emblems were of a rather moralistic character, but this did not mean these emblem books were not entertaining.

As Anna herself pointed out, the emblems "all have a small amusingness to them", which did make the book a proper gift for someone who was going to spend the whole winter in the cold and solitude of the Muiden castle. In that respect, this book was a very considerate gift indeed, and even though Anna herself did have some literary aspirations – she edited one of the later editions of her father's *Sinnepoppen* – the gift was most likely meant as a nice gesture from one person to another without any ulterior literary motives.

Correspondences leave more than just evidence of the books being ordered at the time (as in the case of Badovere) or being offered (as in the case of Anna Roemers Visscher), but also of books being lent out among the correspondents.[124] This is in itself not so remarkable, but what is interesting is the way in which these loans are discussed in these letters and the discursive games that are played out around the themes of loans and gifts.

It seems to have been a convention that whenever a book was sent back to its original owner, the person borrowing the book would apologise for holding onto the book longer than might have been appropriate. This would usually go with a number of excuses and the presumption that the owner of the book would accept these as valid. An example of this is a letter by the earlier mentioned professor Heinsius, with whom Hooft presumably had succeeded in striking up a friendship.[125] Heinsius thanked Hooft for his willingness to lend him a "French booklet" and returned it to him together with one of his own treatises named *De constitutione tragoediae*. He had put this aside in his room for Hooft for a very long time and he hoped Hooft "would receive it in thankfulness".

His excuse for not returning the book to Hooft earlier was that the "cold and hard winter" had refrained him from doing so, and only a visit from their mutual friend Scriverius allowed him to return the book. This seems to be a rather lame excuse: if Heinsius had really wanted to, surely he could have returned the book to Hooft earlier. However, this had probably never been his intention nor had it ever been a problem to Hooft. The book was intended as a loan and not a gift, and both parties were aware of this fact. This, however, did not necessarily mean that there was a specific time limit on the return of the book. Any time would in fact be good time, as long as Hooft could still be convinced that he would ever get his book back within a reasonable time span, and as long as Heinsius could still feel comfortable returning the book. The terms of these loans did not have to be stated explicitly and were the result of implicit and hopefully shared ideas of reasonableness. As Hooft wrote in a letter to Huygens, which accompanied a book that he had borrowed from the latter:[126]

> It seems I have sinned against your courtesy, that should have kindled mine, considering the slowness with which I return the included *Tragiques* to you.

It seems unlikely that Huygens thought Hooft had actually sinned against his courtesy. This was just a manner of speaking. The letter, in the end, was not so much intended to express Hooft's heartfelt apologies for not sending the book back earlier, but an opportunity to discuss the *Tragiques* with Huygens. After these initial niceties, the remainder of the letter was filled with a critical discussion of the book, which was a satirical work by the French, Protestant author Agrippa d'Aubigné.[127]

In other cases, Hooft and the book borrower would agree beforehand on a specific timeframe before which the book had to be returned. This did occasionally lead to some problems. Hooft did send a pointed letter to Jacob van der Burgh, council to the Lord of Brederode.[128] He had apparently borrowed a book from Hooft with the promise of returning it within six days, but as Hooft now claimed, the six days had turned into "six pairs of months". This bothered him, and he preferred not to think about it anymore and just let Van der Burgh keep the book. Hooft said he was about to tell Van der Burgh "as the houseman told the soldier: I offer you the hare to at least bless its ear with a piece of gratitude".

Herewith, Hooft was implying that he would prefer giving the book to Van der Burgh as a gift, because at least then he would have his thankfulness in return while now he was left with nothing – no book and no gratitude. It is hard to judge whether the words Hooft chose for this were meant satirically or were expressions of his actual anger about the book. But it is clear that the way Van der Burgh had dealt with his loan had not been appropriate, and was in fact subjected to jokes or even anger.

Within these literary friendships, it was common to review each other's manuscripts.[129] The manuscript could be either discussed in person or through correspondence. One of the individuals who once criticised one of Hooft's works in a letter was Hugo Grotius, who was at that point still the pensionary of the city of Rotterdam. Hooft and Grotius had met via Bredero, another important writer from that period.[130] Bredero, as he explained in a letter to Hooft, had encountered Grotius at the wedding of mutual friends in Amsterdam and had come to talk about Hooft. Grotius wanted to know about Hooft's "health and well-being" and Bredero had responded "to the best of [his] knowledge".[131] After exchanging these customary courtesies, Bredero mentioned to Grotius that Muiden was only "two miles away" and asked whether it would please Grotius to visit Hooft together with him. According to Bredero, Grotius agreed that this would be a pleasure, after which Bredero sent Hooft a letter to inform him of their intended visit.[132]

Even though it is not clear in the correspondence whether Bredero and Grotius actually did visit Muiden, it seems quite likely that they did, because it is obvious that Hooft and Grotius did come into contact shortly after Bredero's encounter with Grotius at the wedding. Within a month from the wedding in Amsterdam, Grotius sent Hooft a letter that referred to the manuscript of Hooft's *Baeto*. Hooft had obviously either sent Grotius a copy or given him one in person, and he had asked him to review the text and give his honest opinion, which Grotius did. In his letter, Grotius praised the work and "wished [he] could do [Hooft] the service of promoting such laudable work".[133] He did, however, have some criticism about the ending of the tragedy. Grotius suggested that Hooft should opt for an ending in which Baeto was inaugurated and even mentioned where he could find the necessary information.

Grotius's remarks suggest that even though these reviews in letter form were generally full of praise, the task of giving proper criticism to manuscripts was actually one that was taken quite seriously. The reviewer would always make an effort to express the appropriate niceties, but did not refrain from expressing criticism whenever he (or she) thought criticism was in order. The critical remarks could refer to anything from grammar to the structure of the narrative.

Grotius's letter to Hooft not only included praise and criticism of his tragedy, but also a number of "bad poems" Grotius had composed.[134] These poems were offered with the usual humilities as to the poor quality of the offered work and the unworthiness of the giver. This was a literary convention that was generally followed in the seventeenth-century correspondence of the cultural elite.[135] The literary elite made it a habit for the writer of a letter to humiliate himself with respect for the receiver. This was normally done as a means to flatter the receiver, but in the correspondence between Grotius and Hooft this convention was almost a game, in which the two players were involved in a modesty competition. This was the game Hooft played in reaction to Grotius's letter, when he wrote:[136]

> To things that displease you, I thought I could never dare to consciously take pleasure, such as your poems take me to do. Therefore if you reprimand these, so you inform my judgement of their smallness. This makes me doubly obliged to you, for the poems entertain my heart with delight, and your judgement of these my brains with instruction.

With these humble words, Hooft turned Grotius's words of humility into words of instruction. Grotius thereby became Hooft's teacher, while Hooft put himself in the position of being the humble student. Herewith, Hooft offered Grotius a grand compliment, while at the same time beating him at his modesty game. Other than that, Hooft included one of his own poems and thanked Grotius for his criticisms of *Baeto*.

Almost two years later, Hooft again asked Grotius to review a work of his, *Hendrik De Grote*, a biography of Henry IV of France in the Dutch vernacular and, according to Hooft's letter to Grotius, a prelude to his writing the history of the "Fatherland".[137] Hooft asked his "Oracle" whether he should refrain from writing this piece, and expressed his insecurity about the structure of the story, its clarity and its attractiveness. Hooft hoped that Grotius would accept his spontaneous request to be his censor, despite the fact that this would create even more work for him. He explained to Grotius that this request resulted from his acknowledgement of Grotius's "greatness" and his insouciance towards Grotius's benevolence.

Hooft himself in time also became enough of an "oracle" to review the works of other writers. Tesselschade had requested that Hooft read some of her texts. In a letter to her sister Anna, Hooft claimed he could not possibly refuse to do so on the ground that he was "being ordered by the one that may order, and that on behalf of three names, as Tesselschade, as Roemers daughter and as your sister".[138] Naturally, he corrected the text, but – as part of the modesty convention – he claimed his "obedience was a sick one", because it was no good to be ordered to better something, while in fact it would only be made worse by his corrections. He hoped that the reward for his bitter efforts would be that Tesselschade would refrain from asking for his corrections again. And a very modest oracle he was.

Another common gift in literary circles, were laudatory poems. They were obviously meant to compliment an author, but not just that. The poems were also printed with the work itself and thereby functioned as a type of marketing tool. The more honourable the laudatory poems that were included in the publication, the more attractive the book became for a larger public. These laudatory poems were either offered spontaneously, as Hooft did for Heinsius, or offered upon request. It could also be an honour for a lesser-known poet to have his laudatory poem printed along with the work of an important author. In that respect, the laudatory poem could help enhance the reputation of both the writer of the poem and the author of the publication.

As could be expected, Constantijn Huygens had a very charming way of requesting a laudatory poem from Hooft. Huygens claimed that since he would not have published his upcoming book if it weren't for Hooft, the latter was obliged to write a poem of praise. Hooft had convinced him to make his work public, and thus Hooft should be the one to praise his work and explain why it was worthy of publication. Furthermore, Hooft was also requested to ask mutual friends in Amsterdam for their poems of praise under the pretext that these were people who "as a habit shake honorary poems from their sleeves".[139] It seemed unlikely to him that these people would refuse him a piece of poetry that "they were writing by the dozen".[140] Hooft fulfilled Huygens request by sending him a number of laudatory poems and he conventionally apologised to Huygens for their poor quality. Furthermore, he had also asked both Vondel and Reael to contribute to the laudations of Huygens's work with poems. Hooft told Huygens that he could expect something on their behalf.[141]

When Huygens in 1657 was about to publish his book of poetry entitled *Korenbloemen*, he was spontaneously offered a laudatory poem by Alida Bruno (1629-1679), a young woman from Alkmaar who had come into contact with Huygens via her brother who was a tutor of Huygens's children as well as via Tesselschade Roemers Visscher. The latter had moved to Alkmaar after her marriage to Crombalck and she had early on pointed out Alida's talents as a writer to Hooft. The young woman was eager to be taken seriously as a writer and hoped that Huygens would publish these laudatory poems in his *Korenbloemen*. [142]

The letter with which she offered her poems was written in the conventional humble style. She expressed her wish to offer him her poetry on the occasion of the publication of his poetry, and revealed that it had been a struggle to compose something that was worthy of him. Her "flimsy work" turned out to be "beyond hope", because she had written it in a great hurry, since the messenger had been waiting, and she had been disturbed often while writing it. Thus she only saw "the value that his judgement would attach to it".[143] Unfortunately, Huygens did not seem to attach a lot of value to her writings, because they were not published along with his poetry.

This did not imply that he had not appreciated her gesture, but naturally as one of the big poets in the Republic, laudatory poems that were published to praise his work had to be of a certain quality and had to be written by people who belonged to the literary elite. Only then would they contribute to Huygens honour. Even though Alida did manage to have some of her occasional poetry published over time, her reputation was not yet great enough to do honour to Huygens.

It has been suggested that Alido Bruno's humble approach regarding Huygens was typical for women with literary ambitions who addressed men to focus their attention on their writings.[144] Yet this is only true in the sense that this applied to all writers, be it men or women, who wrote to others in the hope of furthering their literary careers. Moreover, humility was a convention within seventeenth-century correspondence as such.

Once a text was finally printed, the author usually received a number of copies from the publisher to offer to his literary friends and other important contacts. These gift copies were thereby also a means of maintaining the literary network of the author. Offering a gift copy of the book was a way of thanking the people that had invested their time in the work by previewing and critiquing it.[145] Others received a copy to attract their attention to the work of the author or to entice benevolence for other reasons.

Naturally, these copies were offered with the conventional expressions of humility. One of the gift copies of Hooft's *Baeto* was sent to Jacob Backer, alderman and later one of Amsterdam's burgomaster. In the accompanying letter, Hooft claimed that "finally the shame was gone, and this book was out in the open: in the hope that the importance of the contents would outweigh the rudeness of the exterior".[146] He ended his letter by saying that he was not expecting Backer's thankfulness, but his forgiveness since his work was in need of mercy from the likes of Backer, which was again a rather modest way of promoting his work.

Another one of the gift copies of *Baeto* was sent to Huygens with the usual modest expressions.[147] Huygens reacted by complimenting the work in a letter to Hooft. Huygens explicitly stated that his words were not just meant as flattery, but that he had enjoyed the work and had never "seen history so well mixed with fables". Although this remark does not necessarily come across as a compliment, it was surely intended as one if one considers the contents of the work. The *Baeto* was indeed a tragedy that mixed both historic facts with literary fiction and, based on the letter, it was a style of writing that Huygens claimed he had thoroughly enjoyed. This had made him all the more eager to read Hooft's *Hendrik de Grote*, which was another historical work about to be published.

When it was published, Huygens naturally received a gift copy of the book. Hooft sent it to him with a letter that again stressed his unworthiness of bothering Huygens, and the rest of the world, with a book of such meagre quality.[148] He did, however, claim that its deficiencies might be helpful for those who were about to take up a work of the same sort, for with Hooft's book they at least were served an example of what mistakes to avoid. Hooft suggested he should at least receive credit for that. Hooft again ended his letter with the wish that the contents of the work would out-weigh the unimportance of its expression.

Another person who received a gift copy of *Hendrik de Grote* was Dirck van Halewijn, who was councilman and alderman of the town of Harderwijk, and had mediated in the process of obtaining the privilege for publishing.[149] Hooft had thanked him for his ef-forts in the letter that accompanied the gift copy. Halewijn reacted to this by saying that he could not possibly accept these words of gratitude, since, according to him, it was only natural that he did what he did and that he would have done even more if it had been possible.[150]

The fact that Halewijn had negotiated for Hooft might suggest that the book was a form of payment or reward, but it was not necessarily experienced this way. Even though a number of the recipients of the gift copies had helped Hooft out during the pro-cess of writing and publishing the book, they still accepted their personal copies as gifts and referred to them as such. Anthonis de Hubert, for instance, thanked Hooft for the *"vereeringe"*, or hon-ouring, of the gift copy.[151]

On the other hand, these gift copies were not entirely free. It seems quite possible that those who had worked on correcting the manuscript of the book or had made the publication of the work possible in other ways, were in fact expecting a gift copy not nec-essarily as payment, but certainly because they were eager to see the final result. Clearly in most cases, the author was more than willing to offer their literary assistants and possible admirers a copy of the work.

Obviously, the exchange of gifts played a very important role in literary networks. The network consisted of individuals with an interest in writing, who would support each other's efforts by cor-recting work, by commenting on its contents, and by lending each other books by other authors as a means of staying up to date with literary practices. These services were not offered for payment, but with the expectation that one's efforts would be reciprocated in the sense that the other would offer similar services, and rewarded in the sense that gift copies would be offered upon publication and laudatory poems would be offered spontaneously or upon request. These practices were beneficial for all of the individuals involved.

The discourse that surrounded the exchange of gifts within these literary networks is largely one of honour, obligation and humility. It was not necessarily the case that these writers actually thought of their own works in such humble terms, but it was certainly a convention to talk about them that way. By requesting literary assistance and support in such humble terms, the other party could feel honoured to be asked this favour and would be more willing to oblige. In that sense, the discourse helped the practice of exchange.

Conclusion

In this chapter, several relationships were discussed in which the exchange of gifts was important. Depending on the character of the relationship, the exchange of gifts therein was made either more or less explicit. Under normal circumstances, gifts were offered and received as a matter of course, without any explicit references to the exchange. Only in more problematic relationships would the rhetoric of the gift come into play. In those cases, the gift, or at least the rhetoric of the gift, was used as a means to force the other individual to behave in a way that brought benefit to the donor. Therewith, the gift became an instrument because by accepting the gift, the recipient – at least in the eyes of the donor – was forced to change his behaviour or fulfil a certain duty. This is the case in the problematic relationship between Herman Verbeeck and his brother and to a certain extent, in the relationship between P.C. Hooft and his servant Aeltje. Still, within these two relationships, the gift may have at the same time been a token of affection. Both Pieter Verbeeck and Hooft may have had the best interests of their brother and servant at heart.

The story of Pieter Hooft and Giacomo Badovere was rather different. It seems Badovere was not sincerely interested in maintaining a social relationship with Hooft. There was something he needed beyond that relationship in itself, namely a mediator that could help him get his money back from Baudius. He used the rhetoric of the gift to tempt Hooft to cooperate, without the intention of offering the gifts at all.

This is quite different from the relationship that David Beck established and tried to maintain with David de Moor. Although this relationship was interesting to Beck because it could potentially provide him with commissions, this did not exclude the fact that the two men actually did appreciate the relationship as such. But in Badovere's case this seems highly unlikely. Even if he had offered Hooft a gift after his mediation efforts, this would still have been an instrument for it most likely would not have been used to maintain a long lasting relationship but just to repay him for services rendered.

Still, these are only a few examples in which the rhetoric of the gift is overtly used. In most relationships, the exchange of gifts went without saying, and as a matter of course. Yet even these exchanges were offered following certain rhetorical conventions. As an example, the letters of the corresponding literary elite were used here to show that "honour", "obligation", and extreme humility were important terms in this respect. However, this terminology of gift exchange was not just typical for the likes of Hooft and Huygens, but is also evident in Dorothea van Dorp's letters and Willem Frederik van Nassau-Dietz's diaries. These were the terms that were conventionally attached to the offering and receiving of gifts in seventeenth-century Holland.

Part IV: Comparison in Time

In the preceding chapters, several aspects of seventeenth-century Dutch gift exchange have been discussed. The goal of this research was to try to understand how gift exchange as a system was organised in seventeenth-century Holland and how it was perceived by individuals in the context of seventeenth-century Dutch society. The general idea was that by taking gift exchange as a means of establishing and maintaining social ties and therewith an important factor in social relationships, gift exchange could help determine whether relationships in this period were as instrumental as they are often perceived by contemporary historians.[1] Or, to put it in other words: Did they perceive their social behaviour as instrumental as we see it?

In order to answer this question, several steps were taken. First, the (possible) practices of exchange in seventeenth-century Holland were analysed and described as a means of discovering what networks individuals were exchanging gifts in; what type of gifts were being exchanged; and on what occasions they exchanged gifts.[2] In the second part, the various meanings gifts could have in seventeenth-century society were considered. The purpose of this was to show how different gifts were perceived; gifts could be appreciated for their symbolic meaning, for their economic value, as a signifier of one's reputation, or as something that brought company and pleasure. In that respect, gifts were not just instruments that were used to obtain something else, but also things that were appreciated in their own right.[3] In part three, the discourses that surrounded gift exchange in this period were examined on the basis of some specific gift-exchange relationships. The role of the gift within these relationships was considered as a way of finding out how gift exchange was discussed and referred to during this period.[4]

In this last chapter, the findings of the earlier chapters on seventeenth-century Dutch gift exchange will be compared to contemporary Dutch gift exchange. This will help explain how both instrumentality and affection are important elements of gift ex-change and social relations in the two periods. Here the practices of and discourses on seventeenth-century exchange will be discussed in comparison to the practices of and discourses on exchange on the brink of the twenty-first-century in the Netherlands on the basis of the Letters to the Future.

The Letters to the Future

These Letters to the Future were already discussed briefly in the prologue.[5] Before getting to the letters themselves it is important to understand what kinds of people wrote these "Letters". Obviously the identities of the writers is not revealed, but they were asked to at least note their sex and year of birth, and their postal codes, which gives us an idea where they lived. Furthermore, it is clear that the writers reveal a lot about themselves in their letters.

On the basis of the 280 letters used here, there are some general remarks that can be made about the writers. In general, they all seem to have quite a lot of free time. Many of the participants did not seem to have full-time jobs. Quite a few of them were elderly people, or at least retired. Others were full-time mothers or at home convalescing.[6] This is not to suggest that these people are inactive as such. Not only do they have busy social lives, many of them seemed to be caring for sick or otherwise deprived people in their environments and a lot seemed to be involved in voluntary work in their communities.[7] Still, it is obvious that one needs some time to spare to write a letter that describes a full day, and in that respect there is a bias in this source material. There are, for instance, very few mothers with full-time jobs represented, and young urban professionals seem to be totally absent. In this respect, the writers of the future are not necessarily representative of Dutch society as a whole.

Another feature of the people that participated is that they enjoyed writing. Many mentioned that they keep diaries, that they occasionally enter writing contests or that they correspond with pen pals abroad.[8] Furthermore, they seem to live life quite consciously: many eat biological foods, a number of them out of principle do not own a car, and seem generally concerned about the world they live in.[9] This was also why it was important to participate in the Letters to the Future project. The writers hoped that the future will produce a better world with more tolerance, less aggression and more concern for the environment.[10] Of course, it is not obvious how their letters would contribute to these goals, but it is this idealism that seems to have enticed these individuals to participate.

Others revealed a clear historical consciousness. Some expressed an appreciation for this project as a means of obtaining sources for future research while others mentioned that they were doing genealogical research as a hobby.[11] In other cases, the historical consciousness was manifested by the grocery store receipts they added so that future researchers can make comparisons, while others wondered whether in the future it will be possible to explain to children what the expression "he who is born a *dubbeltje* can never become a *kwartje*" means after the introduction of the euro.[12] So in general, one might say that people were motivated to write their letters by idealism and a historical consciousness, and in some instances both. As one woman noted: "Moreover, this letter enables me to contribute to both the future and the past and that is quite unique".[13]

Practices of Exchange

Of the one hundred general letters that were selected from the collection randomly, 45 mention the exchange of gifts, and of these 45 letters, 55 instances of gift exchange were mentioned. In the 180 letters that were chosen because they reveal details about festivities and rituals almost all refer to the exchange of gifts in some way or another, be it hospitality or the offering of presents. When it comes to the practices of exchange in twentieth-century Holland, the letters convey similarities and differences with seventeenth-century gift-exchange practices. Generally speaking, the networks, occasions and gifts largely coincide in both periods. However, there are some differences in the importance of certain networks over others, the timing of gift exchange for certain occasions as well as some innovations of occasions, and innovations in the type of gifts exchanged.

Naturally, the findings in the Letters to Future are greatly influenced by the character of the material. The letters describe just one day of one year, and this day was especially picked by the organising committee because is was supposed to be such a normal day. The day, 15 May, was chosen specifically because there was nothing exceptional happening on that day – no elections, no important football match, or anything else that would seriously influence the content of the letters or the number of letters submitted. However, the fact that it just describes one "normal" day, automatically means that some events like calendar feasts are excluded from the descriptions. The exceptions are the few mothers who mentioned Mother's Day that had been celebrated the weekend before and people from the Purmerend area which was celebrating its annual *kermis* that weekend.[14] In as far as these events are described, the mothers received gifts from both their spouses and children, while the *kermis* was described as an event to attend, but not celebrate in the home.[15] One mother wrote that she gave her teenage daughter some money to go to the fair.[16]

Occasions for exchange

When discussing the seventeenth-century material, several different gift opportunities were considered. These were either daily gifts – gifts that could be offered every day of the week without any special reason – or gifts that were related to a rite of passage or a calendar feast. Hospitality could be offered on either of these occasions. As a daily gift it could be offered both spontaneously and as a result of prior planning.

Interestingly enough, the offering of spontaneous hospitality is not one of the major themes in the Letters to the Future. There are naturally some references to offerings of hospitality as a matter of course, but not quite as much as were revealed in David Beck's diary. One man mentioned offering a *"bakkie"*, or a cup of coffee when an acquaintance came by his house.[17] In as far as people do refer to daily hospitality, it usually involved drinks and snacks, whereas David Beck and his circle were also in the habit of sharing meals spontaneously.[18] Spontaneous dinners in contemporary Holland are far less common. In as far as people do have dinners together – not related to a festive occasion – these are usually arranged prior to the event and even these meals were rare.[19] The participants were most likely single or widowed.[20] There is only one instance where it is clear that the meal offered is offered spontaneously, without a prior appointment. This is when an elderly woman is invited over to her friend's house for dinner. She notes that she will have her "nasi goreng with fried egg" some other time.[21] Furthermore, accommodation is mostly offered to young children or to friends and relatives that live abroad.[22] So it seems that the image of spontaneous sociability with family and friends on an almost daily basis is not one that applies to contemporary Dutch society.[23]

However, people in contemporary society are more prone to offer other types of gifts spontaneously. One girl contemplated whether she should offer her sister a gift because she just broke up with her boyfriend and now is heartbroken.[24] She figured a nice gift could help cheer her sister up. Support at times of illness is not only shown through the support itself, but also by the offering of small presents like flowers, fruit and cards.[25]

Rites of passage are still celebrated in much the same manner as they were in the seventeenth century, at least when it comes to the type of gifts offered on these occasions. Marriage, birth and death in twentieth-century Holland are still celebrated with the offering of hospitality, objects, greeting cards and letters and artistic contributions. During weddings, the bride and groom offer hospitality to large groups of people in various ways. After the official ceremony, some couples offer a reception to their close friends and family, and people who they are less intimate with. People who are only invited to the reception for instance include members of the extended family, like aunts and uncles, acquaintances of their parents and colleagues.[26] There are also several letters from parents who had attended the receptions of the friends of their children or others who attended the wedding receptions of children of their friends.[27] The reception usually starts off with coffee and cake and is followed by a few drinks and some snacks.[28] Receptions seldom lasts more than two hours.[29]

The wedding dinner that follows is usually restricted to the inner circle of close friends and the nuclear family. The dinner normally consists of several courses and either takes place in a restaurant or at the venue where the wedding reception takes place.[30] In contrast to seventeenth-century weddings, contemporary wedding dinners are commonly not held in the home of the bride's parents. After dinner, there is normally a party to which a larger group is invited.[31] This group is usually closer to the couple, both in intimate terms and in age, than the people invited to the reception. They are offered drinks and snacks.

The guests are expected to contribute to the festivities by offering gifts. This, however, seems to be a taboo topic, especially for those brides and grooms who describe their wedding day. They do not make any explicit references to gifts except for the fact that they received them, and that there were many or that they were nice.[32] This is only done in general terms. There are no descriptions of specific gifts by brides and grooms. Guests to the wedding, in some cases, do reveal what they gave as a gift and if they do mention it, it usually came in an envelope.[33] The envelope in contemporary Dutch society is a euphemism for money. Some of the writers actually mention the amount of money they gave.[34] Interestingly enough, it seems that the more distant the writer is from the couple, the more likely he or she mentions the gift. The few descriptions of specific gifts in the Letters to the Future are by people who only attended the reception.

People invited for the whole day, did not refer to presents except for the more artistic gifts, like their "A-4tjes" and their "stukjes".[35] The term A-4tje refers to the size of the sheet of paper on which the guests are asked, usually by the master of ceremonies, to write something nice about the couple. This normally results in collages with pictures, poems or anecdotes that are given to the couple as a book in remembrance of their big day. The stukjes are performances by certain groups that attend the wedding on the occasion of the wedding itself. The families of the bride and groom are both likely to prepare a performance, as well as their various groups of friends.

So, even though we have a lot more descriptions of contemporary weddings than for the seventeenth century, there is little more that we can tell about the actual gifts that were offered on the basis of the Letters to the Future. Despite the fact that the writers have the sense that they are providing the future with source material, most of them did not feel that a description of their gifts was appropriate. They generally avoided the topic, especially when the event was emotionally significant to them.

When it comes to the celebration of birth, there is one important difference in contemporary society compared to seventeenth-century Holland. Whereas in the early modern period the christening of the child was the moment for the offering of gifts to the child, in contemporary Holland the gifts are offered right after the delivery, the so-called kraamtijd.[36] In that respect, one can say that the gift moment has moved from the christening to the birth itself. The explanation for this is that it is no longer the christening that makes the child a member of the community, but the fact that it has been born. Furthermore, the child not only receives gifts from the christening witnesses, but from all of the guests who come to visit, although again, those writers who describe visiting a newborn child do not mention the gifts they gave.[37] There are, however, descriptions of what gifts in general are offered on the occasion of a birth. These include mostly clothes and toys.[38] The guests on this occasion are offered coffee and "*beschuit met muisjes*", or biscuits with sugared anise seed, in return.[39] Dinners upon the occasion of a birth are now very uncommon.

Death as a moment for gift exchange is still celebrated in much the same manner as it was in the seventeenth century, except that there seems to be a lot less alcohol involved.[40] The funeral is attended by family, friends, neighbours and professional contacts. After the official ceremonies, the attendees are invited for at the very least coffee and cake, but in some instances they may also be offered a meal consisting of bread rolls and soup.[41] Occasionally, some wine or beer is poured, but it is generally not common to get drunk at funerals, nor would it be appreciated.[42]

Birthdays, as we discussed earlier, were seldom celebrated in seventeenth-century Holland, but in the Letters to the Future, birthdays are the most commonly described gift-exchange event. Unlike weddings, birthdays and birthday gifts are discussed in great detail, both by the people celebrating their birthdays and the people attending. It is the one occasion on which people describe inviting larger groups of people into their house and offering them hospitality. The normal pattern is that guests are first offered coffee and cake, which is followed by drinks (typically wine, beer or soda) and snacks.[43] These snacks usually consist of nuts, crisps and crackers with cheese. People are also more likely to have a special dinner on their birthdays either in their own home or in a restaurant, but this is usually only shared with members of the household and not with other guests.[44] Other people celebrate their birthdays by organising a special outing, like a picnic or an excursion.[45] In return for the hospitality, birthday guests offer gifts. The gifts described in the Letters to the Future, both by givers and recipients, range from CDs and books, to plants and cosmetics.[46] It is also not uncommon to offer money as a gift or gift certificates.[47] Friends and family unable to attend the festivities are expected to either call or send a postcard.[48]

As compared to David Beck's diary, children are an important category in contemporary gift exchange. Their birthdays are celebrated quite extensively, both within the private home and outside. Within the home, the child is sung to by family and receives presents from both parents and siblings. During the actual birthday some other relatives might show up. These guests will be offered coffee and cake and will bring gifts for the child.[49]

Furthermore, the children receive special attention in school for their birthdays. One of the ways it is celebrated in school is by the decoration of a chair. The birthday child is allowed to treat classmates with candy, and he or she can go round to other classes in the school to offer cake to the other teachers.[50] The offering of candy has been the cause for public debate: Officials have tried to encourage parents to bring fruit treats or something else healthy, but presumably in practice this is not a common consideration among either parents or children. As one mother noted, she knows she is supposed to think of healthy treats, but then again, nobody else does.[51]

On a day other than the actual birthday, a special party for the birthday child's friends is usually organised.[52] Children's birthday parties are very important to the parents. Two mothers actually describe the organising of their child's birthday parties in full detail. They make a big effort to put the event together. They do grocery shopping in advance and make sure to buy the train tickets a couple of days before in order to avoid complications on the day of the festivities.[53] The activities that take place on the day itself are also of great significance. One mother specifically mentions that she is taking the children to the museum of natural sciences while the other is planning to take her the children to Madurodam, an open air museum in which the Netherlands is portrayed in miniature.[54] These seem to be very educational and pedagogically sound outings, and might suggest that the Dutch are often very responsible when it comes to children's parties, but this is not necessarily the case. The two mothers who describe these events are women with academic backgrounds and academic level jobs, which probably makes them more prone to organise this type of party. It also seems to make them more conscious of the social significance of these events. One of them is quite nervous about her daughter's birthday party, because "I am aware that what she receives, whom she invites and what she does at the party, also plays a role in her own 'social network'".[55]

Other than birthdays, there are a few other gift exchange occasions mentioned in the Letters to the Future that did not occur in the seventeenth-century material. This is partly because most of the seventeenth-century was produced by protestants. They obviously did not celebrate occasions like Holy Communion and the Sabbath as some of the Letters to the Future writers do. One letter writer mentioned Holy Communion as being celebrated with a party for the family, at which the child who had his or her communion probably received gifts from the guests.[56] Several women described their preparations for the Sabbath in detail. A lot of food is prepared and this is either eaten in their own homes with invited guests or brought to their hostesses when they have been invited to a Sabbath dinner.[57] Other occasions like Mother's day and Father's day are clearly more recent inventions.[58]

In general, one can say that spontaneous hospitality is now less important than it was in the seventeenth century and that, although this cannot be determined on basis of the Letters to the Future, Christian Holidays, especially Christmas, are celebrated festively in contemporary Holland, whereas for David Beck and Willem Frederik these were occasions for reflection. Furthermore, calendar feasts are generally no longer celebrated with the exchange of gifts or the offering of hospitality. The one exception is the celebration of *Sinterklaas* on 5 December, which is still one of the most significant gift-exchange moments in the Dutch calendar year.[59]

Networks of exchange

The Letters of the Future project did not offer as good an opportunity to analyse networks of exchange as David Beck's diary did. Naturally, people do refer to people with whom they maintain social contact, but on the basis of these letters it is impossible to determine what the frequency of contact was with certain groups or the importance of certain networks with certain occasions as compared to others. Still, the letters do offer an opportunity to show that all of the networks that were important in the seventeenth century are still important now.

Moreover, the impression these letters leave is quite different from some of the general ideas that some people have about contemporary western society. Contemporary society is generally regarded as being individualistic, with the family losing its importance, while bonds among friends seem to be replacing family ties.[60] Neighbours are supposedly negligible factors in modern urbanised society, whereas co-workers and colleagues supposedly only play a role in one's working life, and not in one's private life.

In fact, the family is still very important for all the occasions described in the letters. The extended family is invited to weddings, birthdays, funerals and is more likely to be offered accommodations than any other network.[61] A lot of these festivities, however, are also celebrated in the nuclear family circle. In general, these occasions are celebrated within the larger circle of family and friends, but there seems to be a tendency to also create an occasion within the occasion to have a chance to be with the smaller circle that includes the nuclear family and some close friends. This occurs especially on birthdays and weddings; the whole day is celebrated with others, but dinner is an opportunity to be with a smaller circle.[62] As will be shown in the next paragraph, rhetorically people stress the importance of their inner circle. In that sense, people seem to have an inclination for celebrating important events privately, yet without excluding the larger family network from the occasion altogether. Others take these occasions as an opportunity to celebrate exclusively within the small circle of their nuclear family or close friends.[63] This can also be done by organising a short trip.[64]

Friends indeed seem to be of great importance in contemporary Dutch society. They are also invited to all sorts of occasions, but there seems to be a small distinction in the importance of the friendships depending on the life cicle of the friends involved. For children, contact with friends is stimulated by their environment, as was revealed through the birthday parties. The elderly in this sample also tend to spend a lot of time celebrating important events with their circles of friends, this is especially the case for those elderly who are widowed.[65] For these people, it seems that friends have indeed replaced their families. But for adults living in a nuclear family situation, the family still seems to be of great significance. This is not to say that these people do not have friends, but just that these friends have not replaced the family in importance.[66]

Again, like in David Beck's diary, neighbours are not very important in the daily descriptions of the contemporary Dutch. Some might mention that it is nice to have "good neighbours" and others may note that they visited their neighbours on their birthdays, but other than that neighbours are not represented in the Letters to the Future in any great numbers.[67] Neighbours are, however, explicitly mentioned as one of the networks that, together with family, friends and colleagues, are supposed to be invited to funerals.[68] This probably depends on the area in which the deceased lived. Although Zuid- and Noord-Holland are two highly urbanised provinces, within these provinces one can still distinguish between towns and villages. Especially in the more rural villages neighbours are more significant than in towns.

One of the most interesting findings in the Letters to the Future is the importance of gift exchange within the professional environment. As was discussed in the prologue, some authors claimed that throughout history gift exchange has been superseded by market exchange, which implies that as far as there are still remnants of gift exchange in modern society these are not found in the market.[69] Furthermore, there is a general notion that an individual's private and public life are very separated and that the gift only plays a role within one's private life, but this does not seem to be the case at all. The number of descriptions of gift exchange within the professional sphere is enormous. People are offered gifts when they attend openings for professional reasons, for instance.[70] They are offered gifts by their bosses and colleagues when they celebrate their jubilee or when they leave their jobs.[71] On these occasions, employers will also offer hospitality to this employee and his or her co-workers. Employers also offer employees company parties, which usually consist of an activity or excursion and a party afterwards.[72]

Yet gifts in the professional network are not only exchanged on professional occasions, co-workers also play a role in more private occasions. Some people might treat their co-workers to cake or ice-cream on their birthday.[73] Furthermore, colleagues are also invited to weddings or funerals and they are expected to visit and bring presents after the birth of a child.[74] On these occasions, one is not expected to invite all one's co-workers, but at least those one is in direct contact with.

The letters show that the offering of gifts within an environment which is supposed to be ruled by market forces is nothing out of the ordinary. It would be a mistake to think of offerings by superiors as disguised payments, because although there are certain obligatory aspects attached, the gifts are to a large extent expressions of the appreciation of the superior for his employees hard work, dedication and loyalty. For the recipient, these gifts also mean more than just a little extra material wealth; the gifts are also a sign of his reputation within the working environment.

Gifts

What gifts do people in the Letters to the Future mention? And how do these gifts compare to the gifts that were exchanged in seventeenth-century Holland? Again, there seem to be more similarities than differences. The types of gifts exchanged are very similar: objects, hospitality, money, artistic gifts, support and food and drink. There are some interesting features about these gifts in contemporary society, however. As was discussed earlier in this chapter, hospitality remains an important and frequently offered gift. It basically applies to any occasion. Yet the type of hospitality offered has changed. David Beck and his circle exchanged drinks, meals and accommodations, whereas in most of the Letters hospitality is confined to a drink and a small snack. Meals are offered far less frequently and accommodations play almost no role in normal daily life. This could of course be quite different during a popular calendar feast like Christmas.

The objects given and described in the Letters to the Future are usually quite modest. People offer books, CDs, cosmetics, alcohol, plants and flowers, and small pieces of jewellery like cufflinks or a brooch.[75] Objects as gifts in contemporary society are still mostly offered on special occasions, like birthdays, and not just spontaneously. It is disappointing in that respect that brides and grooms do not describe the gifts they received for their wedding. These are most likely the most expensive and meaningful objects, but unfortunately this sample of letters did not reveal anything in this respect.

Somewhat surprisingly, money is also considered an appropriate gift for several occasions. At weddings, guests who don't know the tastes of the newlyweds are likely to give money.[76] By offering the couple money, the couple can then pick a gift they really like, or save up for something more expensive they really need. However, money is also a common gift at birthdays.[77] This is interesting because money is considered an inappropriate gift by many authors on gift-exchange theory. They claim that gifts of money in contemporary society are unsuitable, and have tried to come up with explanations why this is so.[78]

Artistic gifts were already discussed as appropriate wedding gifts. They consist not only of performances and creative sheets of paper. One woman actually described the wedding of her niece for which family and friends of the couple had prepared a slide show, composed several songs and organised a quiz.[79] These artistic gifts are not only offered at weddings, but also wedding anniversaries or anniversaries at work. One man mentioned writing a poem for the 50th wedding anniversary of one of his friends and another composed a song for the 60th birthday of his brother-in-law.[80] As these occasions suggest, artistic gifts are only socially required at big events like weddings, anniversaries and important birthdays. However, short plays and songs and the like are in some social circles replaced by speeches.[81]

Food and drink can be offered spontaneously as well as during a special occasion. One woman described bringing her piano teacher nectarines for no special reason.[82] Others bring cookies when they visit friends.[83] Another woman offered a friend a mango on her birthday.[84] The mayor of a mid-sized town received a box of asparagus and a box of wine after attending the official opening of the new university library.[85] Although food gifts can be offered on any occasion, these examples suggest that the more special the occasion, the more exotic or luxurious the food gifts need to be. Mangos, for instance, are fruits that can be purchased at most supermarkets, but are not common in many households. White asparagus is generally considered a great delicacy and the months of April and May are typical asparagus months. Thus the mayor received a very appropriate gift.

The last gift that needs to be discussed here is support. This is an interesting gift, especially in light of the complaint that contemporary society is individualistic and that people only care about themselves, which suggests that support among individuals in contemporary society would be totally lacking. This is, however, not the case.[86] The writers of these letters actually seem quite supportive of their social environment. This might again be the result of the bias in the participants in this project. They were, after all, mostly quite conscious and idealistic. In fact, the numbers of writers who take care of the sick and elderly, and do volunteer work are probably higher than the Dutch average. Still, they also reveal a willingness to support others with practicalities. They water each others plants during vacations.[87] They help each other out in the shop on busy days.[88] They take care of each other's dogs when they go away for the weekend.[89]

Emotional support is also nothing out of the ordinary. Obviously people still attend funerals, but people are also willing to offer others some comfort on everyday occasions. One woman visited a friend who had smallpox to bring her some fruit. At work, people collected autographs on a greeting card that was sent to a sick co-worker.[90] Adult children called their mother on the date of death of one of their siblings.[91] And of course, let us not forget the teenage girl who contemplated buying a gift for her lovesick sister.

So, all in all, people in contemporary Holland exchange the same types of gifts as people did in the seventeenth century. In as far as gifts have changed these are usually material innovations and not real changes. Of course, roller skates were not available in the seventeenth century, but other types of toys were. Seventeenth-century people naturally could not call each other on the telephone, but they did indeed write each other on special occasions. In that sense, then, not a lot has changed.

There is only one real new category of gifts, which are flowers and plants. In contemporary Holland these can be offered on any occasion, be it birthdays, weddings, funerals and even spontaneously.[92] Naturally, the exchange of plants, bulbs, and flowers among botanists and tulip lovers in the seventeenth century cannot be excluded altogether, but these were obviously not common gifts within general social circles, although there is one example of Hooft sending a May Tree to the sisters Anna and Tesselschade Roemers Visscher on the occasion of the First of May. Unfortunately, one tree fell off the barge and was lost, after which Hooft sent them a new one with a poem detailing the tragic ordeal the first tree had undergone.[93]

Patterns of reciprocity

The Letters to the Future include only one instance in which a writer makes the reciprocal character of a particular exchange of gifts explicit. When one writer mentioned that she went out to a Chinese restaurant that evening with her husband and neighbour, she explained in addition that the three of them go out to dinner approximately once a month. "He treats us because we in turn do

things for him", she adds.[94] As it turns out, these dinners are reciprocations for the fact that the writer and her husband take care
of the neighbour's administrative details. A similar example can
be found in the David Beck's diary. On 3 March 1624, Beck noted
that his friend Breckerfelt came by to offer him a drawing of a
landscape, which he "owed to" Beck because Beck had offered
him a small gift earlier.[95] However, despite these two examples, it
seems clear that reciprocation during both periods was not something that needed to be made explicit. If it weren't for the fact that
Beck described his routines on a daily basis, little would have been
revealed about the reciprocal character of his gift-exchange behaviour.

Since David Beck did describe his gift exchanges for a full year,
it was possible to determine gift-exchange patterns within his social environment. Exchange of gifts between most of the individuals Beck mentions turned out to be balanced. Naturally, it is impossible to come to similar conclusions with the Letters to the
Future. They just describe one day and do not leave much room
to follow the individual's behaviour over a longer period of time.
So, if one invites a person to dinner on 15 May, it is not clear
whether this hospitality will be returned within a certain span of
time, but presumably it will be. Interestingly enough, this does
not mean that nothing can be said about patterns of reciprocity.

In fact, contemporary gift exchange seems to be extremely reciprocal.[96] Again not in the sense that for each gift offered, there
must be a gift of the same form and value returned, but in the
sense that almost all gift moments include a gift from both parties
involved. Gift exchange in contemporary Holland seems to be
characterised by instant reciprocity: a return gift is not delayed
but offered on the same occasion as the first gift was received. On
weddings and birthdays, the guests receive hospitality, while they
are all supposed to offer gifts to the wedding couple or the birthday boy or girl. When people are invited to dinner they bring flowers.[97] In cases of practical support, for instance, the donor is also
often reciprocated for his support instantly. The man who helped
his friend out in the wine bar is offered a bottle of nice wine and
the brother who watched his sister's dog for the weekend was treated to dinner at McDonalds.[98]

It is not that through these return gifts the relationship is balanced and further reciprocation is unnecessary. Of course the
bride and groom will expect an invitation when one of the guests

gets married, as would a birthday boy or girl on the occasion of another friend's birthday. A dinner should not only be reciprocated by a bunch of flowers, but also with a dinner invitation in due time. And the fact that support was rewarded with a gift, does not mean that the person receiving support in this one instance is excused from offering support on another occasion. This does not make the reciprocity a form of repayment either, because they obviously think of these offerings as gifts. Instead it seems that people nowadays seem to feel more obliged to show appreciation for received attentions immediately.

Discourses on Exchange in the Letters to the Future

The writers to the future were asked to describe their day as a means of obtaining source material for future researchers. These descriptions made it possible to analyse popular gifts and important occasions and networks of exchange in Dutch society at the end of the twentieth century. However, one of the purposes of studying this material was to have an opportunity to analyse discourses on exchange in contemporary society. Interestingly, the writers – like David Beck in the seventeenth century – seldom reflect on their gift-exchange practices. They generally stuck to the assignment of describing their day and therewith their gift exchange practices, but without being aware that these gift-exchange practices as such were also of importance to (future) researchers. Although there are a few exceptions, the writers in general do not seem to realise that the way in which they behave socially is also significant to historians and ethnologists. Most of the letters are very descriptive and matter of fact.

There are only two examples in which an awareness of gift exchange as a social practice is manifested. First, there is a description of a birthday that is not just a dry enumeration of hospitality offered and gifts received, but includes a remark to the effect that this is how it is "normally" done and then goes on to describe what people would generally offer their guests at birthday parties. According to this writer guests were offered the following:

> First coffee with piece of cake, afterwards a drink. Mostly wine or beer with something savoury like nuts or crackers with cheese.[99]

The fact that this person referred to coffee and cake, and drinks with snacks is not exceptional. There is an abundance of references to coffee and cake, followed by drinks with nuts and crackers with cheese, even literally.[100] Yet the difference here is that the writer consciously distances herself from the description by adding that this is how it is normally done. She is aware that what she is describing is a pattern that might be of interest to scholars.

The other example is that of the aforementioned mother who is aware that her child's birthday party is important within the child's own social network. Her remark is not one that reveals historical or ethnographic awareness, but one that shows that she is aware of the social implications of gift exchange. She realises that the party that she is organising for her daughter will reflect on her daughter's social identity.

These examples do not exclude the notion that the other writers at times might also be aware of the historic, ethnographic or social implications of their gift-exchange behaviour, but they generally did not make any allusions to this awareness. Considering the purpose of the Letters, one might have expected more reflection on gift exchange as a social practice by the writers, but, again there are very few mentions of any rituals and gift exchange practices. This seems to confirm what social scientists have noted: that gift exchange as a social practice is seldom reflected upon by the subjects participating in the exchange.[101]

Even though the writers did not reflect on their gift-exchange behaviour, they – again like David Beck – did occasionally offer comments on how the exchanges were performed, what the quality of their gifts was, or how they perceived the occasion. These references are largely positive.[102] The "beautiful bouquet of flowers" on a birthday seems highly appreciated. A small child, who had his birthday three days earlier, remarks that he was "still enjoying his presents".[103] A newlywed couple looks back at their big day as being full of "sweet words, splendid songs and lots of presents".[104] And an engagement party at the home of the parents who organised it is judged a "big success".[105] They added that at least 77 guests attended, which is a way of quantifying and emphasising the success of the party. Others also include the number of guests to emphasise of the scale of the hospitality. As one couple noted, "a lot of friends and acquaintances came to congratulate and offer presents", adding that there were 70 guests at their reception, 40 for dinner and 100 at the party, as if they needed to convince themselves of how many "a lot" actually is.[106]

A remark referring to the quality of a gift is made by a woman who comments on the cakes one of her friends from her theatre group had treated them to on the occasion of his birthday. These were obviously no ordinary cakes but pastries from "Maison Kelder", a renowned bakery in The Hague.[107] By mentioning the name of this bakery, the woman shows that she was indeed impressed by either the high quality of the cakes or the great reputation of the shop at which they were purchased.

In any case, these are all examples of gifts that were appreciated, or otherwise judged as impressive, but there are also references to gift-exchanges that emphasise the event's peculiarities. What can we make of a woman's remark that the lunch after a funeral was served in a pub next to the church, for instance?[108] She does not seem particularly offended by the venue, but the fact that she mentioned it at all perhaps means it had some specific significance for her. Of all funerals described in the Letters, this is the only one that mentions the actual setting. Perhaps the concept of a funeral reception in a pub was alien to her, or at least something she associated with "otherness". In fact, the funeral of the brother of her colleague seems to be discussed in such detail in particular because the entire experience was so strange to her. The funeral took place in Brabant, one of the southern provinces of the Netherlands. It included "Holy water, incense, prayers, candles, songs and speeches", or so she noted. To the woman, a practicing Protestant, the funeral was everything one would expect from a typical Roman Catholic funeral in the typically Roman Catholic province of Brabant: a mass with all the known sacred paraphernalia and a lunch in such a profane place as a pub.

One elderly lady went to the inaugural lecture of a female professor, "a young woman only 27 years old", at the University of Rotterdam. After the speech there was a reception at which "the drinks flowed abundantly".[109] This remark might either mean that the lady disapproved of drinking to excess, or that she actually enjoyed it. She only had two glasses of red wine on the occasion, which seems quite modest and suggests that she was not very keen on drinking. Yet in the evening, before she went to bed, she had a whiskey which implies that she does enjoy the occasional drink. The expression she used to characterise the occasion is a common Dutch expression: *"de drank vloeide rijkelijk"*. It means the party had plenty of drinks for everybody, but also suggests the guests were well taken care of by the hosts. In that sense, the remark was benign, but one wonders whether this will be as obvious to future researchers.

Gift exchange in contemporary Holland is not always a positive experience. After having a relatively quiet birthday, a woman stated that she did not quite have the chance to enjoy her company.[110] Although she does not elaborate, it seems that she was so busy serving drinks and providing snacks, that she did not have time to actually spend some time with her guests. Plus inviting one's grandchildren is not just fun and games, or maybe even a bit too much of the two. As one grandmother complains after taking care of her three grandchildren for a couple of nights while her daughter and son-in-law were celebrating their wedding anniversary: "It was very tiring."[111]

Peculiarities of contemporary Dutch gift exchange

Other remarks by other writers point out certain contemporary gift-exchange peculiarities. The preference of celebrating certain events within a more private circle does not only become clear through the organisation of celebratory events as such, but also through certain phrases. People refer to events like a weekend trip for a 50th wedding anniversary or a 65th birthday with the phrase "*met het gezin*", or "with the nuclear family".[112] At one big wedding, the dinner is only for the nuclear family including "*aanhang*", or "partners".[113] This means that besides the wedding couple, their parents and siblings were present, including the partners of these siblings. This is exactly the configuration that constitutes *het gezin* in contemporary Holland: parents, children and partners of the children, and grandchildren.[114]

Another interesting example is the remark that "the hostess paid" for her birthday dinner in a restaurant to which one writer was invited.[115] The dinner, to which the hostess invited several friends, turned out to be a *steen grill* evening in a restaurant.[116] It does seem obvious that a host who invites guests for a special occasion would pay for a dinner. Even the Dutch, who gave meaning to the expression "going Dutch", would agree that an event to which one is invited, should be paid by the host. However, this is not as obvious as it seems, as another example shows. After a birthday dinner at a Chinese restaurant with twelve friends, the invitees of the hostess refused to let her pay for the entire dinner. As one of these friends wrote in her letter: "In the end everybody contributed, because they thought they could not allow the hostess to pay for everything."[117]

Why would these invitees feel awkward about letting the hostess pay for the meal she had invited them to? And why would two writers comment on the question of whether their hostess paid for dinner at all? Supposedly this is not just a matter of money, although eating out in the Netherlands is generally quite expensive. The thing is that eating out on birthdays, at least for the kind of people who wrote Letters to the Future, is generally something one only does with one's nuclear family. Generally speaking, Dutch adults mostly celebrate their birthdays in their own homes. If they do go out to dinner at all, they go out to dinner with their nuclear family and in that case, it is obvious that the head of the household pays.

In these two cases, the dinner took place on the occasion of the birthday of a friend or, more importantly, of a *single* friend. Both women were widowed, divorced or otherwise unmarried, and both thought it would be nice to celebrate their birthdays with a dinner with close friends. However, since this situation is rather out of the ordinary it was obviously not very clear to the invitees how the practicalities, or at least the payment of the bill, of such an event should be organised. This is probably why the first writer noticed who paid for dinner, and what led the second writer to refuse to let the hostess pay. For the Dutch, paying for a dinner for twelve relatives is quite exceptional, let alone paying for a dinner for twelve friends.

Expectations and disappointments

What also becomes clear from the letters is that expectations, and disappointments, play an important role in people's gift exchanges and social relations. People obviously expect certain things from each other, be it gifts or a certain type of behaviour. One man notes that when he called an old colleague to congratulate her on her birthday, she was actually not surprised at all, because she was in fact expecting "either this or a postcard".[118] So, in this instance, the man was in fact living up to her expectations. Other people, however, were seriously disappointed in their friends. The earlier woman who wrote that she did not get to enjoy her own birthday also noted that she had not heard from her best friend on her birthday for the first time in fifty years.[119] She had at least expected a call. Obviously her best friend had failed to live up to the expectations. One way of resolving this type of disappointments is by imposing certain rules with regards to birthdays and other important occasions in one's social circle. One woman remarked that she made a habit of not forgetting birthdays and anniversaries.[120]

This is obviously something that is not expected of men, as is made clear through the observations of a woman who received a telephone call from her brother-in-law on her birthday.[121] She comments on the fact that he remembered her birthday: "Most of the time men are not very good at that, (or they just don't care as much)". She explains that he has become a lot more considerate in this respect since the death of his wife, which seems to mirror Hooft's behaviour after the death of his first wife. Only after her death did he start corresponding with his brother-in-law Joost Baeck on a regular basis.[122] Hooft's correspondence with his son-in-law did not commence until after the death of his stepdaughter. This suggests that, to a large extent, women are responsible for the maintenance of social ties within the family. It is only when a man is alone that he accepts these social obligations.

Sociological research on gift exchange in contemporary society actually confirms that the maintenance of social ties through gifts and attentions is actually the task of women. They both offer and receive most.[123] In that respect, it is not that surprising that most of the descriptions of birthdays and other social events in these letters were written by women. There is probably a majority of letters by women in the whole Letters to the Future collection as such, but doubtless even more so in the 'Rituals and Festivities' section. A sample from the 'Sports and hobbies' category would most likely result in more letters written by men.

But to return to expectations, these do not only come into play during birthdays. Weddings are also expected to be celebrated in a certain manner. Even though the couple might have certain wishes, these in some cases cannot be fulfilled because they are not to the taste of their social environment. Social pressure to satisfy the wishes of the parents is supposedly quite strong. As one woman mentioned after attending the wedding of friends, the couple themselves would have preferred to marry "in silence", meaning with as few guests as possible, but "this was not appreciated by the parents".[124] In fact, this couple ended up having a traditional wedding which included both a reception and a party. This implies that even though the couple is at the centre of the attention on their wedding day in contemporary society, this does not mean that they can decide everything by themselves. In practice this would sometimes mean disappointing so many people that it is not worth the trouble and better to do what is expected.

Another example of expectations and disappointments is one in which a whole family is disillusioned as a result of the behaviour of their social environment. The family consists of a mother, father and three kids.[125] During the day the family received a phone call from one of the friends of their son. The 15th of May was an very warm day following an exceptionally warm week and the family had offered him to have his birthday party in their garden. He called to tell them that he had decided to take them up on the offer of having his birthday party in their backyard that evening. In the afternoon, their son and his friend went downtown to buy groceries for that evening's party.

In the late afternoon, the family received another phone call. This time it is one of the friends of their daughter. He had promised the parents to help with the preparations for their upcoming party on the occasion of their wedding anniversary. The party was to be held the following weekend, but now this friend had decided he could not help them out after all. This was very disappointing news for the family; in the evening, over dinner, they discussed whether to be less kind and less considerate of other people's feelings and wishes. Their disappointment was understandable in light of the fact that they would be kind enough to have their son's friend have his party in their garden. They thought it was a nice thing to do, and they expected that others would do for them what they would do for others. Unfortunately this was not the case.

Cultural Conventions

The cultural conventions of exchange involve both the actual practices of exchange and the discursive practices that surround exchange within a specific cultural environment. The practices of exchange, including the occasions, gifts and networks of exchange, are ruled by convention, which is to say that even though people might experience their gift exchange as free, they are in fact socially obliged to participate in certain gift-exchange rituals. These have thus far been analysed based on the descriptions people in the seventeenth century and twentieth century have left behind of their daily practices. The discursive practices are slightly more difficult to analyse on the basis of these daily descriptions. Though people may comment on their exchange and verbally pass judgement on it in either positive or negative terms in their daily descriptions, these do not leave much room to determine how people are supposed to deal with their gift exchanges by cultural convention.

For the seventeenth century, this could be resolved by taking a closer look at the letters in which the exchange of gifts was discussed by donor and recipient. The correspondence of P.C. Hooft with his literary friends showed that the donor offered his gifts with rhetorical *modesty*. The offered gifts in turn could do *honour* to both the recipient and the donor, who through the gifts were *obliged* to each other. It is exactly these conventions that make the earlier quoted letters by Dorothea van Dorp's so typical for seventeenth-century Dutch culture. She stated that Lady Killigrew would do her a "great honour" by wearing the silver bracelet that Dorothea had offered her. Lady Killigrew would "greatly oblige" Dorothea, who felt "more [like] her servant" than anyone had ever been.[126] It is impossible to find out how deeply this obligation and honour were felt, but what is clear is that Dorothea stuck to convention by expressing her sentiments in these terms.

The Letters to the Future in themselves unfortunately do not reflect on the cultural conventions of contemporary gift exchange. They do not disclose information on how the gift was supposed to be discussed between recipient and donor, nor do they reveal how gift exchange was perceived. Nevertheless, these conventions have in fact already been discussed in the prologue when Komter's definition of gift giving was cited. Although this definition was not intended to describe the conventions of contemporary gift exchange, it does seem to point out some important features of contemporary gift exchange, at least in terms of how this social practice is perceived by the subjects who participate in it. According to Komter, subjects perceive gift giving as – among other things – a *non-reciprocal, altruistic* and *spontaneous activity* and an *expression of personal feelings*.[127]

These are general conventions that apply to gift exchange in contemporary Holland, and therewith most likely also to the writers of the Letters to the Future. Still, the Letters show that the perception of gift exchange in contemporary Holland only coincides to a certain extent with these practices of gift exchange. It is clear, for instance, that even though subjects may not be aware of it, gift exchange in contemporary Holland is extremely reciprocal. Gift exchange in seventeenth-century Holland was as well, but then people allowed for a certain passage of time in which reciprocation was expected. In contemporary Holland, on the other hand, there seems to be a dual pattern of reciprocation. In most instances, a small reciprocation is offered instantly, while at the same time there remains a long-term expectation of future reciprocity. Dinner parties are a good example of this pattern of dual reciprocity: guests invited to dinner show their appreciation instantly by offering the host a bouquet or other small gift. Yet despite this offering they are still expected to invite their hosts to dinner in the future.

The same type of argument also applies to the conventional spontaneity of contemporary gift exchange. Although people feel that they are free to offer a gift at whatever moment they choose, the fact of the matter is that a vast majority of gifts are offered on those occasions that socially require the offering of gifts. The Letters to the Future showed that most gifts were offered at conventional gift exchange moments and only very few were offered spontaneously without any social requirements to do so.[128] This demonstrates that people may experience their gifts on birthdays and weddings as spontaneous gifts, but they in fact follow cultural conventions by offering gifts on exactly these occasions. It would indeed be highly problematic for a person to not offer a gift in these instances. This is an interesting phenomenon: there are cultural conventions that describe on what occasions people should participate in the exchange of gifts, while at the same time there are cultural conventions that prescribe that the discourse on these exchanges should refer to spontaneity and freedom of choice.

Another interesting feature of contemporary gift exchange is the supposed personal character of the gift. Gifts are meant to communicate personal feelings, while the gifts themselves – with few exceptions like wedding performances and speeches – are seldom very personal at all. Most of the gifts described in the Letters to the Future are generic gifts. The most popular gifts seem to be books, CDs, plants and flowers, all of which are presumably purchased in shops and of which there exist at least thousands of other copies.[129] In that respect the gifts are not personal at all. Moreover, a number of people mentioned offering money as a gift, which according to contemporary literature on gift exchange is considered a highly inappropriate gift especially because of its impersonal character.[130]

Still, the gifts may not be personal as such, but people do make certain efforts to personalise them in a way that the gifts do become expressions of the affection for the recipient.[131] This can be done in several ways: The gifts are wrapped to increase the surprise, cards are added to express a few personal words or wishes, and if not in cards then the donor may express conventional sentiments in person when offering the gift.[132]

Money is personalised by referring to something for which the recipient is saving up, or by wrapping it in such a way that it becomes more personal.[133] The money in itself is not made any more personal, but at least it is made appropriate by referring specifically to the recipient or his personal wishes. One woman who attended the wedding of her cousin noted that the couple was offered a big sum of money wrapped in a big calculator made out of concrete. Although this was clearly intended as a way to personalise the money gift, it is unclear how a calculator could refer to any positive personal sentiments towards the recipients.

Gifts can also be made personal by referring to the actual relationship between the donor and recipient. Examples of this are the massaging oil and the sport soap one writer bought for her sports companion and the playing cards and notepad purchased for a bridge partner.[134]

Furthermore, it seems likely that most of the generic gifts that were bought were at least to the personal taste of the recipient. People probably purchased books by a writer and CDs by an artist the recipient likes or at least something in a genre he or she enjoys. And the plants and flowers that are offered as gifts presumably also fit into the lifestyle and colour preferences of the recipient. In that sense, it is not the personal fabrication that makes most contemporary gifts appropriate but the fact that the gift is in some way or form personalised by the donor to suit the recipient.[135] Still, even when the donor does not quite succeed in offering an appropriate, personal gift this is not necessarily disastrous for the relationship as such.[136] As one woman notes after a colleague offered her a fuchsia for her birthday: "Excellent. Not that I like fuchsias that much, but I appreciate the gesture enormously".[137]

Conclusion

What this comparison shows is that gift exchange is indeed an important social phenomenon in both seventeenth-century and contemporary Holland. Although this is hardly ever made explicit, individuals in both periods use gifts to establish and maintain social ties, and in both periods gifts offered are expected to be reciprocated within a certain span of time. Several occasions, from calendar feasts to rites of passage as well as daily happenings, call for the offering of gifts. And depending on the character of the occasion, gifts are expected to be offered within certain social networks, be it a circle of family or friends, or a network of professional contacts. The types of gifts expected also depend on both the occasion and the network of exchange. As was shown, there are some novelties in contemporary gift exchange in terms of gift types and gift moments within the occasions of exchange, but, generally speaking, the systems of exchange are quite similar for both periods.

So without disregarding the peculiarities of gift exchange practices in either of these time periods, it has become clear that the most important difference between seventeenth-century and contemporary gift exchange is the cultural conventions that surround it. Whereas gift exchange in the seventeenth century was supposed to be referred to in terms of honour and obligation, gift exchange in contemporary Holland is supposed to be ruled by spontaneity and personal affections. Although these conventions might deny actual practices this is how gift exchange is supposed to be performed and discussed.

Conclusion

If anything has been clarified over the past few chapters, it has to be the fact that gift exchange is indeed an important social practice. Although human contact is possible without gifts, it is frequently accompanied and enriched by gifts, both in the seventeenth-century and contemporary society.[1] Gifts are exchanged on almost every occasion, sometimes big and splendid gifts are offered, at other times, just a plain cup of coffee. Gifts themselves are instruments: they are used to establish and maintain the social relationships people have. Gifts are employed to initiate social contact and they are used to reaffirm the connection once contact is established.

Still this does not mean that they are solely instruments. Gifts are also signs that have meanings. Gifts are signs of the existence of a relationship, but they can also refer to the ritual status, the social reputation of the recipient, or to the character of the relationship between the donor and the recipient. The signifying quality of the gift is culturally bound. What a gift can mean or cannot mean is governed by cultural conventions. Conventions set the boundaries for the behaviour that is considered appropriate within a gift-exchange relationship, both in terms of practice and the discourse on this practice.

In seventeenth-century Holland, the convention was that gifts were signs of the honour in which the recipient was held, and of the obligatory relationship that the donor and the recipient maintained. They were bound to each other by the expectation of reciprocity. Gifts offered would in time be returned, this was to be expected. Yet when reciprocation would follow and what this would consist of was not made explicit, but was sometimes acknowledged through the discourse of obligation. When offering or receiving a gift, people would in some cases express being obliged to each other, which expression confirmed the relationship that existed between the two parties.

The contemporary discourse on gift exchange in Holland is quite different. The convention prescribes that gifts are offered spontaneously, and when they are offered, the gifts are referred to in terms of affection. Gifts in contemporary Holland are supposed to express the personal feelings that exist between donor and receiver, without referring to a system of exchange. In practice, obligations to participate in gift exchange and expectations of reciprocity are probably as strong in contemporary Holland as they were in the seventeenth century, but this is not supposed to be acknowledged in the terminology that surrounds the exchange of gifts.

This is quite interesting, because it sheds new light on the idea that seventeenth-century terminology had a certain deceptive quality. In fact, it is precisely the contemporary discourse that seems to have the stronger tendency of denying the common features of gift exchange practices. Although the taboo on explicitness as described by Bourdieu applies to both periods in the sense that in both periods terms of reciprocation are not overtly discussed and prices of gifts are generally not made public, the seventeenth-century discourse does acknowledge the obligatory ties that exist between recipient and donor. Seventeenth-century discourse implies that the gift is part of a sequence of gifts, while in contemporary Dutch exchange the gift is supposed to be a spontaneous, singular event that does not relate to other gifts received earlier or expected later.[2]

Does this mean that seventeenth-century individuals were instrumental in maintaining their social relations? Yes, it does indeed, but the same applies to contemporary individuals. Yet seventeenth-century discursive conventions might suggest that they are more instrumental in their maintenance of social ties than contemporary individuals, but even that seems very unlikely. It is obviously difficult if not impossible to measure and compare levels of instrumentality, but if anything should *not* be taken as an accurate gauge, it is the discursive conventions of exchange, as the contemporary material has shown: although the prevailing idea is that gifts should be offered spontaneously without expectations of return, and should express personal sentiments, most gifts are purchased at department stores, offered when convention prescribes, and are usually followed by instant reciprocation. Still contemporary discourse is one of affection.

The question remains how a practice that during both periods has been basically very similar can be discussed so very differently. Although it was not the intention of this research to explain this fact, some explanations – that do not necessarily exclude each other and do need further research – can be suggested. First, one can reason along the lines of Elias's civilisation process.[3] In very general terms, this civilisation process can be clarified as a process in which western civilisation since the Middle Ages has slowly moved from explicitness to implicitness. Whereas people before ate with their hands, over time they started to use knives and forks. Whereas people before would not consider it inappropriate to spit, fart or blow one's nose – without a handkerchief – in public, these types of behaviour through time have become part of the very private sphere. The same can be said about sexuality and aggression: these activities used to be part of everyday public life, whereas in contemporary society they are both hidden and largely restricted. In general, one might say that the pure physical element of all of these activities has either come to be denied through the way they are performed or have come to be performed outside the public eye. According to Elias, these behavioural changes were accompanied by a change in language, or discourse. The same might be said about gift exchange: the very fundament of the gift-exchange system, reciprocity, through time has come to be denied through the way the exchange of gifts is supposed to be discussed.

The second explanation for the difference in discourse during these two periods might be found in the way seventeenth-century and contemporary society are organised. In seventeenth-century Holland, people in need largely depended on their families and friends for survival. Contemporary society is more individualistic with people depending on the welfare state, rather than their family. Since social contacts in seventeenth-century were so vital, the discourse on exchange sometimes needed to be as clear as possible. People needed to know explicitly what they could expect from other individuals in their social network. In that respect, the affectionate discourse on friendship and gift exchange in contemporary society might be one of the luxuries that a well-organised welfare state has to offer.

In any case, gift exchange as a practice is governed by both instrumentality and affection, and these are not mutually exclusive but interdependent.[4] Even though in contemporary discursive practices the existence of instrumentality within relationships is not highly appreciated and often denied, instrumentality is in fact a necessity for relationships to function in a normal way. The maintenance of social relationships largely depends on the instrumental, or reciprocal, character of the relationship. People maintain relationships not out of altruism, but out of self-interest: there is something they want out of their relationships. This want for reciprocity applies both to the activities – like the exchange of gifts – that people venture into and to the feelings they develop within a relationship. Even though one does not necessarily give in order to receive something in return and one does not necessarily love in order to be loved in return, it is preferable when gifts are reciprocated and feelings of love are mutual. It is precisely the fact that both parties want something from each other that the most balanced and rewarding relationships can exist.

This sounds a lot more cynical than it is. Imagine the opposite: A relationship is maintained by person X even though person Y has nothing to offer that is particularly pleasing to person X. In his eyes, person Y is not particularly interesting, funny, intelligent or attractive, but he maintains a relationship with person Y because otherwise it would be sad for person Y. One could say, that this relationship exists because of person X's altruism, which sounds very noble indeed, but one has to wonder whether person Y would appreciate knowing all this.[5] Y would prefer to have a relationship with X not out of pity but because X sincerely liked what Y had to offer. Y would in fact prefer the relationship to be instrumental.[6]

One might say that there is positive and negative instrumentality. It is not only through the offering of gifts that relationships are maintained, which makes gift exchange instrumental, but it is also through the offering of gifts that contact between two individuals – or groups of individuals – is actually established, which makes it not *solely* instrumental. By offering hospitality to friends and family, the individual creates an opportunity to spend time with the people he or she appreciates spending time with, which is obviously a positive type of instrumentality.

A relationship is truly instrumental, in the negative sense, when its sole aim is to get something outside the relationship that is being maintained.[7] In most cases of gift exchange, the goal of the exchange is the maintenance of the relationship as such, even though this sometimes implies that something outside the relationship is being offered or desired. An example can be taken from the seventeenth-century material: Badovere was not interested in maintaining a proper friendly relationship with Hooft, but just remained in contact with him because he needed to get his money back from Baudius. This is what made Hooft, even though he went through some efforts to take care of Badovere's business, feel slightly uncomfortable with the situation. David Beck also went to a lot of trouble to have his cousin appointed as an apothecary in the army, but this was not conceived as being problematic since there was a relationship between the two cousins regardless of the effort requested. That is to say, whereas it seems unlikely that Badovere and Hooft would have remained in contact if the one did not need this favour from the other, the two cousins maintained a relationship anyway and not just because the one might need a favour from the other at some point.

The awareness of the instrumental character of gift exchange is the result of a certain level of analysis. Even in an environment in which implicitness is the rule, some people manage to look at gift exchange with some distance and realise the mechanisms that are at play.[8] In the seventeenth-century, Johan de Brune, pensionary of Zeeland and author of several emblem books, reflected on gift exchange in an objective manner when he stated that "the first gift is the womb of the second", by which he obviously recognised the reciprocal character of gift exchange.[9] Furthermore, he claimed that "benefit is the cement and solder of contemporary friendship", which clearly shows that De Brune saw the instrumental character of social relations.[10] The same can be said for the contemporary mother who realises that her daughter's birthday party is very important within the social network of the child. Unsurprisingly, scholars are trained to look at the world more objectively, and the number of social scientists that realise that contemporary gift exchange is instrumental is high. But then historians have set out to describe instrumentality in social relations as a phenomenon that is typical for the early modern period.

How is that possible? First and foremost, because historians are supposed to only look at the period they are researching. A comparison between two or more countries is allowed by the conventions that govern contemporary history writing, as is a development through time, but a comparison in time is not. Yet it seems unavoidable that a historian needs some reference point when observing a culture that is so distant and yet so close to his own. He is bound to compare it with his own culture, but just not explicitly. And it is in this unconscious comparison that the cultural conventions come into play once more. Naturally, when one looks at the seventeenth century and sees people discussing gifts in terms of mutual obligation, this is a striking point, especially when one comes from an environment in which gifts are referred to in terms of affection.

Another issue that further blurs the historian's view on gift exchange in the early modern period is the notion of the bad gift, or rather the fact that historians deal with written records.[11] Bad gifts are gifts that are either meant to do harm or that go wrong unintentionally. Logically, these are the gifts that are most likely to turn up in written records. Gift exchange is a daily social practice and most of the time dealt with subconsciously, and there are hardly any words wasted on the exchange of gifts when things go well, and most of the time things did go well. However, as was shown in part III, the gift was likely to be explicitly discussed in relationships in which the gift had gone wrong. It is also obvious that the gift exchanges that went wrong show up in judicial records, and not the gift exchanges that went well. Thus, the historian is most likely to run into bad gifts, and might be left with the impression that gift exchange is "inevitably contentious".[12] Still, it seems that David Beck's diary is sufficient proof that a majority of the gifts were exchanged without any problems. When one considers the vast amounts of gifts exchanged within Beck's network alone, between several individuals, upon any type of occasion, and most of the time without any problems, it is clear that gift exchange in general must have been a benign activity.

Nevertheless, there is also a problem with David Beck and I can only discuss this properly by revealing myself as the author of this book. Some people might wonder how representative Beck is of seventeenth-century society. This is a question that I am reluctant to answer, because I am writing cultural history and not social history. The value of research like this is not in the statistical representativeness, but in the interpretation of the behaviour of an individual and its representation within his cultural context. The underlying idea is that this individual is a respected member of several social networks and embedded in his cultural environment, which makes him representative for his social and cultural context at large. Furthermore, the material that this one individual has to offer is placed in the larger context of seventeenth-century society. David Beck's diary is evaluated in comparison to other egodocuments and other types of sources, which I feel is a responsible way for a historian to deal with his material.

The problem with David Beck and I, the author, did not arise until his material was compared to the Letters to the Future. What I found in these letters was a group of people whose individual behaviour was largely consistent with that of the rest of the group, but whose behaviour did make me wonder about the representativeness of the group as a whole. Unlike the seventeenth-century culture, I can comprehend contemporary society through my experience with and my knowledge of it. Yet, what I found were practices of exchange that I recognise as fitting into this society, but that I do not recognise as being my own. For instance, I do celebrate my birthday, but I would not think of serving nuts, crisps and crackers with cheese. My image of self forces me to present myself in a way which includes Turkish bread, olives, *tapenade* and *tzatziki*.[13]

This obviously made me wonder about David Beck's position in seventeenth-century culture. Was he just any ordinary man or was he part of a subculture with exotic gift exchange habits? Did his German background make him very different from the "Dutch" in his environment? These are not problems that can be resolved in this conclusion and they might not even need to be resolved. David Beck may not be the perfect seventeenth-century man, but at least he offered an opportunity to get a glimpse of seventeenth-century gift-exchange practices.

Notes

Notes Introduction

1. Letters by Dorothea van Dorp are taken from Worp, *De briefwisseling van Constantijn Huygens 1608-1687* (The Hague 1911), but are also published in Smits-Veldt and Bakker eds., *In een web van vriendschap. Nederlandse vrouwen uit de zeventiende eeuw* (Amsterdam 1998).

2. Huygens had met Sir Robert and Lady Killigrew during his diplomatic visits to London, between 1621 and 1624. Killigrew was a member of the House of Commons and he and his wife were known for their hospitality to the English cultural elite of this period. See: Blom, *Constantijn Huygens. Mijn leven verteld aan mijn kinderen in twee boeken* (Amsterdam 2003).

3. Dorothea van Dorp: 24-03-1624. Translations of all Dutch quotes to English by the author.

4. Dorothea van Dorp: 23-05-1624.

5. Dorothea van Dorp: 23-05-1624.

6. See: Van Nierop, *Van ridders tot regenten. De Hollandse Adel in de zestiende en de eerste helft van de zeventiende eeuw* (The Hague 1984) 291.

7. Van der Aa, *Biographisch woordenboek de Nederlanden* (unchanged reprint 1969) [1852-1878] VII.

8. See: Wijsenbeek-Olthuis ed. *Het Lange Voorhout. Monumenten, mensen en macht* (Zwolle and The Hague 1998).

9. For a discussion of the women in Huygens's circles see: Keesing, *Het volk met lange rokken. Vrouwen rondom Constantijn Huygens* (Amsterdam 1993).

10. Bourdieu describes this taboo on explicitness in his chapter "The Economy of Symbolic Goods" in *Practical Reason* (Cambridge 1998) 96.

11. Unless otherwise noted, contemporary society specifically means turn of the century (20th to 21st) Dutch society. Yet a number of the conventions ascribed to modern-day Dutch society also apply to Western society as a whole, whereas others can be considered as typical of Dutch society. For instance, the wrapping of presents can be considered as part of western gift-exchange practices as a whole, while the celebration of St. Nicholas Eve with an extensive exchange of gifts is largely specific to Dutch gift-exchange practices.

12. This broad interpretation of what gifts are is largely taken from Komter, *The Gift. An Interdisciplinary Perspective* (Amsterdam 1996) 110.

13. See also: Komter "Reciprocity as a Principle of Exclusion: Gift Giving in the Netherlands", *Sociology* 30, 2 (1996) 305. In this article a similar definition of the gift is proposed.

14. For discussions of this so-called orthodox and revisionist view of family relations and the black and white legends with regard to the history of child-

rearing practices in Dutch history see: Dekker, *Uit de schaduw in 't grote licht. Kinderen in egodocumenten van de Gouden Eeuw tot de Romantiek* (Amsterdam 1995); Haks, "Continuïteit en verandering in het gezin van de vroegmoderne tijd." in *Vijf eeuwen gezinsleven. Liefde, huwelijk en opvoeding in Nederland*, Peeters, Dresden-Coenders and Brandebarg eds. (Nijmegen 1986) 31-56; Van der Heijden, *Huwelijk in Holland. Stedelijke rechtspraak en kerkelijk tucht 1550-1700* (Amsterdam 1998); Roberts, *Through the keyhole. Dutch child-rearing practices in the 17th and 18th century. Three urban elite families* (Hilversum 1998); Sturkenboom, *Spectators van de hartstocht. Sekse en emotionele cultuur in de achttiende eeuw* (Hilversum 1998).

15. Ariès, *L'Enfant et la vie familiale sous l'ancien régime* (Paris 1960); Flandrin, *The Family in Former Times. Kinship, Household and Sexuality* (Cambridge, 1979) [1976]; Shorter, *The Making of the Modern Family* (New York 1975); Stone, *The Family, Sex and Marriage in England 1500-1800* (London, 1977).

16. See: Badinter, *L'Amour en plus. Histoire de l'amour maternel (XVIIe-XIX siè-cle)* (Paris 1980). Also interesting in this respect is Schama's claim that the Dutch in the seventeenth-century were unique in the way they cherished their children: Schama, *The Embarrassment of Riches: An Interpretation of Dutch Culture in the Golden Age* (London and New York 1987) 481-545. This claim has been rejected by Dekker and Groenendijk on the grounds that this was neither unique to the Dutch, nor the seventeenth-century: Dekker and Groenendijk, "The Republic of God or the Republic of children? Childhood and child-rearing after the Reformation. An appraisal of Simon Schama's thesis about the uniqueness of the Dutch case", *Oxford Review of Education* XVII (1991) iii 317-335.

17. On calculated or instrumental friendship, see: Aymard, "Friends and Neighbors" in *A History of Private Life*, Ariès and Duby, eds. (Harvard 1989) [1986] 453; Kooijmans, *Vriendschap en de kunst van het overleven in de zeventiende en achttiende eeuw* (Amsterdam 1997); "Vriendschap. Een 18e-eeuwse familiegeschiedenis", *Tijdschrift voor Sociale Geschiedenis* 28 (1992) 48-65; "Andries & Daniel. Vriendschap in de vroegmoderne Nederlanden", *Groniek. Historisch Tijdschrift* 130 (1995) 8-25; "Kwetsbaarheid en 'koopluider vriendschap'", in *Of bidden helpt? Tegenslag en cultuur in Europa, circa 1500-2000*, Gijswijt-Hofstra and Egmond, eds. (Amsterdam 1997) 61-70. See also the special issue of *Groniek. Historisch Tijdschrift* 132, 1995 on "Vroegmoderne vriendschap".

18. Labrie, "Eenzaamheid en sociabiliteit: Romantische vriendschap in Duitsland", *Groniek*, 68-86.

19. See: Kooijmans, *Vriendschap* and Schmidt, *Om de eer van de familie. Het geslacht Teding van Berkhout 1500-1950, een sociologische benadering* (Amsterdam 1986).

20. See: Macfarlane, *The family life of Ralph Josselin: A seventeenth-century clergyman. An essay in historical anthropology* (Cambridge 1970); Houlbrooke ed. *English Family Life, 1576-1716. An Anthology from Diaries* (Oxford 1988); Pollock, *Forgotten Children. Parent-child Relations from 1500-1900* (Cambridge 1983).

21. Frijhoff and Spies eds., *1650. Bevochten eendracht* (The Hague 1999) 213. Eng. translation: *1650. Hard won Unity*. Transl. Myra Scholz (Assen/ Palgrave 2004)

22. Research related to gift exchange in early modern history: Howell, *The marriage Exchange: Property, Social Place and Gender in the Cities of the Low Countries 1300-1550* (London 1998); McCants, *Civic Charity in a Golden Age: Orphan Care in Early Modern Amsterdam* (Chicago 1997); Muldrew, *The Economy of Obligation: The culture of Credit and Social Relations in Early Modern England* (New York 1998).

23. Davis, *The Gift in Sixteenth-Century France* (Wisconsin 2000). For an overview of research on gift related topics in medieval history, see: Algazi, Groebner, Jussen, eds., *Negotiating the Gift. Pre-Modern Figurations of Exchange* (Goettingen 2003)

24. See the debate on historical anthropology in Kalb, *Focaal. Tijdschrift voor antropologie* 26/27 (1996) "Historical Anthropology: the unwaged debate", and Frijhoff's introduction to historical anthropology in Te Boekhorst, Burke, and Frijhoff, eds. *Cultuur en maatschappij in Nederland 1500-1850. Een historisch-antropologisch perpectief* (Meppel and Amsterdam 1992).

25. See: Dekker, *Lachen in de Gouden Eeuw. Een geschiedenis van Nederlandse humor* (Amsterdam 1997); Knevel, *Het Haagse Bureau. Zeventiende-eeuwse ambtenaren tussen staatsbelang en eigenbelang* (Amsterdam 2001); Schmidt, *Overleven na de dood. Weduwen in Leiden in de Gouden Eeuw* (Amsterdam, 2001); Zijlmans, *Vriendenkringen in de zeventiende eeuw. Verenigingsvormen van het informele culturele leven te Rotterdam* (The Hague 1999).

26. For research on charity and poverty in Early-Modern Netherlands, see: Van Leeuwen, *The Logic of Charity. Amsterdam, 1800-1850* (New York 2000); Spaans, *Armenzorg in Friesland 1500-1800. Publieke zorg en particuliere liefdadigheid in zes Friese steden. Leeuwarden, Bolsward, Franeker, Sneek, Dokkum en Harlingen* (Hilversum and Leeuwarden, 1997); Van der Vlis, *Leven in armoede. Delftse bedeelden in de zeventiende eeuw* (Amsterdam, 2001); Van Wijngaarde, *Zorgen voor de kost. Armenzorg, arbeid, en onderlinge hulp in Zwolle 1650-1700* (Amsterdam, 2000).

27. Kooijmans, *Vriendschap*.

28. Schotel, *Het Oud-Hollandsch Huisgezin der zeventiende eeuw* (Haarlem 1867); *Het maatschappelijk leven onzer vaderen in de zeventiende eeuw* (Amsterdam 1905); Ter Gouw, *De Volksvermaken* (Haarlem 1871).

29. Mauss *Essai sur le Don* [1923]. English translations: Mauss, *The Gift: Forms and Function in Archaic Societies* (New York/London 1967); Mauss, *The Gift: The Form and Reason for Exchange in Archaic Society* (London 1990)

30. Ruffle, "Gift giving with emotions", *Journal of Economic Behaviour & Organization* 39, 4 (1999) 399. For a better understanding of the relationship between sentiments and gift exchange behaviour, see: Van de Ven, *Psychological sentiments and economic behaviour* (Tilburg 2003).

31. Godbout and Caillé, "The world of the gift", *Queens Quarterly* 3 (2000) 368.

32. Macharel, "Dons et réciprocité en Europe", *Archives européennes de sociologie* 24 (1983) 151-166, as cited in Davis, *The Gift in Sixteenth-Century France*, 6. Davis also describes a situation in which three different systems co-existed: the gift mode, the sales mode and the mode of coercion.

33. Davis, *The Gift in Sixteenth-Century France*, 7.

34. Levinson and Ponzetti (eds.), *Encyclopedia of Human Emotions*, "gift giving" written by Komter, 298-301.

35. See, for references to gifts as instruments with which to establish and maintain social ties: Belk, "Gift-giving behaviour" in Jagdish, *Research in*

Marketing (Greenwich 1979) 95-126; Caplow, "Christmas Gifts and Kin Networks", *American Sociological Review* 47, 3 (1982) 383-392; Cheal, "The Social Dimensions of Gift Behaviour", *Journal of Social and Personal Relationships* 3 (1986) 423-493; Ruth and Otnes, et al. (1999). "Gift Receipt and the Reformulation of Interpersonal Relationships" *Journal of Consumer Research* 25, 4 (1999): 385-402; Schmied, *Schenken. Ueber eine Form sozialen Handelns* (Opladen 1996). See, for references to gifts as signs of relationships: Goffman, *Interaction Ritual* (New York 1967) for gifts as tie signs; Godbout and Caillé (2000) "The world of the Gift" describes the gift as "an embodiment of a system of personal relationships". And see: Shuman, "Food Gifts-Ritual Exchange and the Production of Excess Meaning" *Journal of American Folklore*, 113 (2000) 450, in which gifts are seen as "a means to negotiate and display social relationships".

36. Schmied, *Schenken*, 33.

37. Cheal, *The Gift Economy* (London, New York 1988) 137 as cited in Schmied, *Schenken*, 34.

38. Gouldner, "The Norm of Reciprocity: A Preliminary Statement", *American Sociological Review*, 25 2 (1960) 176. Reprinted in Komter, *The Gift*, 49-66

39. On reciprocity, see also the classic texts of Malinowski, "The Principle of Give and Take", *Crime and Custom in Savage Society* (London 1970) 39-45 [1922], reprinted in Komter, *The Gift*. Levi-Strauss, "The Principle of Reciprocity" in Komter, *The Gift* [1949, Eng. trans. 1957] and Schwartz, "The Social Psychology of the Gift", *American Journal of Sociology* 73, 1 (1967) 1-11, also reprinted in Komter, *The Gift*. Furthermore, see: Altman, "Reciprocity of interpersonal exchange" *Journal on the Theory of Social Behaviour* 3 (1973) 249-261; Caplow, "Christmas Gifts and Kin Networks", *American Sociological Review* 47, 3 (1982) 383-392; Komter and Vollebergh, "Gift Giving and the Emotional Significance of Family and Friends" *Journal of Marriage and the Family* 59 (1997) 747-757 and Rider, "A Game-theoretic interpretation of Marcel Mauss' 'The Gift'", *Social Science Journal* 3, 2 (1998) 203-212.

40. Komter, *The Gift*, 110. The distinction between subjective truth and objective reality is made by Bourdieu in "The Work of Time", *The Logic of Practice*, (Cambridge 1990) 104 [1980] and again in *Practical Reason*, 95.

41. Schmied, *Schenken*, 36.

42. Komter, "Reciprocity as a Principle of Exclusion", *Sociology*, 30, 2 (1996) 313; Caplow, "Rule Enforcement Without Visible Means: Christmas Gift Giving in Middletown", *American Journal of Sociology* 89, 6 (1984) 1306-1323.

43. Malinowski, *Crime and Custom*, 40. This part is also quoted in Gouldner, "The Norm of Reciprocity", 170. Malinowksi's statement on these rules of conduct already implies a distinction between subjective experience and objective analysis.

44. Komter, *Sociology*, 313.

45. Giddens as cited in Komter, "Reciprocity as a Principle of Exclusion: Gift Giving in the Netherlands", *Sociology* 30, 2 (1996) 299-316.

46. Caplow, *American Journal of Sociology*, 1306-1323 and Caplow, "Christmas Gifts and Kin Networks", *American Sociological Review* 47, 3 (1982) 383-392.

47. Caplow, *American Journal of Sociology*, 1306.

48. Idem, 1322.

49. Komter, *The Gift*, 110.

50. See again: Bourdieu, *Practical Reason*, 96.

51. More or less the same question is posed in Komter, *The Gift* (1996) 110, and in Davis's introduction to *The Gift in Sixteenth-century France* (2000) 9. I feel entitled to pose and answer the same question since nothing is known about the practices of gift exchange in seventeenth-century Holland and I feel that these practices are a vital starting point. Moreover, this is the most straightforward way of posing the question.

52. In my approach, the discourse on gift exchange includes all of the verbal references to this topic, be it by ordinary individuals or by scholars. I assume that there was a prevailing discourse on seventeenth-century gift exchange, as there is now a on contemporary gift exchange, which was governed by convention. Convention prescribes both what should be done in practice and how it should be discussed and referred to.

53. For diplomatic exchange see: Windler, "Tribute and gift. Mediterranean diplomacy as cross-cultural communication" *Saeculum* 51, 1 (2000) 24-56; Windler, "Tributes and Presents in Franco-Tunesian diplomacy" *Journal of Early Modern History* 4, 2 (2000)169-199.

54. Presser, "Memoires als geschiedbron" in *Winkler Prins Encyclopedie VII* (Amsterdam and Brussels, 1958) 208-210; reprinted in Presser, *Uit het werk van Presser* (Amsterdam 1969) 277-282. See also: Brands, Von der Dunk, and Zwager. "Introductie" *Tijdschrift voor Geschiedenis* 83 (1970) 83 and Dekker, "Egodocumenten: een literatuuroverzicht" *Tijdschrift voor Geschiedenis* 101, (1988) 161.

55. Brands et al., *Tijdschrift voor Geschiedenis*, 145.

56. Von der Dunk, "Over de betekenis van egodocumenten. Een paar aantekeningen als in- en uitleiding", *Tijdschrift voor Geschiedenis*, 83 (1970), 151.

57. An overview of egodocuments in Dutch public collections has been produced by Lindeman, Scherf and Dekker eds., *Egodocumenten van Noord-Nederlanders uit de zestiende tot begin negentiende eeuw. Een chronologische lijst* (Rotterdam 1993). For examples of monographs on Dutch cultural history based on egodocuments see: Baggerman and Dekker, *Kind van de toekomst. De wondere wereld van Otto van Eck, 1780-1798* (Amsterdam 2005); Baggerman, *Een lot uit de loterij. Familiebelangen en uitgeverspolitiek in de Dordtse firma A. Blussé en zoon, 1745-1823* (The Hague 2000); Blaak, *Geletterde levens. Dagelijks leven en schrijven in de vroegmoderne tijd in Nederland 1624-1770* (Hilversum 2004); Dekker, *Uit de schaduw in 't grote licht. Kinderen in egodocumenten van de Gouden Eeuw tot de Romantiek* (Amsterdam 1995); Kooijmans, *Vriendschap en de kunst van het overleven in de zeventiende en achttiende eeuw* (Amsterdam 1997) and *Liefde in opdracht. Het hofleven van Willem Frederik van Nassau* (Amsterdam 2000); Pollmann, *Een andere weg naar God. De Reformatie van Arnoldus Buchelius (1565-1641)* (Amsterdam 2000); Roberts, *Through the keyhole. Dutch child-rearing practices in the 17th and 18th century. Three urban elite families* (Hilversum 1998).

58. Dekker, *Uit de schaduw*, 24-25

59. Dekker, 26-27.

60. Dekker, 27.

61. Dekker, 28.

62. On egodocuments and the development of the self, see: Burke, "Representations of the Self from Petrarch to Descartes" in Porter, ed., *Rewriting the Self: Histories from the Renaissance to the Present*, (London/New York 1997) 17-28; Masuch, *Origins of the Individualist Self: Autobiography and Self-Iden-*

tity in England, 1591-1791 (Cambridge 1997); Davis, "Boundaries and the Sense of Self in Sixteenth-Century France" in Heller and Sosna eds., *Reconstructing Individualism: Autonomy, Individuality and the Self in Western Thought*, (Stanford 1986) 53-63.

63. Frijhoff, *Wegen van Evert Willemsz. Een Hollands weeskind op zoek naar zichzelf 1607-1647* (Nijmegen 1995) 60-61.

64. Dekker, *Uit de schaduw*, 28.

65. Briggs and Burke, *A Social History of the Media* (Cambridge 2002) 44-45.

66. Dekker, 24.

67. Kooijmans, *Vriendschap, Liefde in opdracht*, and "Liefde in opdracht. Emotie en berekening in de dagboeken van Willem Frederik van Nassau," *Historisch Tijdschrift Holland* 30, 4/5 (1998) 231.

68. Briggs and Burke, *A Social History of the Media*, 24.

69. DB: 04-04-1624.

70. Frijhoff and Spies, *1650. Bevochten eendracht*, 168.

71. Van Tricht, *De briefwisseling van Pieter Corneliszoon Hooft* (Culemborg 1976-1979) 11-13.

72. Mostaert, *Nederduijtse Secretaris oft Zendbriefschrijver* (Amsterdam 1635).

73. Van Tricht, *De briefwisseling van Pieter Corneliszoon Hooft*, 15.

74. The manuscript can be found in the library of the municipal archive of The Hague, signature H s 420. The diary is published as David Beck, *Spiegel van mijn leven. Een Haags dagboek uit 1624*, Veldhuijzen ed. (Hilversum 1993).

75. Veldhuijzen, introduction to David Beck, *Spiegel van mijn leven*, 8-10.

76. DB: title page.

77. Ibid.

78. Ibid.

79. "*de voorleser*".

80. DB: 02-02-1624.

81. On social capital see: Kooijmans, *Vriendschap*; Schmidt, *Om de eer van de familie*.

82. Israel, *The Dutch Republic*, 342-343. See also: Lesger, *Handel in Amsterdam ten tijde van de Opstand. Kooplieden, commerciële expansie en verandering in de ruimtelijke economie van de Nederlanden ca. 1550–ca.1630* (Hilversum 2001).

83. For literature on Hooft, see: Dudok van Heel, "De familie van Pieter Cornelisz Hooft" in *Jaarboek van het Centraal Bureau voor Genealogie en het iconografisch Bureau* (1981) 68-108; Jansen, ed., *Omnibus Idem. Opstellen over P. C. Hooft ter gelegenheid van zijn 350ste sterfdag* (Hilversum 1997); Jansen, ed., *Zeven maal Hooft. Lezingen ter gelegenheid van de 350ste sterfdag van P.C. Hooft* (Amsterdam 1998); Van Tricht, *P.C. Hooft* (Arnhem 1951); Haasse and Gelderblom, *Het licht der schitterende dagen. Het leven van P.C. Hooft* (Amsterdam 1981).

84. Hooft, *Henrik de Grote. Zyn leven en bedryf* (Amsterdam 1626); *Neederlandsche histoorien, sedert de ooverdraght der heerschappye van kaizar Karel den Vyfden, op kooning Philips zynen zoon* (Amsterdam 1642). On his historic work, see: Groenveld, *Hooft als historieschrijver. Twee studies.* (Weesp 1981).

85. PC: 1139.

86. Busken Huet, *Het land van Rembrandt*, (Haarlem 1898). For a critique on the concept of the Muiderkring, see: Strengholt, "Over de Muiderkring." in *Een lezer aan het woord. Studies van L. Strengholt over zeventiende-eeuwse Ne-*

derlandse letterkunde, Duits, Leerintveld, Ter Meer and Van Strien, eds. (Muenster 1998) 75-88.

87. See also: Smits-Veldt, *Maria Tesselschade. Leven met talent en vriendschap* (Zutphen 1994).

88. Van Tricht ed. *De briefwisseling van Pieter Corneliszoon Hooft* (3 vols. Culemborg 1976-1979). Part I covers 1599-1630; Part II, 1630-1637; and Part III, 1638-1647. On the culture of correspondence among the Dutch elite, see: Ruberg, *Conventionele correspondentie. Briefcultuur van de Nederlandse elite, 1770-1850* (Nijmegen 2005).

89. Hermanus Verbeeck, *Memoriaal ofte mijn levensraijsinghe* (Hilversum 1999), edited and introduced by Jeroen Blaak. The manuscript can be found in the Stadsbibliotheek Haarlem, hs. 187 A4 en A5.

90. See: Blaak's introduction in the edited autobiography, 9.

91. Ibid.

92. On the Dutch school system, see: Frijhoff and Spies, *1650*, 237-256.

93. Blaak, "Inleiding", 13.

94. Blaak, "Inleiding", 15.

95. HV: 45.

96. "The life of man on earth is a struggle", Job cap. 7 and "Rather dead than alive".

97. Blaak, "Inleiding", 22.

98. Blaak, 25.

99. Willem Frederik kept diaries in office almanacs which have been published by Visser ed., *Gloria Parendi. Dagboeken van Willem Frederik, stadhouder van Friesland, Groningen en Drenthe, 1643-1649, 1651-1654* (The Hague 1995). The manuscript is kept in the Koninklijk Huisarchief, inventory number VIII 3 I-IV, VIII 4 and VIII 2 I-III.

100. Israel, *The Dutch Republic*, 305.

101. Van der Plaat, "Inleiding", in Visser ed. *Gloria Parendi*, x-xi.

102. Ibid., x.

103. Visser, *Gloria Parendi*. His original diaries are kept at the Royal Archives in The Hague and were published by order of the Dutch Historic Association.

104. WF: 320-321.

105. Kooijmans, "Liefde in opdracht. Emotie en berekening in de dagboeken van Willem Frederik van Nassau" in: *Historisch Tijdschrift Holland* 4/5 (1998) 231.

106. WF: 269. Willem Frederik refers to dates using both the Julian calendar, which was still in use in Friesland at the time, and the Gregorian calendar, which was adopted by Holland. An example would be "20/30 Thursday".

107. Mauss makes a similar comparison between archaic society and his own in his *Essai sur le Don*. See: Mauss, *The Gift: Forms and Function in Archaic Societies* (New York/London 1967) especially part IV, 63-82.

108. Similar appeals were made earlier in both Sweden and Denmark, where the response turned out to be even bigger than in the Netherlands.

109. A small collection of these letters was first published in De Jong and Wijers eds., *Brieven aan de toekomst* (Utrecht 1999).

110. Holland and The Netherlands are not the same thing: Holland was just a province of the Dutch Republic, as the provinces Noord- and Zuid-Holland are part of The Netherlands today. When I speak about Holland in this book, I actually mean Holland and not The Netherlands.

111. The letters were processed by the Meertens Institute to properly preserve and catalogue them. This cataloguing system also includes references to the topics that are discussed within the letters.

Notes Part I: Practices of Gift Exchange

1. Davis, *The Gift in Sixteenth-Century France*, 15. On this broad early-modern sense of friendship, see: Davis, 19-20 and Kooijmans, *Vriendschap*, 14-18.
2. In English, the Dutch word *burger* can be translated as burgher, but the word *burgerlijk* is translated as bourgeois, which does not quite cover the meaning of the word. See also: Schama, *Embarrassment of Riches*, 7.
3. Part II will discuss some specific examples of rites of passage gifts and the gift of hospitality in further detail, whereas Part III focuses on a number of specific relationships and networks of exchange. It is in these chapters that the patterns as described here on the basis of the dairy of David Beck will be contextualised.
4. DB: 17-01-1624.
5. DB: 20-09-1624.
6. DB: 02-12-1624.
7. Dekker, *Uit de schaduw*, 43: Likewise, Constantijn Huygens in describing the childhood of his children did not mention their birthdays.
8. Comments on his birthday WF: 23 (1643), 62 (1644), 156 (1645), 265 (1646), 421 (1647), 549 (1648), and 686 (1649). For the period 1651-1654 references to his birthdays are lacking since the diaries only include the first months of the year (1651) or only the first days of the year (1652-1654).
9. WF: 23, 62, 156, 265.
10. WF: 421, 686. In 1648 Willem Frederik did not feel well on his birthday, which might explain the matter of fact account of his birthday.
11. Van Alkemade and Van der Schelling, *Nederlands Displegtigheden vertoonende de plegtige gebruiken aan den Dis, in het houden van maaltijden en het drinken der gezondheden*, 3 vols. (Rotterdam 1732-1735). On Van Alkemade, see: Rooijakkers, "Vieren en Markeren" in *Volkscultuur* (Nijmegen 2000) 174.
12. Van Alkemade, *Nederlands Displegtigheden*, I, 166. Van Alkemade based himself on Calvin's commentary on the evangelistic harmony, in which he discussed the occasion of the birthday of Herodus in Matthew XIV:6.
13. Ibid., 169.
14. WF: 84 (1644).
15. Van Alkemade, I, 175.
16. Interestingly, the likes of P.C. Hooft and Tesselschade Roemers Visscher were in fact celebrating the *verjaring* of their weddings by offering a dinner to friends and family. PC: 606 and PC: 1127. (The Dutch word *verjaring* or *verjaardag* can be translated as both birthday and anniversary.)
17. Bouwman, *Nederlandse gelegenheidsgedichten voor 1700 in de Koninklijke Bibliotheek te 's-Gravenhage. Catalogus van gedrukte gedichten op gedenkwaardige gebeurtenissen in het leven van particuliere personen* (Nieuwkoop 1982).
18. These poems were written for Debora Kivit (508), Ester en Maria van Hoogstraten (611), Mattheus van Nispen (624), and Willemijna Blooteling (637).

19. Davis, *The Gift*, 34.
20. All gift-exchange instances in the diary of David Beck were processed in a database, and analysed accordingly. General remarks on the gift-exchange practices of David Beck and his social environment are based on this database material. Specific examples and incidents are referred to by date of occurrence in the diary.
21. For Dutch eating habits in this period, see: Burema, *De voeding in Nederland van de Middeleeuwen tot de twintigste eeuw* (Assen 1953); Jobse-Van Putten, *Eenvoudig maar voedzaam. Cultuurgeschiedenis van de dagelijkse maaltijd in Nederland* (Nijmegen 1995); Schama, *The Embarrasment of Riches*, 129-188.
22. The one exception to this in the David Beck case will be discussed later.
23. See Jobse-Van Putten, *Eenvoudig maar voedzaam*, 165; foreign visitors have noted that they were only welcome to join a meal upon being invited.
24. DB: 30-09-1624, 05-09-1624.
25. DB: 29-01-1624.
26. DB: 09-12-1624.
27. For example DB: 23-01-1624, 31-03-1624, 10-04-1624, 01-11-1624; DB: 14-03-1624, 11-05-1624, 17-04-1624, 18-04-1624, 28-09-1624.
28. DB: 18-06-1624, 16-06-1624, 09-07-1624.
29. DB: 29-01-1624, 31-01-1624, 06-10-1624.
30. DB: 01-01-1624, 03-03-1624.
31. DB: 31-03-1624, 10-04-1624.
32. DB: 27-09-1624.
33. DB: 28-09-1624.
34. DB: 29-09-1624.
35. DB: 30-09-1624.
36. DB: 03-10-1624.
37. Kooijmans, *Vriendschap*, 173. He interprets sending received gifts as gifts to others as a negative gesture, whereas I do not feel it necessarily implies that someone who sends on presents is a miser, nor that it is not meant well. This is especially the case regarding foodstuffs that cannot be preserved; it just makes sense to make other people happy, if one is not able to enjoy all of the food alone.
38. DB: 08-08-1624. On the growing popularity of psalms in this period, see: Van Deursen, *Bavianen en slijkgeuzen. Kerk en kerkvolk ten tijde van Maurits en Oldenbarnevelt* (Assen 1974) 173; Frijhoff, *Wegen van Evert Willemsz.* 326-332.
39. DB: 29-09-1624.
40. DB: 17-01-1624.
41. DB: 23-02-1624, 09-05-1624, 28-09-1624, 10-11-1624, 29-11-1624.
42. See the first page of Van Alkemade, *Displegtigheden* and 314-331.
43. Roodenburg has pointed out the important social function of drinking in the maintenance of friendship in *Onder censuur*, 338.
44. DB: 27-01-1624. See: Roodenburg, *Onder censuur*, 341.
45. Davis, *The Gift in Sixteenth-Century France*, 53.
46. See for example DB: 25-01-1624, 30-08-1624, 10-11-1624. In these cases, he noted that he had his *portie*, or *maeltyt* at the family member's or friend's home, or he noted that he had been their guest.
47. Schotel's remark that, except for the occasional trip for study, business or visiting relatives, seventeenth-century people rarely travelled and preferred

to stay home is obviously untrue. Schotel, *Het Oud-Hollandsch Huisgezin der zeventiende eeuw* (Haarlem 1867) 2.

48. DB: 04-04-1624.
49. DB: 04-04-1624.
50. DB: 01-08-1624.
51. DB: 17-09-1624.
52. DB: 25-08-1624 till 30-08-1624.
53. Daughter Roeltje was still staying with the wet-nurse at this point. She returned to the household on the 8ᵗʰ of September. Diliane was not too pleased with having the infant in the house as well; David and she argued about her return. (DB: 19-08-1624) It almost seems as if Diliane's trip was meant to compensate for her extra work load.
54. DB: 02-07-1624 till DB: 04-07-1624.
55. DB: 03-07-1624 and DB: 04-07-1624. In September, Eva and two of her children spent another two nights at David's place. DB: 05-09-1624 till 07-09-1624.
56. DB: 18-03-1624.
57. See also: Schotel, *Oude zeden en gebruiken in Nederland* (Leiden, n.d.) 51-52; he describes small amounts of money and drinks as *foy*, yet in Beck's case it is clear that it meant meals. The term *foy* derives from the French *voye*, which means "way". The Dutch still call tips left in restaurants and bars *fooi*.
58. DB: 22-03-1624.
59. *Jonkheer* Josse de Bils, according to Veldhuijzen, *Spiegel van mijn leven*, 237.
60. DB: 28-01-1624, 30-01-1624, 09-02-1624.
61. DB: 22-02-1624, 28-02-1624.
62. DB: 10-03-1624.
63. DB: 11-03-1624.
64. Davis, *The gift in Sixteenth-Century France*, 23. Other references to New Year's Day as an important occasion for the offering of gifts: Ter Gouw, *Volksvermaken*, 109 and Cressy, *Bonfires and Bells: National Memory and the Protestant Calendar in Elizabethan and Stuart England* (London 1989), 16. The latter argues that gift giving on 1 January refers to the biblical gifts offered on Epiphany, which seems unlikely. As Davis points out, it was a tradition that went back to the Romans, *The Gift*, 23. The French word *étrennes* is actually derived from the Roman *strenae*.
65. Bredero, *Moortje*, [Amsterdam 1617] 193; Cats, *Alle de wercken van Jacob Cats* (Amsterdam 1667) 150-151.
66. Van Alkemade, *Nederlands Displegtigheden*,, I, 412.
67. DB: 02-01-1624.
68. Davis, *The Gift*, 24. This is an example of a New Year's gift that was offered by an individual of a lower social class to someone in a higher class, which is similar to Davis's observation that occasionally *étrennes* could also climb up the social ladder.
69. DB: 22-03-1624.
70. DB: 03-03-1624, 11-02-1624.
71. DB: 06-05-1624, 28-09-1624.
72. DB: 24-03-1624.
73. DB: 18-02-1624.
74. DB: 18-02-1624.

75. DB: 19-02-1624.

76. DB: 21-02-1624.

77. Schotel, *Het Oud-Hollandsch Huisgezin*, 393, quotes Lodovido Guicciardini, an Italian nobleman who, in his descriptions of the Netherlands, said that the Dutch were in the habit of inviting family and friends to make good cheer, and that they were not averse to travelling 25 to 40 miles to join the party.

78. WF: 325, 332, 346 and 742.

79. In English, Shrove Tuesday can actually be referred to as "Pancake Tuesday". See also: Cressy, *Bonfires and Bells*, 18. Like Cressy, I also do not wish to go into carnival in terms of "hierarchical inversion, theatrical mimesis, reaffirmative reintegration, liminal transgression, or latent control". I feel that in keeping with the focus of this research it is sufficient to note that *vastelavond*, as it is described by David Beck, was an occasion for socialising and hospitality.

80. Considering the contention of some historians that love of one's children was not highly developed in this early-modern period, it is interesting to note that children were often actually invited on their own account.

81. For literature on the fair in the Netherlands, see: Keyser, "Kermis in Nederland tot het einde van de 19e eeuw." *Nederlands Volksleven* 28 (1978) 73-80; Strouken, ed. "Kermis; special issue" of *Volkscultuur*, 5, 1988; Van Zoonen, "De kermis in de 17de eeuw (1572-1700)" (Hoorn 1996).

82. Rooijakkers, *Rituele Repertoires*, 395.

83. Haks, *Huwelijk en gezin in Holland*, 80.

84. DB: 26-04-1624.

85. Rooijakkers, *Rituele Repertoires*, 401, has also pointed out this connection between the *kermis*, family visits, and cleaning.

86. DB: 30-04-1624, 01-05-1624. St. James – Jacob in Dutch – was the patron saint of the parish church in The Hague and May 1st was the day of his commemoration (as well as of St. Philip). According to Cressy, *Bonfires and Bells*, 21-22, the celebration of May Day in early-modern England was sanctioned by the church because it was associated with the commemorations of both Saint Philip and Saint James, but the May rituals, like raising of the Maypole, were of pagan origin. On Maypoles see also: Schotel, *Het Oud-Hollandsch Huisgezin der zeventiende eeuw* (Haarlem 1867) 203-205.

87. DB: 04-05-1624 till 09-05-1624.

88. DB: 05-05-1624.

89. WF: 135.

90. DB: 06-05-1624.

91. DB: 09-05-1624.

92. DB: 12-05-1624. The *Haagse kermis* is still a household name in parts of the contemporary Netherlands. For a discussion of the Haagse kermis, see also: Wijsenbeek-Olthuis ed., *Het Lange Voorhout*, 70-72.

93. DB: 23-05-1624.

94. According to Van der Aa's *Biographisch Woordenboek*, Johannes Meurs (1579-1639), or Meurskens as Beck called him, was a professor of Greek and history at the University of Leiden during this period. In 1625, he was appointed to the University of Soro in Denmark.

95. DB: 27-05-1624.

96. PC : 983.

97. DB: 12-06-1624.

98. DB: 16-06-1624. Beck uses the expression *"goede sier maken"* whenever he is well received by his hosts. This seems to have been a common expression; it is also used in other seventeenth-century egodocuments. The English equivalent would be "good cheer".

99. DB: 19-09-1624.

100. DB: 21-09-1624.

101. DB: 23-09-1624.

102. DB: 22-09-1624.

103. DB: 29-05-1624.

104. DB: 19-06-1624.

105. DB: 26-09-1624.

106. For a discussion of the international ox trade in the early-modern period see: Gijsbers, *Kapitale ossen. De internationale handel in slachtvee in Noordwest-Europa* (Hilversum 1999).

107. Jobse-Van Putten, *Eenvoudig maar voedzaam*, 171, suggests that this is a general trend in Dutch feasting during this period. People preferred food quantity over quality, and were especially keen on drinking.

108. DB: 14-01-1624. Interestingly enough, Beck also mentions a *harst* dinner at the beginning of the year. On 14 January, he was invited by Jan Willemsz Swaertveger and his wife to attend their *harst* dinner. *"Ende waren naer de gelegenheijt des tyts te zamen goede dingen ende zoet in stilligheijt ende modestie"*. It is not quite clear what the occasion was, nor what led them to celebrate is such a silent and modest manner.

109. References to the ox market in David Beck's diary. DB: 28-10-1624: "great ox market, therefore no school"; DB: 04-11-1624, 11-11-1624, 18-11-1624, 25-11-1624. On 11 November Beck notes that it is the last ox market of the year, but the following week Beck orders some meat, and the week after that he is again invited to a *harst* dinner.

110. DB: 28-10-1624.

111. Schotel, *Het Oud-Hollandsch Huisgezin*, 375-376. Schotel describes the rituals of the slaughter season, yet does not refer to this period or the meals as *harst*.

112. This is translated by Schama as "The Wise Cook or Painstaking Housholder", *Embarrassment of Riches*, 158.

113. This can be translated as "Dutch Slaughter Time".

114. Witteveen ed., *De verstandighe kock, of sorghvuldige huys-houdster* (Amsterdam 1993) Facsimile reprint of the 1670 edition.

115. DB: 06-11-1624.

116. DB: 10-11-1624.

117. DB: 16-11-1624.

118. DB: 16-11-1624.

119. DB: 13-11-1624.

120. DB: 18-11-1624.

121. DB: 18-11-1624.

122. DB: 05-12-1624. See also DB: 05-01-1624, when the Winter King of Bohemia was celebrating Epiphany. In this case, Beck also referred to the Catholic character of the celebration; *"S. Excellentie [...] hielen ten dage (op zyn Roomsch) drie Cooningen-Avont"*.

123. DB: 05-12-1624. Schotel, *Het Oud-Hollandsch Huisgezin*, 217, confirms that the celebration of St. Nicholas Eve in seventeenth-century Holland was quite tumultuous. Roodenburg, *Onder censuur*, 33, refers to complaints about these stalls to the authorities.

124. Van Leer, *Geven rond Sinterklaas* (Amsterdam 1995) 49.

125. Ter Gouw, *Volksvermaken*, 259-260; Schotel, *Het Oud-Hollandsch Huisgezin*, 217, 319; Van Leer, *Geven rond Sinterklaas*, 50-52; Rooijakkers, *Rituele repertoires*, 451-459, discusses the Reformed aversion to the Epiphany, St. Martin and *Sinterklaas*.

126. DB: 06-12-1624.

127. Bredero, *Moortje*, 192-193.

128. Van Leer, *Geven rond Sinterklaas*, 50.

129. Cressy, *Bonfires and Bells* offers an interesting insight into how pagan, Catholic and Protestant ritual calendars intermingled in early-modern England.

130. Veldhuijzen in introduction of Beck, *Spiegel van mijn leven*, 12.

131. DB: 07-04-1624, 16-05-1624, 26-05-1624.

132. DB: 07-04-1624.

133. DB: 27-03-1624. Cressy. *Bonfires and Bells*, 19; in early-modern England, Easter was the favourite occasion for taking communion. According to Van Deursen it was one of the tasks of the schoolmaster to provide catechism, *Bavianen en slijkgeuzen*. 161.

134. Davis specifically describes the Christian holidays as moments for charitable offerings, *The Gift*, 25-26.

135. DB: 24-12-1624 till 29-12-1624.

136. DB: 28-12-1624.

137. See: WF: 94, 139, 141,190, 226, 232, 235, 319, 374, 393 for references to Christian holidays in the diary of Willem Frederik. WF: 319 refers to Christmas; Willem Frederik had dinner alone that evening.

138. This confirms Roodenburg's suggestion that festivities like *vastelavond* were probably celebrated more and more within the confines of private homes. *Onder censuur*, 332.

139. DB: 18-03-1624.

140. DB: 28-03-1624.

141. DB: 31-03-1624.

142. DB: 03-04-1624.

143. DB: 18-04-1624.

144. DB: 06-05-1624.

145. The marriage ritual and wedding gifts will be discussed in further detail in Part II.

146. DB: 04-04-1624.

147. Hufton, *The prospect Before Her: A History of Women in Western Europe* (New York 1998) 186.

148. Schotel, *Het Oud-Hollandsch Huisgezin*, 25.

149. KB, hss 129 D 16, Dagboek Pieter Teding van Berkhout, 06-04-1670.

150. DB: 04-04-1624.

151. The Dutch word for these dinners was *kraammaal*. The word *kraam* refers to everything that has to do with childbirth and for which there is – as far as I know – no single English word. For instance: *kraambezoek* means maternity visit, and *kraamheer* means father of the new-born child.

152. Schotel, *Het Oud-Hollandsch Huisgezin*, 27. Other traditions that surrounded birth described by Schotel are the offering of the *kindermaanstick* to the neighbourhood children that came to see the new-born child and the hanging of a *kloppertje* which indicated the sex of the child on the door. There is no hint of these traditions in Beck's descriptions.

153. PC: 795.

154. PC: 799.

155. DB: 08-04-1624. Veldhuijzen suggests that the term *compeer* is used to refer to a specific type of friend who serves as a role model and in some cases, is also someone in the same line of business. Beck's use of the term, however, suggests that he used it to refer both to godfathers and godchildren. (But he also used the term *peet* for both male and female christening witnesses.) Beck used the term *gevaertje* for the wife of his *compeer* Matthijs Muller. Aymard in "Friends and Neighbors", 469, discusses the French term *compérage*, the English *godchild* and the German *Gevatter* and *Gevatterin*. He did not explicitly distinguish between a christening witness (godparent) and a person with the same godparent either.

156. DB: 11-04-1624. In Jaccomijntje's case, Beck used the term *petemoey*, which means godmother.

157. All christenings of relatives of the Becks and other relations were checked in the Delft archives.

158. DTB Delft inv. nr. 55 Doopboek Nieuwe Kerk folio 2.

159. DB: 15-04-1624.

160. DB: 10-12-1624; Beck commemorates in his diary that his wife had died one year ago.

161. DB: 08-01-1624.

162. DB: 23-01-1624.

163. DB: 10-10-1624.

164. DB: 07-02-1624.

165. DB: 11-02-1624.

166. DB: 30-08-1624.

167. See also: Noordegraaf and Valk, *De Gave Gods. De pest in Holland vanaf de late middeleeuwen* (Baarn 1988).

168. DB: 01-08-1624.

169. DB: 27-08-1624.

170. DB: 27-08-1624 and 28-08-1624.

171. DB: 02-06-1624, 13-09-1624 and 07-10-1624.

172. DB: 29-08-1624.

173. DB: 30-09-1624.

174. DB: 01-10-1624.

175. DB: 01-10-1624.

176. DB: 22-09-1624.

177. DB: 13-06-1624, 31-08-1624, and 01-09-1624.

178. DB: 08-03-1624.

179. DB: 06-03-1624.

180. DB: 29-07-1624.

181. For example, DB: 13-11-1624.

182. Ter Gouw, *De Volksvermaken*, 549.

183. Schotel, *Het maatschappelijk leven onzer vaderen in de zeventiende eeuw* (Amsterdam 1905) 390.

184. DB: 23-02-1624 and 29-11-1624.
185. DB: 29-01-1624.
186. This is the Crispijn van den Queeborn (1604-1652) who is still known as an artist from this period.
187. DB: 24-09-1624.
188. Van Alkemade, *Nederlandse Displegtigheden*. Vol I, 330.
189. Idem, 331.
190. DB: 09-08-1624.
191. That this type of support can in some cases be considered a (disputable) gift, will be shown in chapter III.
192. DB: 08-05-1624.
193. DB: 04-06-1624.
194. DB: 06-06-1624.
195. DB: 07-06-1624.
196. DB: 09-06-1624.
197. DB: 27-05-1624.
198. DB: 23-06-1624.
199. DB: 27-06-1624.
200. DB: 13-12-1624.
201. DB: 05-04-1624.
202. DB: 06-04-1624.
203. DB: 25-07-1624.
204. DB: 22-08-1624.
205. DB: 17-05-1624.
206. Poems as dinner invitation, DB: 16-02-1624/18-02-1624, 12-06-1624; poems as wedding gifts, DB: 26-04-1624, 17-07-1624; poems to friends and patrons in Amsterdam, DB: 26-01-1624, 25-06-1624, 18-11-1624, 20-12-1624.
207. See: Frijhoff, "Burgerlijk dichtplezier in 1650?" *Spiegel der Letteren* 43-3 (2001) 248-269.
208. DB: 26-01-1624. In light of this research, it is interesting to note that the copies of poems Christina Poppings sent to Beck were poems written by P.C. Hooft on the occasion of Tesselschade Roemers Visscher's marriage to Allard Crombalck. The other gossip was that Anna Roemers Visscher had "also been the bride".
209. DB: 26-01-1624.
210. DB: 17-07-1624.
211. See: Schenkeveld-van der Dussen, "Poëzie als gebruiksartikel; gelegenheidsgedichten in de zeventiende eeuw", in *Historische Letterkunde*, Spies, ed. (Groningen 1984) 75-92.
212. De Jong and Wijers, eds. *Brieven aan de toekomst* (Utrecht 1999), 61.
213. DB: 13-01-1624.
214. DB: 01-10-1624.
215. DB: 30-09-1624, 22-11-1624. Jobse-Van Putten, *Eenvoudig maar voedzaam*, 88.
216. Jobse-Van Putten, *Eenvoudig maar voedzaam*, 87.
217. Roeltje returned home, DB: 08-09-1624. On sugar trade in the seventeenth-century see: Poelwijk, *"In dienste vant suyckerbacken"*. *De Amsterdamse suikernijverheid en haar ondernemers, 1580-1630* (Hilversum 2003).
218. DB: 03-10-1624.

219. DB: 22-07-1624.

220. DB: 17-02-1624.

221. This also shows through the correspondences of P.C. Hooft and Maria van Reigersberch.

222. DB: 26-09-1624.

223. Haks discusses the importance of neighbours in *Huwelijk en gezin in Holland in de 17de en 18de eeuw* (Assen 1982), 48, 58. He also refers to *Haagse Buurtbrieven*, 62. Jacobs has written an interesting article on neighbours, social capital and gifts: Jacobs, "Sociaal kapitaal van buren. Rechten, plichten en conflicten in Gentse gebuurten (zeventiende-achttiende eeuw)" *Volkskundig Bulletin* 22-2 (1996): 149-176.

224. Davis, *The Gift in Sixteenth-century France*, 20-21.

225. Ter Gouw, *De Volksvermaken*, 549; Schotel, *Het maatschappelijk leven onzer vaderen*, 390; Roodenburg, "Naar een etnografie van de vroegmoderne stad: de "gebuyrten" in Leiden en Den Haag" in *Cultuur en maatschappij in Nederland 1500-1850, een historisch-antropologisch perspectief*, Te Boekhorst, Burke and Frijhoff, eds., (Amsterdam/Heerlen 1992) 239, the most important obligations neighbours in a neighbourhood had towards each other were related to birth, marriage and death.

226. Roodenburg, "Naar een etnografie van de vroegmoderne stad" 229.

227. DB: 06-06-1627.

228. See: Jacobs, "Sociaal kapitaal van buren", 149; Roodenburg, "Naar een etnografie van een vroegmoderne stad", 239. Neighbours in The Hague were obligated to attend funerals.

Notes Part II: Gifts and Meanings

1. In fact, the use of the term mourning is unnecessary in this respect, since contemporary ethnologists also count funerals on the list of "celebrations". Celebration, to them, is any event that is celebrated ritually. See: Rooijakkers, "Vieren en Markeren", 183.

2. Van Gennep, *Les Rites de Passage* (Chicago 1960) [1909]. Interesting research on this topic has been published by: Boissevain, *Revitalizing European Rituals* (London 1992); Muir, *Ritual in Early Modern Europe* (Cambridge 1997); Rooijakkers, *Rituele repertoires* (Nijmegen 1994). These authors all deal with rituals that connect to life's important events and events connected to the yearly calendar.

3. Muir, *Ritual in Early Modern Europe*, 16, distinguishes between calendrical rites and rites of passage.

4. For literature on marriage in early-modern Holland, see: Haks, *Huwelijk en gezin in Holland in de 17de en 18de eeuw. Processtukken en moralisten over aspecten van het laat 17de- en 18de-eeuwse gezinsleven* (Assen 1982); Van der Heijden, *Huwelijk in Holland. Stedelijke rechtspraak en kerkelijk tucht 1550-1700* (Amsterdam 1998); Roodenburg, *Onder censuur. De kerkelijke tucht in de gereformeerde gemeente van Amsterdam, 1578-1700* (Hilversum 1990).

5. JC: 51.

6. Ibid.

7. Art historian Wayne Franits discusses "images of domestic virtue" in order to describe ideal-typical behaviour for Dutch women in this period by following the structure of Cats's *Houwelick*; Franits *Paragons of Virtue* (Cambridge,1993).

8. See: Cats, *Huwelijk*, Sneller and Thijs, eds. (Amsterdam 1993), epilogue, 197.

9. JC: 69.

10. Ibidem.

11. See: De Mare, "The Domestic Boundary as Ritual Area in Seventeenth-Century Holland" in *Urban Rituals in Italy and the Netherlands: Historical Contrasts in the Use of Public Space, Architecture and the Urban Environment*, De Mare and Vos, eds. (Assen 1993); De Mare, "De keuken als voorstelling in het werk van Simon Stevin en Jacob Cats" in *Van alle markten thuis: vrouwen- en genderstudies in Nederland*, Bouw, De Bruijn and Van der Heiden, eds. (Amsterdam 1994). De Mare uses literature, architectural and visual sources to argue that the house in seventeenth-century Holland was the woman's domain. One of the sources that is central to her argument is Cats's *Houwelick*.

12. See: Van Deursen, *Mensen van klein vermogen. Het kopergeld van de Gouden Eeuw* (Amsterdam 1996) [1991] 19; Frijhoff, et al. *1650*, 191.

13. Kooijmans has discussed the strategic quality of Dutch marriages for both the civic elites, *Vriendschap en de kunst van het overleven*, 32 and for stadholder Willem Frederik, *Liefde in opdracht. Het hofleven van Willem Frederik van Nassau* (Amsterdam 2000) 17, 19. Although these are two well-written and interesting books, I do not agree with his line of reasoning that affection within social relations in this period was solely a means of hiding the instrumental nature of the relationship. See, for example, his conclusion in *Vriendschap*, 326-329.

14. Haks, *Huwelijk en gezin in Holland*, 140. Van Deursen has also showed this for Graft and environment in *Een dorp in de polder. Graft in de zeventiende eeuw* (Amsterdam 1994), 228.

15. PC: 262.

16. PC: 264. The words she used according to Hooft were "*ick wenschte dat ik genegenheit hadde om te trouwen*". *Genegenheid* can mean both affection and inclination. Since she had already confessed her affections for Hooft, it seems she regretted her unwillingness to marry him despite these affections.

17. Van Tricht, *De Briefwisseling*, part I, 621.

18. PC: 263.

19. PC: 264.

20. PC: 264.

21. PC: 265.

22. Van Tricht, *De Briefwisseling*, part I, 631.

23. PC: 272, 273, 276, 277.

24. PC: 912, 928, 1037.

25. Schmidt, *Overleven na de dood. Weduwen in Leiden in de Gouden Eeuw* (Amsterdam 2001) 90-91, 219-220.

26. Another point is that even though people nowadays supposedly marry for love it does not necessarily make marriages happier nor more successful.

27. See: Bilker, "De huwelijken van Nassau-Dietz" in *Nassau uit de schaduw van Oranje*, Groeneveld, Huizinga and Kuiper, eds. (Franeker 2003) 73-74; Kooijmans, *Liefde in opdracht*, 17; Visser, ed., *Gloria Parendi*, introduction x.
28. WF: 85, 275, 276.
29. Visser ed. *Gloria Parendi*, introduction ix.
30. WF: 554.
31. WF: 293.
32. This was Sophie van Haren, daughter of Willem van Haren. See also: Kooijmans, *Liefde in opdracht*, 122-127.
33. WF: 599.
34. WF: 754.
35. JC: 72.
36. JC: 73.
37. JC: 80.
38. HY: 11.
39. DB: 08-03-1624.
40. JC: *Alle de Wercken*, 279.
41. For descriptions of how weddings were celebrated, see: Van Boheemen, ed. *Kent, en versint. Eer datje mint. Vrijen en trouwen 1500-1800* (Apeldoorn and Zwolle 1989); Spierenburg, ed. *In de jonkheid gaan. Over vrijen en trouwen 1500-1800. Themanummer Jeugd en samenleving*, 19, (1989) 609-736. For knowledge on the rituals of marriage, Dutch historians are still indebted to Schotel, *Het Oud-Hollandsch Huisgezin der zeventiende eeuw*, (Haarlem 1867).
42. For engagements see Schotel, *Oud-Hollandsch huisgezin*, 249.
43. Sweerts, *De tien vermakelijkheden van het huwelijk*, Grootes and Winkelman, eds. (Amsterdam 1988) [1678].
44. HS: 20.
45. Cats, *Alle de Wercken*, 288.
46. HS: 19 and 25.
47. See: Alkemade, *Nederlandse Displegtigheden*, II, 301-305. Sarti, *Europe at Home*, 153, also stresses the importance of hierarchy at the table, as does Muir, *Ritual in Early Modern England*, 131.
48. HS: 26.
49. DB: 01-04-1624.
50. Schotel, *Oud-Hollandsch huisgezin*, 256.
51. Alkemade, *Displegtigheden*, I, 193-194, 196. Burema also refers to the sumptuary laws, *De voeding in Nederland*, 99. These laws were far less common in the Dutch Republic than elsewhere.
52. Cats: 295.
53. Cats: 299.
54. PC: 1207, 1209, 1210.
55. Alkemade, *Displegtigheden*, I, 533.
56. See also: Heal, *Hospitality in Early Modern England* (Oxford 1990).
57. Other authors have discussed the ritual of *het schutten van de bruid*. This can be described as a type of forced gift exchange because the bride would be abducted by neighbourhood youngsters and would only be returned to the groom after he offered them (money for) drinks. See: Haks, *Huwelijk en gezin in Holland*, 67; Van der Heijde, *Huwelijk in Holland*, 211-212; Rooijakkers, *Rituele repertoires*, 347; Schotel, *Het Oud-Hollandsch huisgezin* 283-285.

58. Examples of counter-weddings in Hooft: PC: 736, 889.
59. See for example HV: 85-86.
60. Cats: 289.
61. Cats: 293.
62. This seems to have been common in most parts of Europe, see Sarti, *Europe at Home*, 45.
63. Dibbits, *Vertrouwd bezit. Materiële cultuur in Doesburg en Maassluis 1650-1800* (Nijmegen 2001), 104. On the linen cupboard, see: Dibbits, "Between society and Family values. The Linen cupboard in early modern households." In *Private Domain, Public Inquiry. Families and Lifestyles in the Netherlands and Europe, 1550 to the Present*, Schuurman and Spierenburg, eds. (Hilversum 1996) 125-145. Schotel confirms the importance of the linen cupboard, *Oud-Hollandsch huisgezin*, 121. Franits discusses the meaning of linen on seventeenth-century paintings and emblems in *Paragons of Virtue*, 104.
64. Roemer Visscher, *Sinnepoppen* (Amsterdam 1614) 32.
65. HS: 35.
66. But it is fair to assume that they did. A French series of prints that eventually became popular in the Dutch Republic shows the different stages of married life. One of these prints is a depiction of a number of women offering gifts, such as pots and pans, to a young bride. It seems unlikely that this print would have appealed to the Dutch if this was a ritual they were themselves not familiar with. (The "Boijmans Van Beuningen Documentation system for paintings and prints" was used to trace images of weddings and the like.)
67. For references to poems as (wedding) gifts, see: Schotel, *Maatschappelijk leven*, 259; Frijhoff, "Burgerlijk dichtplezier in 1650?" *Spiegel der Letteren* 43-3 (2001) 248-269. For wedding gifts in general see: Van Boheemen et al., *Kent en versint*, 173.
68. Idem, 174.
69. Schotel refers to engraved and painted glass as a popular gift, *Oud-Hollandsch huisgezin*, 9.
70. PC: 279. Schotel also refers to this gift in his *Oud-Hollandsch huisgezin*, 125-126.
71. For the poems Hooft received on the occasion of his wedding, see PC: 272, 273, 274, 276.
72. PC: 273.
73. RB: 570-572.
74. We have now moved into the field of "material culture". Material culture can be both a topic and a source for historical research. In the first case, the material life of the past is the main theme, which can also be researched through non-material sources. In the second case, material culture is a source for research on culture in more general terms, which is the case here. For important work on material culture in both the Netherlands and internationally, see: Adshead, *Material Culture in Europe and China 1400-1800* (London/ New York 1997); Brewer and Porter, eds. *Consumption and the World of Goods* (London and New York 1993); Dibbits, *Vertrouwd bezit. Materiële cultuur in Doesburg en Maassluis 1650-1800* (Nijmegen 2001); Kamermans, *Materiële cultuur in de Krimpenerwaard in de zeventiende en achttiende eeuw: ontwikkeling en diversiteit* (Wageningen 1999); Laan, *Drank en*

drinkgerei. Een archeologisch en cultuurhistorisch onderzoek naar de alledaagse drinkcultuur van 18ᵉ-eeuwse Hollanders (Amsterdam 2003); Molendijk ed., Materieel Christendom. Religie en materiële cultuur in West-Europa (Hilversum 2003); Roche, Histoire des choses banales. Naissance de la consommation XVIIe-XVIIIe siècle (Paris 1997); Sarti, Europe at Home. Family and Material Culture 1500-1800 (New Haven and London 2002); Schuurman, Materiële cultuur en levensstijl. Een onderzoek naar de taal der dingen op het Nederlandse platteland in de 19e eeuw (Wageningen 1989); Schuurman, De Vries and Van der Woude. Aards geluk. De Nederlanders en hun spullen van 1550 tot 1850 (Amsterdam 1997); Weatherhill, Consumer Behaviour and Material Culture in Britain 1660-1760 (London and New York 1993); Wijsenbeek-Olthuis, Achter de gevels van Delft. Bezit en bestaan van rijk en arm in een periode van achteruitgang (1700-1800) (Hilversum 1987).

75. See, on the history of these villages in the seventeenth century: Van Deursen, Een dorp in de polder. Graft in de zeventiende eeuw. Amsterdam, 1994.

76. See: Pre-industriële gebruiksvoorwerpen 1150-1800, (catalogue Museum Boijmans Van Beuningen) (Rotterdam); Klijn, Loodglazuuraardewerk in Nederland. De collectie van het Nederlands Openluchtmuseum, (catalogue) (Arnhem 1995). For this type of pots, see also: Thoen, "Grafter kookpotten en hertrouwende weduwen. Connotaties van een zeventiende-eeuws gebruiksvoorwerp" Volkskundig Bulletin 23.2 (1997)107-126 and Thoen, "'Soo krijght altemet de gescheurde pot een deghelijck decksel...' Zeventiende-eeuwse slibaardewerken kookpotten uit Graft: object, methode en betekenis" (Erasmus University Rotterdam 1996) unpublished M.A. thesis.

77. Quintessens. Wetenswaardigheden over acht eeuwen kookgerei, (exhibition catalogue Museum Boijmans Van Beuningen) (Rotterdam 1992).

78. On hutspot, see: Jobse-van Putten, Eenvoudig maar voedzaam, 149-150, 163, 205.

79. See: Vreeken, Kunstnijverheid Middeleeuwen en Renaissance, (catalogue Museum Boijmans Van Beuningen). (Rotterdam 1994) and Ruempol and Van Dongen, eds. Pre-industriële gebruiksvoorwerpen 1150-1800 (Rotterdam)

80. See: Van Lennep and Ter Gouw, Het boek der opschriften. Een bijdrage tot de geschiedenis van het Nederlandsche volksleven (Amsterdam 1869).

81. See: the collections of Museum Boijmans van Beuningen in Rotterdam and the Nederlands Openlucht Museum in Arnhem. These two museums have the largest collections of pre-industrial utensils in The Netherlands.

82. Marriage registers of Graft and De Rijp, Regionaal Archief Alkmaar.

83. Johan Le Francq van Berkhey, Natuurlyke historie van Holland, vol. 3, Handelende over de volksgewoonten en landseigen plegtigheden der Hollanderen (Amsterdam 1769), part 2, 974. On Le Francq van Berkhey as a proto-etnologist, see: Frijhoff, "Volkskundigen voor de volkskunde?" Volkskundig Bulletin 20/3 (1994).

84. See, for example, the Rapenburg inventories. See also, Dibbits, Vertrouwd bezit, 128.

85. Johannes Luyken, Het leerzaam huisraad, Amsterdam 1710

86. For literature on Dutch emblems, see: De Jongh, Zinne- en minnebeelden in de schilderkunst in de zeventiende eeuw (1967), Meertens, Nederlandse emblemata (Leiden 1983); Porteman, Inleiding tot de Nederlandse emblemataliteratuur (Groningen 1977).

87. Johannes and Caspar Luyken, *Spiegel van 't menselyck bedryf* (Amsterdam 1704) 144-145.

88. For the meaning of the "cleaning of the pot" in early-modern Netherlandish paintings and prints see: Becker, "Are these girls really so neat? On Kitchen Scenes and Method" in *Art in History, History in Art*, eds Freedberg and De Vries (Santa Monica 1991), 139-161.

89. Johannes Luyken, *Het leerzaam huisraad* (Amsterdam 1710) 14-15.

90. JC: 70.

91. Visscher, Roemer. *Sinnepoppen*. Amsterdam, 1614, 50.

92. Cats, Jacob. *Spiegel van den ouden en nieuwe tyd*. Amsterdam, 1632, 104.

93. In the iconography of seventeenth-century genre painting, the theme of the dog in the pot is usually explained as being an example of the bad training or upbringing that the children that also crowd these depictions must have had. However, considering the paintings and prints that show this theme in connection with children it seems more likely that the dog and the pot refer to the sexual act of which the children are the result.

94. Another emblem in which Cats connects the cooking pot to inappropriate female sexual activity is "*De kanne gaet soo lange te water, totse eens breeckt*", also printed in the *Spiegel van den ouden en nieuwe tyd*, 120.

95. HS: 49.

96. See: Franits, *Paragons of Virtue*, 195.

97. I am aware of the ongoing debate in art history on seventeenth-century genre paintings and how their meaning should be interpreted. Although I am not an expert, I feel visual material (both emblems and paintings) can be used as a source for historic research since it offers an idea of the associative framework of the seventeenth-century individual. Without the assumption of being complete, the following works give an idea of the debate: Alpers, *The Art of Describing* (Chicago/London 1983); Bedaux, *The Reality of Symbols* ('s-Gravenhage and Maarssen 1990); Falkenburg, "Recente visies op zeventiende-eeuwse Nederlandse schilderkunst" *Theoretische geschiedenis* 18 (1991) 119-140; Hecht, "Dutch 17th-century genre painting: a reassessment of some current hypothesis" *Simiolus* 21 (1992) 83-93; De Jongh ed. *Tot Lering en Vermaak* (Amsterdam 1976); De Jongh, "De iconologische benadering van de zeventiende-eeuwse Nederlandse schilderkunst" in *De Gouden Eeuw in perspectie*, Grijzenhout and Van Veen, eds., 299-330 (Nijmegen and Heerlen 1992); Miedema, "Over iconologie en de betekenis van schilderijen" *Theoretische geschiedenis* 25 (1998) 168-183; Sluijter, "Belering en verhulling? Enkele 17de-eeuwse teksten over de schilderkunst en de iconologische benadering van Noordnederlandse schilderijen uit deze periode" *De zeventiende eeuw* 4 (1988) 3-28. For readings on iconology and history see: Falkenburg, "Iconologie en historische antropologie: een toenadering" in *Gezichtspunten*, Halbertsma and Zijlmans, eds., (Nijmegen 1993); Freedberg and De Vries eds., *Art in History, History in Art* (Santa Monica 1991).

98. An interesting article on the kitchen and the female virtues: Corbeau, "Pronken en koken. Beeld en realiteit van keukens in het vroegmoderne Hollandse binnenhuis" *Volkskundig Bulletin* 19.3 (1993) 354-379.

99. Sarti, *Europe at Home*, 70, describes spindle and distaff as an appropriate wedding gifts fit to the bride, since they were symbols of good wife- and motherhood.

100. Deursen, *Bavianen en slijkgeuzen*. 136-137; Rooijakkers, *Rituele repertoires*, 431-441; Cressy, *Birth, Marriage and Death. Ritual, Religion and the Life-Cycle in Tudor and Stuart England* (Oxford 1997) 97; Hufton, *The Prospect before her. A History of Women in Western Europe* (New York 1998) 192-193.

101. Roodenburg, *Onder censuur*, 88.

102. Cressy, *Birth, Marriage and Death*, 161.

103. Justinus van Nassau (1559-1631) was the bastard son of William of Orange.

104. HY: 17. Huygens autobiography was written in Latin.

105. Frijhoff, *Wegen van Evert Willemsz.*, 134-135, offers an analysis of Dutch naming practices for this period. For naming practices of the Dutch overseas see: Tebbenhoff, "Tacit rules and hidden family structures: naming practices and godparentage in Schenectady, New York, 1680-1800" *Journal of Social History* 18 (1985) 567-585.

106. DTB Delft inv.nr. 55 Doopboek Nieuwe Kerk folio 2

107. DTB Delft inv.nr. 7.

108. DTB Delft, HGA, GAR. For the period from approximately 1615 to 1680, a total of 72 children could be related to David Beck, and his relatives and friends. In 65 of these records the name of the godparents was actually noted. A broad time period was chosen in order to analyse whether the choice of godparentage evolved over time, from one generation to the next.

109. DTB Delft, HGA GAR. Of the 65 names that were possible to trace, only three godchildren were named after their godfather and none were named after their godmother. A number of 13 children were either named after their parents, grandparents or predeceased siblings.

110. DTB Delft, HGA and GAR.

111. DTB Delft inv. nr. 7, 8, 54, 55.

112. DTB Delft inv. nr. 8.

113. Beck, *Spiegel van mijn leven*, 264. Other authors have argued that this was the usual reasoning behind the choice of godparents, but other than schoolmaster Du Rieu, David Beck and his social circle do not leave any evidence to this effect.

114. Huygens, *Het dagboek van Constantijn Huygens*, Unger, ed. (Amsterdam 1885), bijlage: Aantekeningen van Christiaan Huygens den Ouden, 3.

115. HY: 16.

116. Davis, *The Gift in Sixteenth-Century France*, 27, Kooijmans, *Vriendschap en de kunst van het overleven*, 94.

117. Kooijmans, idem.

118. Beck: 09-08-1624

119. See Schotel, *Oud-Hollandsch huisgezin*, 50-57.

120. RB: 115-118, 571-577, 746-748 etc.

121. PC: 1134.

122. Later, the parents of the child sent Hooft and his wife a letter in order to thank them for the gift. PC: 1135.

123. RB: 571-577.

124. HD: bijlage A, 3.

125. HD: bijlage A, 3-4.

126. HD: bijlage A, 4.

127. HD: bijlage A3-4.

128. Huygens, *Mijn jeugd*, Heesakkers ed. (Amsterdam 1994) 17.

129. Frijhoff, *Evert Willemsz*, 139.

130. According to Schotel the *pillegift* was only brought to the pawn bank in cases of utmost necessity, *Het Oud-Hollandsch huisgezin*, 57.

131. DB: 30-09-1624 and 22-10-1624.

132. For literature on death in the early-modern period see Koslofsky's introduction to *The Reformation of the Dead. Death and Ritual in Early Modern Germany, 1450-1700* (London/ New York 2000).

133. DB: 07-02-1624 and 11-02-1624.

134. Huygens's letters as cited in: Smits-Veldt and Bakker eds., *In een web van Vriendschap* (Amsterdam 1999) 17-18.

135. PC: 203.

136. Web: 92. Year: 1612.

137. HY: 103-104. Elisabeth Huygens died 8th May 1612.

138. HY: 103.

139. Huygens, *Korenbloemen*, Van Strien ed., 42.

140. HY: 104.

141. The linguistic aspects of these letters are discussed in: Kaper, *Liever geen bloemen. Over dood en rouw in de 17de eeuw* (Culemborg 1984) 23-41.

142. See: Brandt's biography of Hooft, dedicated to Huygens.

143. DB: 23-02-1624.

144. Huygens, *Korenbloemen*, ed. Van Strien, 31-32.

145. Brandt, *Het leven van Vondel*, 58.

146. Sneller and Van Marion, *De gedichten van Tesselschade Roemers* (Hilversum 1994) 60.

147. On occasional poetry in seventeenth-century Holland see: Schenkeveld-van der Dussen "Poëzie als gebruiksartikel; gelegenheidsgedichten in de zeventiende eeuw" in *Historische Letterkunde*, ed. Spies (Groningen 1984) 75-92. For conventions in occasional poetry see: Nieuweboer, "Medeleven volgens voorschrift en verzen op bestelling. Achttiende-eeuwse gelegenheidsgedichten" *Literatuur. Tijdschrift over Nederlandse Letterkunde* 1- 3 (1986) 15-22.

148. Christina van Erp died 6 June, 1624.

149. PC: 206.

150. PC: 207.

151. PC: 631.

152. PC: 633.

153. PC: 636.

154. PC: 637.

155. PC: 641.

156. Sneller and Van Marion, *De gedichten van Tesselschade Roemers* (Hilversum 1994) 30.

157. Huygens, *Korenbloemen*, Van Strien, ed. (Amsterdam 1996) 21.

158. Idem, 61.

159. Heal, *Hospitality in Early Modern England* (Oxford 1990) 344, 355, 376, 386. On hospitality see also: Heal, "The idea of hospitality in Early Modern England" *Past and Present* 102 (1987) 66-93 and O'Sullivan, *Hospitality in medieval Ireland, 900-1500* (Dublin 2004). For hospitality as a gift, see: Heal, *Hospitality*, 21; Du Boulay, "Strangers and gifts: hostility and hospitality in rural Greece" *Journal of Mediterranean Studies* 1 (1991) 37-53 and Simpson-Herbert, "Women, food and hospitality in Iranian society" *Canberra Anthropology* 10 (1987) 24-34.

160. Heal, *Hospitality*, 3, makes the same distinction between food, drink and accommodation as elements of hospitality.
161. For example: DB: 03-01-1624, 03-03-1624, 10-03-1624.
162. For example: DB: 18-02-1624, 15-06-1624, 16-06-1624, 20-06-1624, 28-10-1624, 10-11-1624.
163. For example: DB: 08-02-1624, 18-02-1624, 15-07-1624, 21-07-1624, 05-08-1624, 12-08-1624, 19-09-1624, 27-09-1624, 14-11-1624, 17-11-1624, 25-11-1624.
164. Heal, *Hospitality*, 5, stresses the mandatory quality of hospitality. This is largely the result of the social groups that are central to her research; the elite, especially aristocratic elite, had a social and moral obligation to provide hospitality on specific occasions. These were occasions that connected to the ritual year (70-79) and to rites of passage (80-86). A failure to be generous could result in damage to one's reputation.
165. Cressy also discusses hospitality on the occasion of rites of passage such as marriage, birth and death: *Birth, Marriage and Death. Ritual, Religion and the Life-Cycle in Tudor and Stuart England* (Oxford 1997). On pages 365-367, 197-228 and 443-449 respectively.
166. Krausman Ben-Amos also points out that these ritual occasions were occasions "for sociability and conviviality" that cemented ties within the community, "Gifts and favors: informal support in Early Modern England" *The Journal of Modern History* 72- 2 (2000) 316.
167. For requests for foodstuff see: Part III.
168. See: HS: 25; Cats: 317 and Alkemade, *Nederlands Displegtigheden*, II, 301-307.
169. For Dutch literature on honour in the early-modern period see: Van de Pol, "Prostitutie en de Amsterdamse burgerij: eerbegrippen in een vroegmoderne stedelijke samenleving" in *Cultuur en maatschappij in Nederland 1500-1850. Een historisch-antropologisch perspectief*, eds te Boekhorst, Burke and Frijhoff, (Meppel/Amsterdam 1992) 179-218; Roodenburg, "Eer en oneer ten tijde van de Republiek. Een tussenbalans" *Volkskundig Bulletin* 22 (1996) 129-149; Rooijakkers, *Eer en schande. Volksgebruiken van het oude Brabant.* (Nijmegen 1995); Schmidt, *Om de eer van de familie*; De Waardt, "Inleiding: naar een geschiedenis van de eer" *Leidschrift* 12 (1996) 7-19; De Waardt, "De geschiedenis van de eer en de historische antropologie" *Tijdschrift voor Sociale Geschiedenis* 23 (1997) 334-354.
170. See epilogue.
171. Heal, "The idea of hospitality in Early Modern England" *Past and Present* 102 (1987) 68.
172. See part I.
173. For example: 17-02-1624, 30-08-1624, 27-10-1624.
174. See part III.
175. DB: 16-09-1624, 18-10-1624.
176. For example: DB: 15-03-1624, 11-04-1624.
177. DB: 04-01-1624.
178. DB: 21-10-1624.
179. DB: 31-03-1624, 07-05-1624, 02-06-1624, 16-06-1624, 04-07-1624 08-07-1624, 14-07-1624, 02-08-1624, 04-08-1624, 080-08-1624, 16-08-1624, 06-09-1624, 08-09-1624, 13-09-1624, 14-09-1624, 21-09-1624.

180. DB: 14-01-1624, 09-02-1624, 28-02-1624, 11-03-1624, 02-06-1624, 21-04-1624, 22-05-1624, 10-06-1624, 12-06-1624, 24-09-1624, 27-10-1624, 28-10-1624, 10-10-1624, 15-11-1624, 04-12-1624.
181. DB: 28-05-1624, 30-05-1624, 19-09-1624.
182. Heal, "The idea of hospitality", 69, has pointed out that it was the head of the household who was to take the initiative in offering hospitality.
183. DB: 03-03-1624.
184. DB: 20-03-1624.
185. DB: 03-10-1624, 09-10-1624, 17-10-1624.
186. DB: 22-09-1624, 29-09-1624, 30-09-1624, 03-10-1624, 24-10-1624.
187. DB: 13-11-1624, 01-09-1624, 13-06-1624.
188. DB: 26-04-1624, 19-1-1624.
189. DB: 15-01-1624.
190. DB: 16-01-1624, 20-01-1624.
191. DB: 19-11-1624, 26-04-1624.
192. DB: 06-02-1624.
193. DB: 16-02-1624 and 06-02-1624 respectively.
194. DB: 18-02-1624.
195. DB: 29-05-1624, 28-06-1624.
196. DB: 02-06-1624, 30-06-1624.
197. DB: 15-11-1624.
198. On wet nursing in early-modern Holland see: Dekker, *Uit de schaduw*, 142-155; Kloek, Van Oostveen, and Teeuwen, "Nederlandse moralisten over moederschap en min (1600-1900)" *Volkscultuur* 8, (1991) 20-39; Roberts, *Trough the keyhole*, 78-86.
199. For example, DB: 28-02-1624, 30-06-1624.
200. DB: 19-02-1624, 07-05-1624.
201. DB: 23-12-1624. The infant was returned to the Beck household on 08-09-1624.
202. Although Beck does mention that Hooft was in The Hague to bring some scoundrels to court. DB: 25-02-1624
203. PC: 385.
204. PC: 385.
205. PC: 387.
206. PC: 388.
207. Hooft's concerns about christening and funeral wines were discussed earlier. See: part I.
208. PC: 389, dated 13 September 1630.
209. PC: 391.
210. PC: 391.
211. PC: 392.
212. PC: 393.
213. PC: 394.
214. PC: 395.
215. PC: 395.
216. PC: 399.
217. PC: 399.
218. PC: 405.
219. PC: 405.
220. PC: 412.

221. DB: 21-02-1624, 05-05-1624, 07-05-1624.

222. DB: 10-10-1624.

223. According to Davis, *The Gift in Sixteenth-Century France*, 27-29, marriage is the most symmetrical of gift-exchange occasions. I believe this is true in the sense that all parties (parents, couple, guests) participate in the offering of gifts, but not in terms of the value of the gifts offered. However, Davis does include dowries in her discussion, whereas I do not since the types of sources that I use seldom reveal any information on this topic. For dowries and marriage exchange in the legal sense, see: Fair Bestor, "Marriage transactions in Renaissance Italy and *Mauss's Essay on the Gift*" *Past and Present* 164 (1999) 6-46; Howell, *The marriage exchange. Property, social place and gender in the cities of the Low Countries 1300-1550* (London 1998).

224. See also: Krausman Ben-Amos, "Gifts and favors: informal support in Early Modern England" *The Journal of Modern History* 72- 2 (2000) 316.

Notes Part III: Terms and Conditions of Exchange

1. Veluwenkamp's book on Dutch trade with Archangel does not mention Verbeeck's brother: Veluwenkamp, *Archangel. Nederlandse ondernemers in Rusland 1550-1785* (Amsterdam 2000). Wijnroks, *Handel tussen Rusland en de Nederlanden 1560-1640. Een netwerkanalyse van Antwerpse en Amsterdamse kooplieden, handelend op Rusland* (Hilversum 2003) also deals with Dutch-Russian trade.

2. HV: 52.

3. HV: 54.

4. HV: 61.

5. HV: 62.

6. HV: 66-67.

7. HV: 82.

8. HV: 78.

9. HV: 80.

10. HV: 83-84.

11. HV: 86.

12. HV: 86.

13. HV: 82.

14. Haks, *Huwelijk en gezin in Holland*, 128-129.

15. Haks, *Huwelijk en gezin in Holland*, 131-132, showed that the norm of equal marriage was not always practiced. In 1750, he calculated that a lot more people chose marriage partners for other social classes, than could have been expected on the basis of what Dutch moralists were writing at the time.

16. HV: 87. Schotel *Het Oud-Hollandsch huisgezen*, 19, points out that a 'luercorf' was a gift that was offered to a pregnant woman on behalf of her mother-in-law or the future godparents of the child.

17. HV: 98 and HV: 100.

18. HV: 101.

19. HV: 102.

20. HV: 103.

21. HV: 106.
22. On wet nursing, see part II b.
23. HV: 106.
24. HV: 112-113.
25. HV: 115.
26. HV: 137.
27. HV: 117.
28. David Beck did the same: depending on someone's social status he either refers to first names, or last names with occupation.
29. HV: 143.
30. HV: 146.
31. The idea of possession over generations was indeed important in this period. Several authors like De Brune (*Banketwerck* I-148) and Cats – *Alle de wercken*, 601) were debating the question of whether one should have a will or whether one should give while one is still alive. That this was an issue of importance becomes clear through the story of Vondel. He had already passed his belongings on to his daughter while he was still quite young. This turned out to be very problematic because he lived beyond the age of 90, while his daughter had already passed away. Coornhert, on the other hand, believed that one could only give during one's life, because after death one cannot possess anything and thus cannot give. He claimed that a will was actually a form of theft from those who stood to inherit the property. Coornhert, *Weet of Rust. Proza van Coornhert*, Bonger and Gelderblom, eds. (Amsterdam 1993).
32. HV: 169.
33. HV: 196.
34. HV: 178.
35. HV: 182.
36. HV: 212.
37. HV: 226.
38. On the theme of informal support, see: Krausman Ben-Amos, "Gifts and favors: informal support in Early Modern England", *The Journal of Modern History* 72-2 (2000) 295-338. She distinguishes between material and immaterial support. The first is the support needed for sheer survival, the latter determines the quality of life and can consist of social contacts, protection, information, emotional support, 297.
39. See, for the idea of social capital in early modern Holland: Kooijmans, *Vriendschap en de kunst van het overleven* and Schmidt, *Om de eer van de familie*.
40. A pure gift is a gift for which nothing – no other gift, nor good behaviour – is expected in return.
41. For charity in connection to concepts of gift exchange, see: Van Leeuwen, *The Logic of Charity*.
42. In fact, research on poor relief reveals that the expectation of good behaviour is an important motivation for offering the relief. It was not offered to all of the poor, but only to the "deserving poor", which implies that even though they were poor they were living according to moral or social standards. See, for example: Van der Vlis, *Leven in armoede*.
43. DB: 03-02-1624.
44. DB: 07-02-1624.

45. DB: 09-02-1624.
46. DB: 18-02-1624.
47. DB: 08-02-1624.
48. For a discussion of trust in more economic terms, see: Muldrew, *The Economy of Obligation. The Culture of Credit and Social Relations in Early Modern England* (New York 1998) and Muldrew, "Zur Anthropologie des Kapitalismus. Kredit, Vertrauen, Tausch und die Geschichte des Marktes in England 1500-1750", *Historische Anthropologie* 6 (1998) 167-199.
49. On the instrumental character of friendship, see again: Kermode, "Sentiment and Survival", *Journal of Family History*; Kooijmans, *Vriendschap en de kunst van het overleven*); Kooijmans, "Vriendschap. Een 18e-eeuwse familiegeschiedenis", *Tijdschrift voor Sociale Geschiedenis*; Kooijmans, "Andries & Daniel. Vriendschap in de vroegmoderne Nederlanden", *Groniek. Historisch Tijdschrift*; Kooijmans, "Kwetsbaarheid en 'koopluider vriendschap'", in *Of bidden helpt? Tegenslag en cultuur in Europa, circa 1500-2000*, eds. Gijswijt-Hofstra and Egmond, (Amsterdam 1997) 61-70.
50. On the historic development of friendship, see: Aymard, "Friends and Neighbors" in *A History of Private Life*; Labrie, "Eenzaamheid en sociabiliteit: Romantische vriendschap in Duitsland", *Groniek* (1995) 68-86; and Spierenburg, "Vriendschap tussen messentrekkers?", *Groniek* (1995) 42-56.
51. DB: 26-08-1624.
52. DB: 06-05-1624.
53. Beck, *Spiegel van mijn leven*, introduction by Veldhuijzen, 11.
54. Beck, *Spiegel van mijn leven*, register by Veldhuijzen, 239.
55. Ibid.
56. Van Tricht, *De Briefwisseling van Pieter Corneliszoon Hooft*, part I, comments with letter 3.
57. Hooft's accounts of his travels are published as: Hooft, *Reis-heuchenis*, De Lange and Huijskes, eds. (Amsterdam 1991). His grand tour is discussed in: Frank van Westrienen, *De Groote Tour. Tekening van een educatiereis door Nederlanders in de zeventiende eeuw* (Amsterdam 1983). His son Arnout Hellemans Hooft also kept notes on his grand tour, which were published by: Grabowsky and Verkruijsse, eds. *Arnout Hellemans Hooft. Een naekt beeld op een marmore matras seer schoon. Het dagboek van een "grand tour" (1649-1651)* (Hilversum 2001).
58. PC: 3.
59. See, for example: PC: 84, 689, 728, 730, 908, 911, 1021, 1030.
60. DB: 04-04-1624 and Teding van Berkhout: see part I.
61. MvR: 76, 118, 122, 167, 169, 173, 178, 182, 291, 293, 325, 326. She also received requests for clothing and furniture from other people via her brother Nicholas: MvR: 69, 112, 170, 174, 176, 178, 182, 199. See also Rogge's introduction in Rogge, ed. *Brieven van en aan Maria van Reigersberch* (Leiden 1902) 27.
62. MvR: 123, 182, 185.
63. PC: 4 and 6.
64. PC: 6 (08-01-1601).
65. PC: 6.
66. For a biography on Baudius: Grootens, *Dominicus Baudius. Een levensschets uit het Leidsche Humanisten-milieu, 1566-1631* (Nijmegen 1942).
67. See, also: Van Tricht, *De briefwisseling*, part I, 95.

68. PC: 10 (18-10-1608).
69. PC: 9 (16-03-1608).
70. PC: 14 (24-01-1609).
71. PC: 19 (25-01-1611).
72. PC: 21 (07-06-1611).
73. PC: 21.
74. PC: 39 (09-08-1612).
75. PC: 39.
76. It is not clear when Badovere died exactly, but it was probably prior to 1620. See Van Tricht, *De briefwisseling van Pieter Corneliszoon Hooft*, 73-74.
77. Krausman Ben-Amos, "Gifts and Favors", also discusses the relationship between masters and servants in this respect, 310-314.
78. Haks, *Huwelijk en gezin in Holland*, 168-169, describes the mutual obligations of master and servant in seventeenth-century Holland. De Jong stresses the fact that for elite families, servants were a practical necessity as well as something that added to their status: De Jong, *Een deftig bestaan* (Amsterdam and Dieren 1987) 152-156. According to him, relations among masters and servants in Holland were in general quite good. For more literature on servants in early modern Holland, see: Carlson, *Domestic service in a changing city economy: Rotterdam 1680-1780* (Madison 1993); Faber, "Vrouwen van de rekening. Kindermoordzaken ten tijden van de Republiek te Amsterdam en in Friesland" in *Soete minne en helsche boosheit. Seksuele voorstellingen in Nederland, 1300-1850*, Hekma and Roodenburg, eds. (Nijmegen 1988); Jongejan, *Weeldeboden en werkboden. Huispersoneel in Goes in de achttiende en begin van de negentiende eeuw* (Veere 1984).
79. This was also a theme in one of the emblems by Cats discussed in part II, where the servant was punished for leaving "her pot" open.
80. Haks, 171.
81. PC: 322.
82. PC: 322.
83. PC: 322.
84. PC: 322.
85. PC: 882.
86. WF: 104.
87. On patronage, see below.
88. DB: 22-03-1624. Beck referred to this dinner with the word *foy*, which, as noted earlier, was during this period generally used for farewell meals.
89. Schotel already pointed out that schoolmasters were in the habit of doing writing jobs for others. He also referred to both copying works and the actual writing of poetry. Unfortunately, in his case, it is not clear on what sources he based this information: Schotel, *Oud-Hollandsch huisgezin*, 254.
90. DB: 26-01-1624.
91. DB: 27-06-1624.
92. DB: 07-07-1624.
93. Other source material offers the same patterns of exchange. See, for instance, Hooft's correspondence and the biographies of Vondel and Hooft by Geerard Brandt. See also Ann Goldgar's very interesting book on "The Republic of Letters", in which the exchange of gifts and services is described as an important feature of this scholarly network: Goldgar, *Impolite learning. Conduct and community in the Republic of Letters 1680-1750* (New

Haven/London 1995). Stegeman also describes expected modes of behaviour within this "Republic of Letters": Stegeman, *Patronage en dienstverlening. Het netwerk van Theodorus Janssonius van Almeloveen (1657-1712) in de Republiek der Letteren* (Nijmegen 1996). For the link between patronage and gift giving, see: Kettering, "Gift-giving and patronage in early modern France", *French History* 2 (1988) 131-151.

94. I find the use of the concept of disguise in the practices of individuals highly problematic, since disguising something is an act and the term suggests that things are disguised intentionally. The term therewith almost implies that we, as historians, can pass moral judgement on individuals in the past for not being sincere. I think it makes more sense to accept the historic individual's own judgement of his own practices. If they refer to their offerings as gifts, I presume to them these were gifts.

95. DB: 27-05-1624, 30-08-1624, 08-09-1624, 14-09-1624, 22-09-1624, 23-09-1624, 24-09-1624.

96. DB: 04-11-1624.

97. DB: 28-11-1624.

98. For the printed version of this poem, see: Beck, Spiegel van mijn leven, 280-281.

99. On books as gifts, see: Davis, "Beyond the market: books as gifts in sixteenth-century France", *Transactions of the Royal Historical Society* 5- 33 (1983) 69-88.

100. See also: Goldar, *Impolite learning*, 235.

101. PC: 1139.

102. This seems to have been a conventional gift; Goldgar also mentions silver basins as a gift from royalty in reciprocation of a dedication, *Impolite learning*, 235.

103. PC: 1142.

104. Brandt, *Het leven van Pieter Corn. Hooft*, Leendertz, ed. (The Hague 1932) [1677]; Brandt, *Het leven van Joost van den Vondel*, Leendertz, ed. (The Hague 1932) [1682].

105. Brandt, *Het leven van Vondel*, introduction.

106. Ibid. 68.

107. Ibid.

108. Ibid.

109. Ibid.

110. Ibid.

111. Brandt, *Het leven van Vondel*, 40.

112. Worp ed., *De briefwisseling van Constantijn Huygens*, 23-05-1624.

113. Lunsingh Scheurleer, Fock and Van Dissel, eds. *Het Rapenburg. Geschiedenis van een Leidse gracht.* (Leiden 1988, 1989, 1990) 288-289.

114. Smits-Veldt, ed. *In een web van vriendschap*, 51.

115. Stadholder Willem Frederik describes the story of an admiral who refused his chain, after which the authorities decided to offer his wife jewels instead; WF: 52.

116. PC: 18.

117. PC: 18.

118. Also important in this respect are the *rederijkers* and their chambers of rhetoric. For an overview of recent literature on rhetoricians, see: Van Dixhoorn, "In een traditie gevangen? Hollandse rederijkerskamers en rederij-

kers in de recente literatuurgeschiedschrijving", *Tijdschrift voor geschiedenis* 112-3 (1999) 385-406. Moser has written a book on the changing position of Netherlandish rethoricians in the early modern period: *De strijd voor rhetorica. Poëtica en positie van rederijkers in Vlaanderen, Brabant, Zeeland en Holland tussen 1450 en 1620* (Amsterdam 2001). For the activities of a *rederijkerskamer* in Rotterdam, see: Zijlmans, "Rederijkerskamer de Blauwe Acolyen" in her book *Vriendenkringen in de zeventiende eeuw* (The Hague 1999) 19-42.

119. See Spies, "Betaald werk? Poëzie als ambacht inde zeventiende eeuw", *Holland* 23 (1991) 210-225.

120. Ibid.

121. Although the network that is described here is not a "Republic of Letters" in the scholarly sense of the word, in its functions, these literary circles share a lot of features with the "Republic of Letters". On the "Republic of Letters", see: Bots and Waquet. *La République des Lettres* (Paris 1997); and again, Goldgar, *Impolite learning: Conduct and Community in the Republic of Letters 1680-1750*.

122. Goldgar discusses the "Republic of Letters" as a community in which the exchange of gifts and services is or vital importance to its existence, *Impolite learning*, 19-26. To her, the "Republic of Letters" can be seen as a reciprocal community in which it was "exactly that expectation of return that kept the system in cooperation".

123. PC: 74.

124. For lending within the "Republic of Letters", see: Goldgar, 16. Dutch humanist Vossius even had a special booklet where he kept notes on whom he had lent books out to, which was published by Rademaker and Tuynman, eds. *Het uitleenboekje van Vossius* (Amsterdam 1962).

125. PC: 80.

126. PC: 199.

127. Van Tricht, *Briefwisseling*, I, p. 477.

128. PC: 860.

129. See also Goldgar, *Impolite learning*, 225.

130. PC: 95.

131. PC: 95.

132. PC: 97.

133. PC: 97.

134. PC: 97.

135. Bredero in his dedication in *Moortje*, 100, insisted that only the giver of a gift and how the gift was offered were important: "*Men moet niet aenmercken hoe groot de ghiften zyn, maer wie die, en hoe ze gegeven worden.*"

136. PC: 98.

137. PC: 127.

138. PC: 187.

139. PC: 214.

140. Ibid.

141. PC: 215.

142. Smits-Veldt, *In een web van vriendschap*, 132.

143. Ibid., 71.

144. Ibid., 133.

145. Goldgar also interprets gift copies as a means of showing gratitude, *Impolite learning*, 42.

146. PC: 222.
147. PC: 225.
148. PC: 227.
149. PC: 228.
150. PC: 228. Others who received gift copies of *Hendrik de Grote* were Willem de Groot (Hugo de Groot's brother), Constantijn Huygens, Adriaen van Blijenburgh, Anthonis de Hubert, Cornelis van der Mijle, Nicolaas Cromhout, and Grotius, all of whom were important regents.
151. PC: 232.

Notes Part IV: Comparison in Time

1. See: prologue.
2. See: part I: Practices of Gift Exchange.
3. See: part II: Gifts and Meanings.
4. See: part III: Terms and Conditions of Exchange.
5. A lot of writers, for some reason, did not know that their letters were going to be used for research prior to 2098. They were actually released for research after conservation and cataloguing routines were completed. I find this quite problematic, since this means I am using material that people did not know was going to be accessible so soon. It is unclear where this assumption comes from however, because I have looked through all the press material and there is no suggestion that the letters would not be disclosed prior to 100 years later. However, people could indicate on the form, whether they preferred their letters to remain closed for 25, 50 or 100 years. This should also have been an indication to the writers that if they did not specify, their letters could be opened sooner.
6. Within the sample of the first 50 letters, that were taken randomly, a majority of the writers were retired, unemployed, or full-time mothers. See BadT: 1, 2, 4, 6, 8, 9, 11, 12, 14, 17, 18, 20, 21, 25, 28, 29, 30, 32, 33, 34, 36, 38, 42, 43, 46, 49, 50.
7. See for example BadT: 4, 9, 24, 28, 33, 34, 41, 44, 46. See for solidarity: Komter, *Solidariteit en de gift. Sociale banden en sociale uitsluiting* (Amsterdam 2003).
8. See for example BadT: 3, 5, 26, 24, 34, 36, 43, 46, 49.
9. See for example BadT: 48, 49.
10. See for example BadT: 23, 24, 30, 32, 35, 36, 47.
11. See for example BadT: 38, 42, 47, 404.
12. BadT: 12074, A *kwartje* is a quarter of the guilder, the former Dutch currency, and a *dubbeltje* is ten guilder cents.
13. BadT: 2015.
14. On Mother's Day see BadT: 24, 49, 50, 65, 219, 404, 3380. On fairs see BadT: 151, 160, 12098. There is also mention of Father's Day BadT: 160.
15. BadT: 151.
16. BadT: 160.
17. BadT: 18.
18. BadT: 14.
19. BadT: 1431, 12066.

20. BadT: 1431, 12066.
21. BadT: 11341.
22. Accommodations offered to children: BadT 12084, 12014, 11368. Accommodations offered to people living abroad: BadT 12111, 12075, 12067.
23. This does not coincide with other findings regarding hospitality in the contemporary Netherlands. See, for instance: Van Leer and Komter, "Gastvrijheid, of de kunst van het ontvangen" in *Het geschenk over de betekenissen van het geven*, Komter, ed. (Amsterdam 1997) and the article by Komter and Schuyt in *Trouw* 1993: "Geven in Nederland". They claim that hospitality is offered on quite a grand scale in the contemporary Netherlands and more to friends than family. Of course, their research is much more representative, but I wanted to stick to what I could find on this topic within the context of the sources.
24. BadT: 428.
25. Support at illness, BadT: 12083, 11340. Support at illness through gifts, BadT: 22, 50, 120.
26. BadT: 409, 525, 2182, 2205, 11382, 11393, 11524, 11979.
27. BadT: 89, 409, 11344.
28. BadT: 2182, 11979.
29. BadT: 409, 11394, 11524.
30. BadT: 408, 2205, 11382, 11524, 12082.
31. BadT: 408, 11382, 11524.
32. BadT: 11382, 11524. One explanation for this may be the use of "wedding lists" by the couple. This is a system in which the couple leaves a list of preferred gifts at a department store from which the guests can choose the gifts that they would like to offer. The gifts are then delivered by the department store to the couple's home after the wedding. However, it would seem to me that the couples who participated in the Letters to the Future project seldom belong to the kind of people who would have wedding lists.
33. BadT: 89, 12082.
34. BadT: 11344.
35. BadT: 408, 555, 2205, 11382.
36. See also BadT: 12083.
37. BadT: 11911.
38. BadT: 12072, 12083
39. BadT: 11982.
40. This is to a certain extent the result of the fact that the provinces of Zuid- and Noord-Holland are central in this study. As will be shown later, funerals in the province of Brabant are still associated with the consumption of alcohol.
41. BadT: 12111, 15911, 2193, 11539.
42. BadT: 15911.
43. Hospitality on birthdays BadT: 2, 28, 37, 41, 65, 112, 173, 175, 181, 398, 1448, 1471, 11970, 11982, 12014, 4012, 3856, 4719, 16521, 11905, 11366.
44. Dinners within the home on birthdays BadT: 171, 11982, 14777. Dinners outside of the home BadT: 11959, 11522, 11539.
45. Outings on birthdays BadT: 12063, 850, 2688.
46. Gifts on birthdays BadT: 40, 41, 49, 12063, 12087, 112, 173, 181, 198, 398, 555, 13344, 12014, 14777, 2688, 2198, 11522, 11911, 11344, 11355, 11365, 11366.

47. Money as a gift on birthdays BadT: 65, 188. Gift tokens BadT: 12066, 1471.
48. Cards and phone calls on birthdays BadT: 13, 20, 112, 1450, 13860, 16521, 3563, 2198, 11344, 11366.
49. BadT: 181.
50. BadT: 12040.
51. BadT: 12040.
52. BadT: 175, 1448.
53. BadT: 850.
54. BadT: 11365, 850.
55. BadT: 11365.
56. BadT: 424.
57. BadT: 177, 207, 413, 2386. On the social meaning of Sabbath dinners, see: Shuman, "Food Gifts, Ritual Exchange and the Production of Excess Meaning." *Journal of American Folklore* 113, 450 (2000) 495-508.
58. Again: on Mother's Day BadT: 24, 49, 50, 65, 219, 404, 3380 and Father's Day BadT: 160.
59. For literature on the celebration of *Sinterklaas* in contemporary Holland, see: Helsloot, "Sinterklaas en de komst van de kerstman" *Volkskundig Bulletin* 22 (1996) 299-329; Van Leer, *Geven rond Sinterklaas. Een ritueel als spiegel van veranderende relaties* (Amsterdam 1995); Van Leer, "Wie gelooft er nog in Sinterklaas? Een ritueel geschenkenfeest als spiegel van veranderende relaties" *Volkskundig Bulletin* 22 (1996) 239-262; Van Leer, "Wederkerigheid in een surprise. Sinterklaasgeschenken vanuit historisch-sociologisch perspectief" in *Het geschenk. Over de verschillende betekenissen van het geven*, Komter, ed. (Amsterdam 1997).
60. For a discussion of the supposed decline of importance of family relations, see: Osborne and Williams, "Determining patterns of exchanges and expanded family relationships", *International Journal of Sociology of the Family* 6 (1976) 198-199.
61. Osborne and Williams, "Determining Patterns of Exchanges and Expanded Family Relationships" *International Journal of Sociology of the Family* 6 (1976) also conclude that extended family relations are an important feature of family life in contemporary society. For a discussion of gift giving within the family, and especially among generations, see: Komter and Vollebergh, 'Intergenerational solidarity. Family ties under strain?', *Sociale Wetenschappen* 41, 3 (1998) 25-37.
62. BadT: 408, 535, 2688, 2205, 11382, 11524, 11905, 11929.
63. BadT: 11968, 11899, 11539.
64. BadT: 195, 11968.
65. BadT: 12066, 11959, 11970, 14777, 11522.
66. For a discussion on gift exchange within family and friendship networks, see: Komter and Vollebergh, "Gift Giving and the Emotional Significance of Family and Friends" *Journal of Marriage and the Family* 59 (1997) 747-757. They claim that gift giving among friends is more likely to be accompanied by feelings of affection, while exchange within the family network is the result of social obligation.
67. BadT: 33, 175.
68. BadT: 11539.
69. Ruffle also stresses the importance of gift giving in commercial relations. See: Ruffle, "Gift giving with emotions" *Journal of Economic Behaviour &*

Organization 39, 4 (1999) 400. As do Klamer and Van Staveren, "Geven is geen ruilen. De gift in de economie" in *Het geschenk*, ed. Komter (Amsterdam 1997)108-120 and Offer, "Between the gift and the market: the economy of regard", *Economic History Review* 3 (1997) 450.

70. BadT: 12110.

71. Jubilees and farewells BadT: 49, 171, 173, 11895, 11527, 885

72. Company parties BadT: 2183, 11368.

73. Birthday treats at the workplace BadT: 37, 12043.

74. Colleagues and rites of passage BadT: 555, 15911, 2205, 11382, 11911.

75. Objects as gifts BadT: 8, 65, 112, 198, 398, 885, 11982, 12014, 13344, 14777, 2198, 11522.

76. Money as a wedding gift BadT: 29, 89, 12082.

77. Money as a birthday gift BadT: 65, 188, 398.

78. See: Belk and Coon, "Can't buy me love: dating, money and gifts", *Advances in consumer research* 18 (1991) 521-527; Burgoyne and Roth, "Constraints on the use of money as a gift at Christmas: the role of status and intimacy", *Journal of Economic Psychology* 12 (1991) 47-69; Cameron, "The unacceptability of money as a gift and its status as a medium of exchange", *Journal of Economic Psychology* 10 (1989) 253-255; Webley and Wilson, "Social relationships and the unacceptability of money as gift", *Journal of Social Psychology* 129 (1989) 85-91; Zelizer, *The social meaning of money* (New York 1994). Caplow on the other hand claims that can be an appropriate gift as long as it is offered 'intergenerational and downwards', "Christmas Gifts and Kin Networks", *American Sociological Review* 47, 3 (1982) 386.

79. BadT: 11979.

80. BadT: 12013 and 11992.

81. BadT: 11382.

82. BadT: 11522.

83. BadT: 11362.

84. BadT: 12014.

85. BadT: 12110.

86. See also: Komter and Vollebergh, "Intergenerational solidarity. Family ties under strain?", *Sociale Wetenschappen* 41, 3 (1998) 25-37, in which support among different categories of social relations is discussed.

87. BadT: 12097.

88. BadT: 12060.

89. BadT: 12064.

90. BadT: 120.

91. BadT: 213.

92. BadT: 22, 41, 49, 398, 404, 1471, 12066, 12074, 12111, 12014, 13344, 2198, 11379, 11911, 11344, 11363, 11366.

93. PC: 174.

94. BadT: 20.

95. DB: 03-03-1624.

96. Reciprocity is not only important within the system of gift exchange, but also in social relations as such, as Altman shows in: "Reciprocity of interpersonal exchange", *Journal on the Theory of Social Behaviour* 3 (1973) 249-261. On reciprocal disclosure in intimate relations, see: Rubin, "Lovers and other strangers: the development of intimacy in encounters and relationships", *American Scientist* 62 (1974) 182-190.

97. BadT: 12066.
98. BadT: 12060, 12064.
99. BadT: 4012.
100. See, for example, BadT: 398, 11366, 16521, 11982, 12014. This is also offered at other festivities celebrated within the home as, for example, a 46th wedding anniversary, BadT: 554.
101. See prologue.
102. BadT: 13344.
103. BadT: 13381. He literally wrote: "*En ik geniet nog van me caudotjes*".
104. BadT: 11382.
105. BadT: 154.
106. BadT: 11524. The numbers confirm the system of having many acquaintances at the reception, intimate family and friends for dinner, and a big party for a larger circle of friends, family and acquaintances.
107. BadT: 12017.
108. BadT: 15911.
109. BadT: 15134. The woman is not very well informed: This professor, in fact, was already in her forties when she accepted the chair.
110. BadT: 12014.
111. BadT: 12084.
112. BadT: 195, 11968, 11899. I am obviously not a linguist but it seems telling in this respect that the Dutch language has one term to refer to the nuclear family (= gezin) and another to refer to the family at large (= familie).
113. BadT: 408.
114. See, for reference to "*gezin plus aanhang*" also BdT: 11929.
115. BadT: 11959.
116. *Steengrillen* is a social activity where a heated stone is placed in the centre of the table. The dinner guests can prepare their own food on the heated stone.
117. BadT: 11522.
118. BadT: 16521. Postcards are naturally also a type of gift, see: Jaffe, "Packaged sentiments. The social meanings of greeting cards", *Journal of Material Culture* 4, 2 (1999) 115-141. On the symbolic and social meaning of Christmas cards, see: Searle-Chatterjee, "Christmas Cards and the Construction of Social Relations in Britain Today", in *Unwrapping Christmas*, ed. Miller (Oxford 1993) 176-192.
119. BadT: 12014.
120. BadT: 89.
121. BadT: 1471.
122. Joost Baeck was married to Christina van Erp's sister.
123. See, for instance: Komter, "Vrouwen geschenken en macht. De betekenis van giftuitwisseling door vrouwen in een westerse samenleving" in *Van alle markten thuis: vrouwen- en genderstudies in Nederland*, eds. De Bouw, De Bruijn and Van der Heiden (Amsterdam 1994) 95-109; Areni, Kiecker and Palan, "Is it better to give than to receive? Exploring gender differences in the meaning of memorable gifts", *Psychology & Marketing* 15, 1 (1998) 81-109; McGrath, "Gender differences in gift exchanges. New directions from projections", *Psychology & Marketing* 12, 5 (1995) 371-393.
124. BadT: 11394.
125. BadT: 4719.

126. Dorothea van Dorp: 23-05-1624. See also the introductory paragraph of the prologue.

127. Komter, *The Gift*, 14 and 110. Schuyt and Komter conducted extensive research on people's perceptions on gift giving for the daily newspaper, the *Trouw*. See: Komter and Schuyt. "Geven in Nederland.", *Trouw* (1993). See also: Komter, "Reciprocity as a Principle of Exclusion: Gift Giving in the Netherlands., *Sociology* 30, 2 (1996) 305-306. See also: Sherry, McGrath and Levy, "The dark side of the gift", *Journal of Business Research* 28, 3 (1993) 228.

128. These exceptions have been discussed earlier.

129. On this topic see: Mooney and Brabant, "Off the Rack. Store bought Emotions and the Presentation of Self", *Electronic Journal of Sociology* 3, 4 (1998) 1-11 and Jaffe, "Packaged sentiments. The social meanings of greeting cards", *Journal of Material Culture* 4, 2 (1999) 115-141. Both articles explain how greeting cards, despite of the fact they are purchased 'of the rack', can still function as personal gifts.

130. See again: Belk and Coon, "Can't buy me love: dating, money and gifts"; Burgoyne and Roth, "Constraints on the use of money as a gift at Christmas: the role of status and intimacy", *Journal of Economic Psychology* 12 (1991) 47-69; Cameron, "The unacceptability of money as a gift and its status as a medium of exchange", *Journal of Economic Psychology* 10 (1989) 253-255; Webley and Wilson, "Social relationships and the unacceptability of money as gift", *Journal of Social Psychology* 129 (1989) 85-91.

131. Caplow's "wrapping rule", "gift selection rule", "scaling rule", and "fitness rule" are interesting in this respect see: Caplow, "Rule Enforcement Without Visible Means: Christmas Gift Giving in Middletown" *American Journal of Sociology* 89, 6 (1984) 1306-1323.

132. Examples of wrapping gifts BadT: 12063, 12087.

133. BadT: 188 and 12082 respectively. See also: Offer, "The Economy of Regard", 454.

134. BadT: 173, 1471.

135. According to Sherry et al. "the ideal gift is the union of the right persons and the right objects", *Journal of Business Research*, 240.

136. On the different effects of gifts on social relationships, see: Ruth, Otnes and Brunel, "Gift receipt and the reformulation of interpersonal relationships" *Journal of Consumer Research* 25, 4 (1999) 385-402.

137. BadT: 2198.

Notes Conclusion

1. Naturally, if one were to define speech as a gift and communication as a kind of gift system, human contact would indeed be impossible without the exchange of gifts.

2. See again: Bourdieu, "The Economy of Symbolic Goods" in *Practical Reason* (Cambridge 1998) 96.

3. See: Elias, *Het civilisatieproces. Sociogenetische en psychogenetische onderzoekingen* (Utrecht 1990) [1939].

4. For the interdependency of violence and cooperation, see: Rider, "A game-theoretic interpretation of Marcel Mauss's "The Gift"", *Social Science Journal* 35, 2 (1998) 207.

5. As Gouldner states: "there is an altruism in egoism made possible through reciprocity". Gouldner, "The Norm of Reciprocity: A Preliminary Statement", *American Sociological Review* 25, 2 (1960) 173.

6. Laidlaw argues along the same lines. According to him, a pure gift can only be offered to someone with whom one is maintaining a personal tie. See: Laidlaw, "A free gift makes no friends", *Journal of the Royal Anthropological Institute* 6, 4 (2000) 617-634.

7. This is when gift exchange becomes corruption. On corruption in early modern politics, see: Huiskamp, "Tussen centrum en periferie. Giften en corruptie in de vroegmoderne politiek", *Volkskundig Bulletin* 21 (1995) 27-58; Knevel, *Het Haagse Bureau. Zeventiende-eeuwse ambtenaren tussen staatsbelang en eigenbelang* (Amsterdam 2001).

8. Smart also argues that individuals might be aware that others try to obligate them to offer gifts. Smart, "Gifts, bribes and *guanxi*: a reconsideration of Bourdieu's social capital", *Cultural Anthropology* 8 (1993) 395.

9. De Brune I: 44. See: Verkruijsse ed., *Johan de Brune de Oude (1588-1658). Een Zeeuws literator en staatsman uit de zeventiende eeuw* (Middelburg 1990).

10. De Brune I: 25.

11. See : Sherry et al., "The dark side of the gift" *Journal of Business Research* 28, 3 (1993) 229.

12. Davis, *The gift in sixteenth-century France*, 124.

13. As Schwartz rightly argued the gift is "a generator of identity"; Schwartz, "The Social Psychology of the Gift", *American Journal of Sociology* 73, 1 (1967) 2.

Sources

Alkemade, K., and P. van der Schelling. *Nederlandse Displegtigheden vertoonende de plegtige gebruiken aan den Dis, in het houden van maaltijden en het drinken der gezondheden* (Rotterdam 1732-1735) 3 vols.

Beck, David. *Spiegel van mijn leven. Een Haags dagboek uit 1624.* Edited byVeldhuijzen (Hilversum 1993).

Berkhey, Johan Le Francq van. *Natuurlyke historie van Holland.* vol. 3, *Handelende over de volksgewoonten en landseigen plegtigheden der Hollanderen* (Amsterdam 1769).

Boijmans Van Beuningen Documentatiesysteem voor Prenten en Schilderijen.

Brandt, Geeraardt. *Het leven van Pieter Corn. Hooft.* Edited by Leendertz. (The Hague 1932) [1677].

Brandt, Geeraardt. *Het leven van Joost van den Vondel.* Edited by Leendertz. (The Hague 1932) [1682].

Cats, Jacob. *Alle de wercken van Jacob Cats* (Amsterdam 1667).

Cats, Jacob. *Huwelijk.* Edited by Sneller and Thijs (Amsterdam 1993).

Cats, Jacob. *Spiegel van den ouden en nieuwe tyd* (Amsterdam 1632).

Doop-, trouw-, en begraafboeken of the municipal archives of Delft, The Hague, Rotterdam and Alkmaar.

Heesakkers, C. (ed.). *Constantijn Huygens. Mijn jeugd.* (Amsterdam 1994).

Letters to the Future. Meertens Instituut, Amsterdam 1998.

Lunsingh Scheurleer, Th., W. Fock, and A. van Dissel (eds.). *Het Rapenburg. Geschiedenis van een Leidse gracht* (Leiden 1988, 1989, 1990).

Luyken, Jan. *Goddelyke liefdesvlammen* (Amsterdam 1691).

Luyken, Jan. *Spieghel van het menselyck bedrijf* (Amsterdam 1694).

Rogge, H. (ed.). *Brieven van en aan Maria van Riegersberch* (Leiden 1902).

Sweerts, Hieronymus. *De tien vermakelijkheden van het huwelijk.* Edited by Grootes and Winkelman (Amsterdam 1988) [Amsterdam 1678].

Tricht, H. van (ed.). *De briefwisseling van Pieter Corneliszoon Hooft* (Culemborg 1976-1979).

Unger, J. (ed.) *Dagboek van Constantijn Huygens* (Amsterdam 1885).

Verbeeck, Hermanus. *Memoriaal ofte mijn levensraijsinghe,1621-1681.* Edited by Blaak (Hilversum 1999).

Visscher, Roemer. *Sinnepoppen* (Amsterdam 1614).

Visser, J. (ed.). *Gloria Parendi. Dagboeken van Willem Frederik, stadhouder van Friesland, Groningen en Drenthe 1643-1649, 1651-1654, Nederlandse historische bronnen* (Den Haag 1995).

Witteveen, J. (ed.). *De verstandighe kock, of sorghvuldige huys-houdster.* (Amsterdam 1993) [facsimile 1670].

Worp, J.A. (ed.). *De briefwisseling van Constantijn Huygens (1608-1687)* vol. I (The Hague 1911).

Literature

Aa, A. van der (ed.). *Biographisch woordenboek der Nederlanden* (Haarlem 1969) [1852-1878].

Adshead, S. *Material Culture in Europe and China 1400-1800* (London and New York 1997).

Algazi, G., V. Groebner, and B. Jussen (eds.). *Negotiating the gift. Pre-modern figurations of exchange* (Goettingen 2003).

Alpers, S. *The Art of Describing: Dutch Art in the Seventeenth Century* (Chicago and London 1983).

Altman, L. 'Reciprocity of interpersonal exchange', *Journal on the Theory of Social Behaviour* 3 (1973) 249-261.

Areni, C., P. Kiecker, and K. Palan. 'Is it better to give than to receive? Exploring gender differences in the meaning of memorable gifts', *Psychology & Marketing* 15, 1 (1998) 81-109.

Ariès, Ph. *L'Enfant et le vie familiale sous l'ancien regime* (Paris 1960).

Aymard, M., 'Friends and Neighbors' in: Ph. Aries and G. Duby (eds.). *A History of Private Life. Passions of the Renaissance* (Harvard 1989) [1986], 447-491.

Badinter, E. *L'Amour en plus. Histoire de l'amour maternel (XVIIe-XIXe siècle)* (Paris 1980).

Baggerman, A., and R. Dekker. *Kind van de toekomst. De wondere wereld van Otto van Eck (1780-1798)* (Amsterdam 2005).

Baggerman, A. *Een lot uit de loterij. Familiebelangen en uitgeverspolitiek in de Dordtse firma A. Blussé en zoon, 1745-1823* (Den Haag 2000).

Becker, J. 'Are these Girls Really so Neat? On Kitchen Scenes and Method' in: D. Freedberg and J. de Vries (eds.). *Art in History, History in Art: Studies in Seventeenth-Century Dutch Culture* (Santa Monica 1991) 139-161.

Bedaux, J.B. *The Reality of Symbols. Studies in the Iconology of Netherlandish Art 1400-1800* (The Hague and Maarssen) 1990.

Belk, R. 'Gift-giving Behavior' in: E. Shet Jagdish (ed.). *Research in Marketing* (Greenwich 1979) 95-126.

Belk, R.W., and G.S. Coon. 'Can't buy me love: dating, money and gifts', *Advances in Consumer Research* 18 (1991) 521-527.

Ben-Amos, I. Krausman. 'Gifts and favors: Informal support in Early Modern England', *The Journal of Modern History* 72, 2 (2000) 295-338.

Bestor, J. Fair. 'Marriage transactions in Renaissance Italy and *Mauss's Essay on the Gift*', *Past and Present* 164 (1999) 6-46.

Museum Boijmans van Beuningen. *Quintessens. Wetenswaardigheden over acht eeuwen kookgerei (Exhibit Catalogue)* (Rotterdam 1992).

Bilker, B. 'De huwelijken van Nassau-Dietz' in: S. Groeneveld, J. Huizinga and Y. Kuiper, (eds.). *Nassau uit de schaduw van Oranje* (Franeker 2003) 71-88.

Blaak, J. *Geletterde levens. Dagelijks lezen en schrijven in de vroegmoderne tijd in Nederland 1624-1770* (Hilversum 2004).

Blom, R. *Constantijn Huygens. Mijn leven verteld aan mijn kinderen in twee boeken.* (Amsterdam 2003).

Boekhorst, P. te, P. Burke, and W. Frijhoff (eds.). *Cultuur en maatschappij in Nederland 1500-1850. Een historisch-antropologisch perpectief* (Meppel and Amsterdam 1992).

Bogaers, L. 'Geleund over de onderdeur. Doorkijkjes in het Utrechtse buurtleven van de vroege Middeleeuwen tot in de zeventiende eeuw', *Bijdragen en mededelingen betreffende de geschiedenis der Nederlanden* 112 (1997) 336-363.

Boheemen, P. van (ed.). *Kent, en versint. Eer datje mint. Vrijen en trouwen 1500-1800* (Apeldoorn/Zwolle) 1989.

Boissevain, J. *Revitalizing European Rituals* (London 1992).

Boone, M. 'Dons et pots-de-vin, aspects de sociabilite urbaine au bas Moyen Age. Le cas de gantois pendant la periode bourguignonne', *Revue de Nord* 278 (1988) 471-488.

Bots, H., and F. Waquet. *La République des Lettres* (Paris 1997).

Boulay, J. du. 'Strangers and gifts: hostility and hospitality in rural Greece', *Journal of Mediterranean Studies* 1 (1991) 37-53.

Bourdieu, P. *Practical Reason: On the Theory of Action* (Cambridge 1998).

Bourdieu, P. 'The work of time' in: A. Komter (ed.). *The Gift. An Interdisciplinary Perspective* (Amsterdam 1996) 135-147.

Bouw, C., J. de Bruijn, and D. van der Heijden (eds.). *Van alle markten thuis. Vrouwen- en genderstudies in Nederland* (Amsterdam 1994).

Bouwman, J. *Nederlandse gelegenheidsgedichten voor 1700 in de Koninklijke Bibliotheek te 's-Gravenhage. Catalogus van gedrukte gedichten op gedenkwaardige gebeurtenissen in het leven van particuliere personen* (Nieuwkoop 1982).

Brands, M., H. von der Dunk, and H. Zwager. 'Introductie', *Tijdschrift voor Geschiedenis* 83 (1970).

Brewer, J., and R. Porter (eds.) *Consumption and the World of Goods* (London and New York 1993).

Briggs, A., and P. Burke. *A Social History of the Media: From Gutenberg to the Internet* (Cambridge 2002).

Burema, L. *De voeding in Nederland van de Mideeleeuwen tot de twintigste eeuw* (Assen 1953).

Burgoyne, C.B., and D.A. Roth. 'Constraints on the use of money as a gift at Christmas: the role of status and intimacy', *Journal of Economic Psychology* 12 (1991) 47-69.

Burke, P. 'Representations of the Self from Petrach to Descartes' in: R. Porter (ed.). *Rewriting the Self: Histories from the Renaissance to the Present* (London and New York 1997) 17-28.

Cameron, S. 'The unacceptability of money as a gift and its status as a medium of exchange', *Journal of Economic Psychology* 10 (1989) 253-255.

Caplow, T. 'Christmas Gifts and Kin Networks', *American Sociological Review* 47, 3 (1982) 383-392.

Caplow, T. 'Rule Enforcement without Visible Means: Christmas Gift Giving in Middletown', *American Journal of Sociology* 89, 6 (1984) 1306-1323.

Carlson, M. *Domestic Service in a Changing City Economy: Rotterdam 1680-1780* (Madison, WI 1993).

Cheal, D. *The Gift Economy* (London and New York 1988).

Cheal, D. 'The Social Dimensions of Gift Behaviour', *Journal of Social and Personal Realtionships* 3 (1986): 423-493.

Corbeau, M. 'Pronken en koken. Beeld en realiteit van keukens in het vroegmoderne Hollandse binnenhuis', *Volkskundig Bulletin* 19, 3 (1993) 354-379.

Cressy, D. *Birth, Marriage and Death: Ritual, Religion and the Life-Cycle in Tudor and Stuart England* (Oxford 1997).

Cressy, D. *Bonfires and Bells: National memory and the Protestant calendar in Elizabethan and Stuart England* (London 1989).

Davis, N. 'Beyond the market: books as gifts in sixteenth-century France', *Transactions of the Royal Historical Society* 5, 33 (1983) 69-88.

Davis, N. 'Boundaries and the Sense of Self in Sixteenth-Century France' in: T. Heller and M. Sosna (eds.) *Reconstructing Individualism: Autonomy, Individuality and the Self in Western Thought* (Stanford 1986) 53-63.

Davis, N. *The Gift in Sixteenth-Century France* (Madison, WI 2000).

Dekker, J., and L. Groenendijk. 'The Republic of God or the Republic of children? Childhood and child-rearing after the Reformation. An appraisal of Simon Schama's thesis about the uniqueness of the Dutch case', *Oxford Review of Education* 12, 3 (1991) 317-335.

Dekker, R. 'Egodocumenten: een literatuuroverzicht', *Tijdschrift voor Geschiedenis* 101, (1988) 161-189.

Dekker, R. *Lachen in de Gouden Eeuw. Een geschiedenis van Nederlandse humor* (Amsterdam 1997).

Dekker, R. *Uit de schaduw in 't grote licht. Kinderen in egodocumenten van de Gouden Eeuw tot de Romantiek* (Amsterdam 1995).

Deursen, A.Th. van. *Bavianen en slijkgeuzen. Kerk en kerkvolk ten tijde van Maurits en Oldenbarnevelt* (Assen 1974).

Deursen, A.Th. van. *Een dorp in de polder. Graft in de zeventiende eeuw* (Amsterdam 1994).

Deursen, A.Th. van. *Mensen van klein vermogen. Het kopergeld van de Gouden Eeuw* (Amsterdam 1996) [1991].

Dibbits, H. 'Betweeen society and Family values. The Linen cupboard in early modern households' in: A. Schuurman and P. Spierenburg (eds.) *Private Domain, Public Inquiry. Families and lifestyles in the Netherlands and Europe, 1550 to the present* (Hilversum 1996) 125-145.

Dibbits, H. *Vertrouwd bezit. Materiële cultuur in Doesburg en Maassluis 1650-1800.* (Nijmegen 2001).

Dixhoorn, A. van. 'In een traditie gevangen? Hollandse rederijkerskamers en rederijkers in de recente literatuurgeschiedschrijving', *Tijdschrift voor geschiedenis* 112, 3 (1999) 385-406.

Dunk, H, von der. 'Over de betekenis van Ego-documenten. Een paar aantekeningen als in- en uitleiding', *Tijdschrift voor Geschiedenis* 83 (1970) 147-161.

Dussen, M. Schenkeveld-van der. 'Poëzie als gebruiksartikel; gelegenheidsgedichten in de zeventiende eeuw' in: M. Spies (ed.), *Historische Letterkunde* (Groningen 1984) 75-92.

Elias, J.E. *De vroedschap van Amsterdam 1578-1795* (Haarlem 1903-1905).

Elias, N. *Het civilisatieproces. Sociogenetische en psychogenetische onderzoekingen* (Utrecht 1990) [1939].

Faber, S. 'Vrouwen van de rekening. Kindermoordzaken ten tijden van de Republiek te Amsterdam en in Friesland', in: G. Hekma and H. Roodenburg (eds.) *Soete minne en helsche boosheit. Seksuele voorstellingen in Nederland, 1300-1850* (Nijmegen 1988).

Falkenburg, R. 'Iconologie en historische antropologie: een toenadering' in: M. Halbertsma and K. Zijlmans (eds.) *Gezichtspunten. Een inleiding in de methoden van de kunstgeschiedenis* (Nijmegen 1993).

Falkenburg, R. 'Recente visies op zeventiende-eeuwse Nederlandse schilderkunst', *Theoretische geschiedenis* 18 (1991) 119-140.

Flandrin, J. L. *The Family in Former Times: Kinship, Household and Sexuality* (Cambridge 1979) [1976].

Franits, W. *Paragons of Virtue: Women and Domesticity in Seventeenth-Century Dutch Art.* (Cambridge 1993).

Freedberg, D., and J de Vries (eds.). *Art in History, History in Art: Studies in Seventeenth-Century Dutch Culture* (Santa Monica 1991).

Frijhoff, W. 'Burgerlijk dichtplezier in 1650?', *Spiegel der Letteren* 43-3 (2001) 248-269.

Frijhoff, W. 'Volkskundigen voor de volkskunde?', *Volkskundig Bulletin* 20, 3 (1994).

Frijhoff, W. *Wegen van Evert Willemsz. Een Hollands weeskind op zoek naar zichzelf 1607-1647* (Nijmegen 1995).

Frijhoff, W., and M. Spies (eds.). *1650. Bevochten eendracht, Nederlandse cultuur in Europese context* (The Hague 1999).

Gennep, A. van. *Les Rites de Passage* (Chicago 1960) [1909].

Gijsbers, W. *Kapitale ossen. De international handel in slachtvee in Noordwest-Europa.* (Hilversum 1999).

Godbout, J.T., and A. Caille. 'The world of the gift', *Queens Quarterly* 107, 3 (2000) 366-372.

Goffman, E. *Interaction Ritual* (New York 1967).

Goldgar, A. *Impolite Learning: Conduct and Community in the Republic of Letters 1680-1750* (New Haven/ London 1995).

Gouldner, A. 'The Norm of Reciprocity: A Preliminary Statement', *American Sociological Review* 25, 2 (1960) 161-178.

Gouw, J ter. *De Volksvermaken* (Haarlem 1871).

Grabowsky, E., and P. Verkruijsse (eds.). *Arnout Hellemans Hooft. Een naekt beeld op een marmore matras seer schoon. Het dagboek van een 'grand tour' (1649-1651)* (Hilversum 2001).

Groenveld, S. *Hooft als historieschrijver. Twee studies* (Weesp 1981).

Grootens, P. *Dominicus Baudius. Een levensschets uit het Leidsche Humanistenmilieu, 1566-1631* (Nijmegen 1942).

Haasse, H., and A.J. Gelderblom. *Het licht der schitterende dagen. Het leven van P.C. Hooft.* (Amsterdam 1981).

Haks, D. 'Continuiteit en verandering in het gezin van de vroeg-moderne tijd' in: H. Peeters, L. Dresden-Coenders and T. Brandenbarg (eds.). *Vijf eeuwen gezinsleven. Liefde, huwelijk en opvoeding in Nederland* (Nijmegen 1986) 31-56.

Haks, D. *Huwelijk en gezin in Holland in de 17de en 18de eeuw. Processtukken en moralisten over aspecten van het laat 17de- en 18de-eeuwse gezinsleven* (Assen 1982).

Heal, F. *Hospitality in Early Modern England* (Oxford 1990).

Heal, F. 'The idea of hospitality in Early Modern England', *Past and Present* 102 (1987) 66-93.

Hecht, P. 'Dutch 17th-century genre painting: a reassessment of some current hypothesis', *Simiolus* 21 (1992) 83-93.

Heel, S.A.C Dudok van. 'De familie van Pieter Cornelisz Hooft', *Jaarboek van het Centraal Bureau voor Genealogie en het Iconografisch Bureau* (1981) 68-108.

Heijden, M. van der. *Huwelijk in Holland. Stedelijke rechtspraak en kerkelijk tucht 1550-1700* (Amsterdam 1998).

Hekma, G. (ed.) *Soete minne en helsche boosheit. Seksuele voorstellingen in Nederland 1300-1850* (Nijmegen 1988).

Helsloot, J., 'Sinterklaas en de komst van de kerstman', *Volkskundig Bulletin* 22 (1996) 299-329.

Houlbrooke, R. (ed.). *English Family Life, 1576-1716: An Anthology from Diaries* (Oxford 1988).

Howell, M.C. *The Marriage Exchange: Property, Social Place and Gender in the Cities of the Low Countries, 1300-1550* (Chicago 1998).

Huet, C. Busken. *Het land van Rembrand. Studiën over de Noordnederlandse beschaving in de zeventiende eeuw* (Haarlem 1898).

Hufton, O. *The Propect before Her: A History of Women in Western Europe* (New York and London 1998) [1995].

Huiskamp, R. 'Tussen centrum en periferie. Giften en corruptie in de vroegmoderne politiek', *Volkskundig Bulletin* 21 (1995) 27-58.

Israel, J. *The Dutch Republic: Its Rise, Greatness and Fall 1477-1806* (Oxford 1995).

Jacobs, M. 'Sociaal kapitaal van buren. Rechten, plichten en conflicten in Gentse gebuurten (zeventiende-achttiende eeuw)', *Volkskundig Bulletin* 12, 2 (1996) 149-176.

Jaffe, A. 'Packaged sentiments: The social meanings of greeting cards', *Journal of Material Culture* 4, 2 (1999) 115-141.

Jansen, J. (ed.). *Omnibus Idem. Opstellen over P.C. Hooft ter gelegenheid van zijn 350ste sterfdag* (Hilversum 1997).

Jansen, J. (ed.) *Zeven maal Hooft. Lezingen ter gelegenheid van de 350ste sterfdag van P.C. Hooft* (Amsterdam 1998).

Jong, A. de, and C. Wijers (eds.). *Brieven aan de toekomst* (Utrecht 1999).

Jongejan, M. *Weeldeboden en werkboden. Huispersoneel in Goes in de achttiende en begin van de negentiende eeuw* (Veere 1984).

Jongh, E, de. 'De iconologische benadering van de zeventiende-eeuwse Nederlandse schilderkunst' in: F. Grijzenhout and H. van Veen, eds., *De Gouden Eeuw in perspectief. Het beeld van de Nederlandse zeventiende-eeuwse schilderkunst in later tijd* (Nijmegen and Heerlen 1992) 299-330.

Jongh, E. de (ed.). *Tot Lering en Vermaak. Betekenissen van Hollandse genrevoorstellingen uit de zeventiende eeuw* (Amsterdam 1976).

Jongh, E. de. *Zinne- en minnebeelden in de schilderkunst in de zeventiende eeuw* (s.l. 1967).

Kalb, D. 'Historical Anthropology: the unwaged debate', *Focaal. Tijdschrift voor antropologie* 26/27 (1996).

Kamermans, J. *Materiële cultuur in de Krimpenerwaard in de zeventiende en acht-tiende eeuw: ontwikkeling en diversiteit* (Wageningen 1999).

Kaper, R. *Liever geen bloemen. Over dood en rouw in de 17de eeuw* (Culemborg 1984).

Keesing, E. *Het volk met lange rokken. Vrouwen rondom Constantijn Huygens* (Amsterdam 1993).

Kermode, J. 'Sentiment and Survival: Family and Friends in Late Medieval English Towns', *Journal of Family History* 24, 1 (1999) 6-18.

Kettering, S. 'Gift-giving and patronage in early modern France', *French History* 2 (1988) 131-151.

Keyser, M. 'Kermis in Nederland tot het einde van de 19e eeuw', *Nederlands Volksleven* 28 (1978) 73-80.

Klamer, A., and I. van Staveren. 'Geven is geen ruilen. De gift in de economie' in: A. Komter (ed.). *Het geschenk. Over de verschillende betekenissen van geven* (Amsterdam 1997) 108-120.

Klijn, E. *Loodglazuuraardewerk in Nederland. De collectie van het Nederlands Open-luchtmuseum* (Catalogue) (Arnhem 1995).

Kloek, E., G. van Oostveen, and N. Teeuwen. 'Nederlandse moralisten over moe-derschap en min (1600-1900)', *Volkscultuur: tijdschrift voor tradities en verschijnselen* 8 (1991) 20-39.

Knevel, P. *Het Haagse Bureau. Zeventiende-eeuwse ambtenaren tussen staatsbelang en eigenbelang* (Amsterdam 2001).

Komter, A. *Solidariteit en de gift. Sociale banden en sociale uitsluiting* (Amsterdam 2003).

Komter, A. 'Gift Giving' in: D. Levinson and J. Ponzetti (eds.) *Encyclopedia of Human Emotions* (1999) 298-301.

Komter, A. (ed.). *The Gift. An Interdisciplinary Perspective* (Amsterdam 1996).

Komter, A. (ed.). *Het geschenk. Over de verschillende betekenissen van geven* (Amsterdam 1997).

Komter, A. 'Reciprocity as a Principle of Exclusion. Gift Giving in the Netherlands', *Sociology* 30, 2 (1996) 299-316.

Komter, A. 'Vrouwen geschenken en macht. De betekenis van giftuitwisseling door vrouwen in een westerse samenleving' in: C. Bouw, J. de Bruijn and D. van der Heiden (eds.). *Van alle markten thuis: vrouwen- en genderstudies in Nederland* (Amsterdam 1994) 95-109.

Komter, A., and K. Schuyt. 'Geven in Nederland', *Trouw* (1993).

Komter, A., and W. Vollebergh. 'Gift Giving and the Emotional Significance of Family and Friends', *Journal of Marriage and the Family* 59 (1997) 747-757.

Komter, A., and W. Vollebergh. 'Intergenerational solidarity. Family ties under strain?', *Sociale Wetenschappen* 41, 3 (1998) 25-37.

Kooijmans, L. 'Andries & Daniel. Vriendschap in de vroegmoderne Nederlan-den', *Groniek. Historisch Tijdschrift* 130 (1995) 8-25.

Kooijmans, L. 'De dagboeken van Joan Huydecoper', *Nederlands Archievenblad* 100 (1996) 49-69.

Kooijmans, L. 'Kwetsbaarheid en "koopluider vriendschap"' in: M. Gijswijt-Hof-stra and F. Egmond (eds.). *Of bidden helpt? Tegenslag en cultuur in Europa, circa 1500-2000* (Amsterdam 1997) 61-70.

Kooijmans, L. 'Liefde in opdracht. Emotie en berekening in de dagboeken van Willem Frederik van Nassau', *Historisch Tijdschrift Holland* 30, 4/5 (1998) 231-255.

Kooijmans, L. *Liefde in opdracht. Het hofleven van Willem Frederik van Nassau.* (Amsterdam 2000).

Kooijmans, L. *Vriendschap en de kunst van het overleven in de zeventiende en achttiende eeuw* (Amsterdam 1997).

Kooijmans, L. "Vriendschap. Een 18e-eeuwse familiegeschiedenis", *Tijdschrift voor Sociale Geschiedenis* 28 (1992) 48-65.

Koslofsky, C. *The Reformation of the Dead. Death and Ritual in Early Modern Germany, 1450-1700* (London and New York 2000).

Laan, C. *Drank en drinkgerei. Een archeologisch en cultuurhistorisch onderzoek naar de alledaagse drinkcultuur van de 18e-eeuwse Hollanders* (Amsterdam 2003).

Labrie, A. "Eenzaamheid en sociabiliteit: Romantische vriendschap in Duitsland", *Groniek* (1995) 68-86.

Laidlaw, J. "A free gift makes no friends", *Journal of the Royal Anthropological Institute* 6, 4 (2000) 617-634.

Leer, M van. *Geven rond Sinterklaas. Een ritueel als spiegel van veranderende relaties* (Amsterdam 1995).

Leer, M van. "Wederkerigheid in een surprise. Sinterklaasgeschenken vanuit historisch-sociologisch perspectief" in: A. Komter (ed.). *Het geschenk. Over de verschillende betekenissen van het geven* (Amsterdam 1997).

Leer, M. van. "Wie gelooft er nog in Sinterklaas? Een ritueel geschenkenfeest als spiegel van veranderende relaties", *Volkskundig Bulletin* 22 (1996) 239-262.

Leer, M. van, and A. Komter. "Gastvrijheid, of de kunst van het ontvangen" in: A. Komter (ed.). *Het geschenk over de betekenissen van het geven* (Amsterdam 1997).

Leeuwen, M. van. "Logic of Charity: Poor Relief in Pre-Industrial Europe", *Journal of Interdisciplinary History* 24 (1994) 589-613.

Lennep, J. van, and J. ter Gouw. *Het boek der opschriften. Een bijdrage tot de geschiedenis van het Nederlandsche volksleven* (Amsterdam 1869).

Lesger, C. *Handel in Amsterdam ten tijde van de opstand. Kooplieden, commerciële expansie en verandering in de ruimtelijke economie van de Nederlanden ca. 1550-ca. 1630* (Hilversum 2001).

Levi-Strauss, C. "The principle of reciprocity" in: A. Komter (ed.). *The Gift. An Interdisciplinary Perspective* (Amsterdam 1996) 18-26.

Lindeman, R., Y. Scherf and R. Dekker (eds.). *Egodocumenten van Noord-Nederlanders uit de zestiende tot begin negentiende eeuw. Een chronologische lijst* (Rotterdam 1993).

Lis, C. "Neighbourhood and social change in West-European cities: sixteenth to nineteenth centuries", *International Review of Social History* 38 (1993) 1-30.

Macfarlane, A. *The Family Life of Ralph Josselin: A Seventeenth-Century Clergyman. An Essay in Historical Anthropology* (Cambridge 1970).

Macharel, C. "Dons et réciprocité en Europe", *Archives européennes de sociologie* 24 (1983) 151-166.

Malinowski, B. "The Principle of Give and Take" in: *Crime and Custom in Savage Society* (London 1970) 39-45.

Mare, H. de. "De keuken als voorstelling in het werk van Simon Stevin en Jacob Cats" in: C. Bouw, J. de Bruijn and D. van der Heiden (eds.), *Van alle markten thuis: vrouwen- en genderstudies in Nederland* (Amsterdam 1994).

Mare, H. de. "The Domestic Boundary as Ritual Area in Seventeenth-Century Holland" in: H. de Mare and A. Vos (eds.). *Urban Rituals in Italy and the Netherlands. Historical contrasts in the use of public space, architecture and the urban environment* (Assen 1993).

Masuch, M. *Origins of the Individualist Self: Autobiography and Self-Identity in England, 1591-1791* (Cambridge 1997).

Mauss, M. *The Gift: Forms and Functions of Exchange in Archaic Societies* (New York and London 1967) [1923-24].

McCants, A. *Civic Charity in a Golden Age. Orphan Care in Early Modern Amsterdam* (Chicago 1997).

McGrath, M.A. "Gender differences in gift exchanges – New directions from projections", *Psychology & Marketing* 12, 5 (1995) 371-393.

Meertens, P.J. *Nederlandse emblemata. Bloemlezing uit de Noord- en Zuidnederlandse emlblemataliteratuur van de zesteinde en zeventiende eeuw* (Leiden 1983).

Miedema, H. "Over iconologie en de betekenis van schilderijen", *Theoretische geschiedenis* 25 (1998) 168-183.

Miller, D. *Unwrapping Christmas* (Oxford 1993).

Molendijk, A.L. (ed.). *Materieel Christendom. Religie en materiële cultuur in West-Europa.* (Hilversum 2003).

Mooney, L., and S. Brabant. "Of the Rack. Store bought Emotions and the Presentation of Self", *Electronic Journal of Sociology* 3, 4 (1998) 1-11.

Moser, N. *De strijd voor rhetorica. Poëtica en positie van rederijkers in Vlaanderen, Brabant, Zeeland en Holland tussen 1450 en 1620* (Amsterdam 2001).

Muir, E. *Ritual in Early Modern Europe, New Approaches to European History* (Cambridge 1997).

Muldrew, C. *The Economy of Obligation: The Culture of Credit and Social Relations in Early Modern England* (New York 1998).

Muldrew, C. "Zur Anthropologie des Kapitalismus. Kredit, Vertrauwen, Tausch und die Geschichte des Marktes in England 1500-1750", *Historische Anthropologie* 6 (1998) 167-199.

Nierop, H. van. *Van ridders tot regenten. De Hollandse Adel in de zestiende en de eerste helft van de zeventiende eeuw* (The Hague 1984).

Nieuweboer, A. "Medeleven volgens voorschrift en verzen op bestelling. Achttiende-eeuwse gelegenheidsgedichten", *Literatuur. Tijdschrift over Nederlandse Letterkunde* 1, 3 (1986) 15-22.

Noordegraaf, L., and G. Valk. *De Gave Gods. De pest in Holland vanaf de late middeleeuwen* (Baarn 1988).

Offer, A. "Between the gift and the market: the economy of regard", *Economic History Review* 3 (1997) 450-476.

Osborne, R., and J. Williams. "Determining Patterns of Exchanges and Expanded Family Relationships", *International Journal of Sociology of the Family* 6 (1976) 197-209.

O'Sullivan, C. *Hospitality in medieval Ireland, 900-1500* (Dublin 2004).

Peeters, H., L. Dresen-Coenders, and T. Brandenbarg (eds.). *Vijf eeuwen gezinsleven. Liefde, huwelijk en opvoeding in Nederland* (Nijmegen 1988).

Poelwijk, A. *"In dienste vant suyckerbacken". De Amsterdamse suikernijverheid en haar ondernemers, 1580-1630* (Hilversum 2003).

Pol, L. van de. "Prostitutie en de Amsterdamse burgerij: eerbegrippen in een vroegmoderne stedelijke samenleving" in: P. te Boekhorst, P. Burke and W. Frijhoff (eds.). *Cultuur en maatschappij in Nederland 1500-1850. Een historisch-antropologisch perspectief* (Meppel and Amsterdam 1992) 179-218.

Pollmann, J. *Een andere weg naar God. De Reformatie van Arnoldus Buchelius (1565-1641).* (Amsterdam 2000).

Pollock, L. *Forgotten Children: Parent-Child Relations from 1500-1900* (Cambridge 1983).

Porteman, K. *Inleiding tot de Nederlandse emblemataliteratuur* (Groningen 1977).

Presser, J. "Memoires als geschiedbron" in: *Winkler Prins Encyclopedie VIII* (Amsterdam and Brussels 1958) 208-210.

Presser, J. "Memoires als geschiedbron" in: J. Presser (ed.). *Uit het werk van J. Presser* (Amsterdam 1969) 277-282.

Putten, J. Jobse-van. *Eenvoudig maar voedzaam. Cultuurgeschiedenis van de dagelijkse maaltijd in Nederland* (Nijmegen 1995).

Rademaker, C., and P. Tuynman (eds.). *Het uitleenboekje van Vossius* (Amsterdam 1962).

Rider, R. "A game-theoretic interpretation of Marcel Mauss's 'The Gift'", *Social Science Journal* 35, 2 (1998) 203-212.

Roberts, B. *Through the keyhole. Dutch child-rearing practices in the 17th and 18th century. Three urban elite families* (Hilversum 1998).

Roche, D. *Histoire des choses banales. Naissance de la consommation XVIIe-XVIIIe siècle* (Paris 1997).

Roodenburg, H. "Eer en oneer ten tijde van de Republiek. Een tussenbalans", *Volkskundig Bulletin* 22 (1996) 129-149.

Roodenburg, H. "'Freundschaft', 'Bruederlichkeit' und 'Einigkeit'": Staedtische Nachbarschaften im Westen der Republik' in: T. Dekker (ed.). *Ausbreitung buergerlicher Kultur in die Niederlanden und Nordwestdeutschland* (Munster 1991).

Roodenburg, H. "Naar een etnografie van de vroegmoderne stad: de 'gebuyrten' in Leiden en Den Haag" in: P. te Boekhorst, P. Burke and W. Frijhoff (eds.). *Cultuur en maatschappij in Nederland 1500-1850, een historisch-antropologisch perspectief* (Amsterdam/Heerlen 1992) 219-243.

Roodenburg, H. *Onder censuur. De kerkelijke tucht in de gereformeerde gemeente van Amsterdam, 1578-1700* (Hilversum 1990).

Rooijakkers, G. *Eer en schande. Volksgebruiken van het oude Brabant* (Nijmegen 1995).

Rooijakkers, G. *Rituele repertoires. Volkscultuur in oostelijk Noord-Brabant 1559-1853* (Nijmegen 1994).

Rooijakkers, G. "Vieren en Markeren" in: *Volkscultuur* (Nijmegen 2000) 173-230.

Ruberg, W. *Conventionele correspondentie. Briefcultuur van de Nederlandse elite, 1770-1850* (Nijmegen 2005).

Rubin, Z. "Lovers and other strangers: the development of intimacy in encounters and relationships", *American Scientist* 62 (1974) 182-190.

Ruempol, A., and A. van Dongen. *Pre-industriële gebruiksvoorwerpen 1150-1800* (Rotterdam n.d.)

Ruffle, B.J. "Gift giving with emotions", *Journal of Economic Behaviour & Organization* 39, 4 (1999) 399-420.

Ruth, J.A., C.C. Otnes, and F.F. Brunel. "Gift receipt and the reformulation of interpersonal relationships", *Journal of Consumer Research* 25, 4 (1999) 385-402.

Sarti, R. *Europe at Home. Family and Material Culture 1500-1800* (New Haven/London 2002).

Schama, S. *The Embarrassment of Riches: An Interpretation of Dutch Culture in the Golden Age* (London 1987).

Scheurleer, Th. Lunsingh, C.W. Fock, and A. van Dissel (eds.). *Het Rapenburg. Geschiedenis van een Leidse gracht* (Leiden 1988, 1989, 1990).

Schmidt, A. *Overleven na de dood. Weduwen in Leiden in de Gouden Eeuw* (Amsterdam 2001).

Schmidt, C. *Om de eer van de familie. Het geslacht Teding van Berkhout 1500-1950, een sociologische benadering* (Amsterdam 1986).

Schmied, G. *Schenken. Ueber eine Form sozialen Handelns* (Opladen 1996).

Schotel, G.D.J. *Het maatschappelijk leven onzer vaderen in de zeventiende eeuw.* (Amsterdam 1905).

Schotel, G.D.J. *Het Oud-Hollandsch Huisgezin der zeventiende eeuw* (Haarlem 1867).

Schotel, G.D.J. *Oude zeden en gebruiken in Nederland* (Leiden n.d.)

Schuurman, A. *Materiële cultuur en levensstijl. Een onderzoek naar de taal der dingen op het Nederlandse platteland in de 19e eeuw: de Zaanstreek, Oost-Groningen, Oost-Brabant.* (Wageningen 1989).

Schuurman, A., J de Vries, and A. van der Woude (eds.). *Aards geluk. De Nederlanders en hun spullen van 1550 tot 1850* (Amsterdam 1997).

Schwartz, B. "The Social Psychology of the Gift", *American Journal of Sociology* 73, 1 (1967) 1-11.

Searle-Chatterjee, M. "Christmas Cards and the Construction of Social Relations in Britain Today" in: D. Miller, (ed.), *Unwrapping Christmas* (Oxford 1993) 176-192.

Sherry, J.F., M.A. McGrath, and S.J. Levy. "The dark side of the gift", *Journal of Business Research* 28, 3 (1993) 225-244.

Shorter, E. *The Making of the Modern Family* (New York 1975).

Shuman, A. "Food gifts- Ritual exchange and the production of excess meaning", *Journal of American Folklore* 113, 450 (2000) 495-508.

Simpson-Herbert, M. "Women, food and hospitality in Iranian society", *Canberra Anthropology* 10 (1987) 24-34.

Sluijter, E.J. "Belering en verhulling? Enkele 17de-eeuwse teksten over de schilderkunst en de iconologische benadering van Noordnederlandse schilderijen uit deze periode", *De zeventiende eeuw* 4 (1988) 3-28.

Smart, A. "Gifts, bribes and *guanxi*: a reconsideration of Bourdieu's social capital", *Cultural Anthropology* 8 (1993) 388-408.

Smits-Veldt, M. *Maria Tesselschade. Leven met talent en vriendschap* (Zutphen 1994).

Smits-Veldt, M., and M. Bakker (eds.). *In een web van vriendschap. Nederlandse vrouwen uit de zeventiende eeuw* (Amsterdam 1998).

Sneller, A.A., and O. van Marion (eds.). *De gedichten van Tesselschade Roemers* (Hilversum 1994).

Spaans, J. *Armenzorg in Friesland 1500-1800. Publieke zorg en particuliere liefdadigheid in zes Friese steden. Leeuwarden, Bolsward, Franeker, Sneek, Dokkum en Harlingen* (Hilversum and Leeuwarden 1997).

Spierenburg, P. (ed.). *In de jonkheid gaan. Over vrijen en trouwen 1500-1800. Themanummer Jeugd en samenleving* 19 (Amersfoort 1989) 609-736.

Spierenburg, P. "Vriendschap tussen messentrekkers? De tafelrand van zeventiende- en achttiende-eeuws Amsterdam", *Groniek* (1995) 42-56.

Stegeman, S. *Patronage en dienstverlening. Het netwerk van Theodorus Janssonius van Almeloveen (1657-1712) in de Republiek der Letteren* (Nijmegen 1996).

Stone, L. *The Family, Sex and Marriage in England 1500-1800* (London 1977).

Strengholt, L. "Over de Muiderkring" in: H. Duits, A. Leerintveld, T. ter Meer and A. van Strien (eds.). *Een lezer aan het woord. Studies van L. Strengholt over zeventiende-eeuwse Nederlandse letterkunde* (Muenster 1998) 75-88.

Strouken, I. (ed.). *Kermis; special issue Volkscultuur*, 5, 1988.

Tebbenhoff, E. "Tacit rules and hidden family structures: naming practices and godparentage in Schenectady, New York, 1680-1800", *Journal of Social History* 18 (1985) 567-585.

Thoen, I. "Grafter kookpotten en hertrouwende weduwen. Connotaties van een zeventiende-eeuws gebruiksvoorwerp", *Volkskundig Bulletin* 23, 2 (1997) 107-126.

Thoen, I. "'Soo krijght almtemet de gescheurde pot een deghelijck decksel...' Zeventiende-eeuwse slibaardewerken kookpotten uit Graft: object, methode en betekenis.". (Unpublished M.A. thesis Erasmus University 1996).

Tricht, H.W. van. *P.C. Hooft* (Arnhem 1951).

Veluwenkamp, J. *Archangel. Nederlandse ondernemers in Rusland 1550-1785* (Amsterdam 2000).

Ven, J. van de. *Psychological sentiments and economic behaviour* (Tilburg 2003).

Verkruijsse, P. (ed.). *Johan de Brune de Oude (1588-1658). Een Zeeuws literator en staatsman uit de zeventiende eeuw* (Middelburg 1990).

Vlis, I. van der. *Leven in armoede. Delftse bedeelden in de zeventiende eeuw* (Amsterdam 2001).

Vreeken, H. *Kunstnijverheid Middeleeuwen en Renaissance (Catalogue)* (Rotterdam 1994).

Waardt, H de. "De geschiedenis van de eer en de historische antropologie", *Tijdschrift voor Sociale Geschiedenis* 23 (1997) 334-354.

Waardt, H. de. "Inleiding: naar een geschiedenis van de eer", *Leidschrift* 12, (1996) 7-19.

Weatherhill, L. *Consumer Behaviour and Material Culture in Britain 1660-1760* (London and New York 1993).

Webley, P., and R. Wilson. "Social relationships and the unacceptability of money as gift", *Journal of Social Psychology* 129 (1989) 85-91.

Westrienen, A. Frank van. *De Groote Tour. Tekening van een educatiereis door Nederlanders in de zeventiende eeuw* (Amsterdam 1983).

Wijngaarde, H. van. *Zorgen voor de kost. Armenzorg, arbeid, en onderlinge hulp in Zwolle 1650-1700* (Amsterdam 2000).

Wijnroks, E. *Handel tussen Rusland en de Nederlanden 1560-1640. Een netwerkana-lyse van de Antwerpse en Amsterdamse kooplieden, handelend op Rusland* (Hilversum 2003).

Wijsenbeek-Olthuis, Th. *Achter de gevels van Delft. Bezit en bestaan van rijk en arm in een periode van achteruitgang (1700-1800)* (Hilversum 1987).

Wijsenbeek-Olthuis, Th. (ed.). *Het Lange Voorhout. Monumenten, mensen en macht* (Zwolle and The Hague 1998).

Windler, C. "Tribute and gift: Mediterranean diplomacy as cross-cultural communication", *Saeculum* 51, 1 (2000) 24-56.

Windler, C. "Tributes and presents in Franco-Tunesian diplomacy", *Journal of Early Modern History* 4, 2 (2000) 169-199.

Zijlmans, J. *Vriendenkringen in de zeventiende eeuw. Verenigingsvormen van het informele culturele leven te Rotterdam* (The Hague 1999).

Zoonen, A van "De kermis in de 17de eeuw (1572-1700)" in: *"Stap op en laat je wegen". De geschiedenis van 550 jaar Hoornse kermis* (Hoorn 1996).

Index of Subjects